BOOKS THAT COOK

Books That Cook

The Making of a Literary Meal

Edited by

JENNIFER COGNARD-BLACK

and

MELISSA A. GOLDTHWAITE

With a Foreword by

MARION NESTLE

NEW YORK UNIVERSITY PRESS
New York and London

NEW YORK UNIVERSITY PRESS
New York and London
www.nyupress.org

Library of Congress Cataloging-in-Publication Data
Books that cook : the making of a literary meal / edited by Jennifer Cognard-Black and Melissa A. Goldwaite ; with a foreword by Marion Nestle.
pages cm   Includes bibliographical references and index.
ISBN 978-1-4798-3021-3 (cloth)
1. Cooking. 2. Cooking in literature. 3. Food in literature. I. Cognard-Black, Jennifer, 1969– editor of compilation. II. Goldthwaite, Melissa A., 1972– editor of compilation.
III. Nestle, Marion, writer of preface.
TX714.B64128   2014
641.5—dc23   2014006080

New York University Press books are printed on acid-free paper, and their binding materials are chosen for strength and durability. We strive to use environmentally responsible suppliers and materials to the greatest extent possible in publishing our books.

Manufactured in the United States of America

10 9 8 7 6 5 4 3 2 1

To our Books That Cook students, who share our consuming passion for the literatures of food.

One wants
in a fantastic time
the certainty of
chicken popping in grease
the truth of potatoes. . . .

—from "Sunday Dinner" by Lucille Clifton

CONTENTS

FOREWORD

Sparking an avalanche of interest in writings about food is the simple fact that everyone eats. Years ago as a young biology teacher, I quickly discovered that students are willing to study anything if it relates to food. I could use food as an entry point to teach the principles of digestive physiology, the biochemistry of metabolism, and how nutrients function in health. And I could also use food to teach how governments regulate, the principles and practices of democratic societies, and anything else I wanted to about history, sociology, anthropology, or just about any other disciplinary area of study. Food, as my NYU department likes to explain, is a lens through which to view and analyze the most important political, economic, and cultural problems facing today's globalized world. And students, we professors soon find out, eat it up.

In 1996, a far-sighted dean at New York University took a leap of faith and allowed my department (known, amazingly, as Home Economics until 1990) to begin offering undergraduate, master's, and doctoral programs in Food Studies. Only one other such program existed at the time, the Julia Child–inspired Gastronomy program at Boston University. Rather than Gastronomy, we chose to name our program Food Studies in a deliberate effort to command the academic respectability afforded to other NYU "studies" programs—Women's Studies, Liberal Studies, Media Studies, French Studies, and Africana Studies, for example.

A set of programs in hotel management had just been transferred from the department to another school at NYU, leaving a large tuition gap. I had been traveling for some years with a group of food writers, chefs, and academics and could feel their hunger—a frequent and appropriate metaphor in *Books That Cook*—for credible, research-based information about the history of food and about food itself. Academics and their graduate students yearned for more rigorous training in the analysis and interpretation of the role of food in society, approached from their various disciplinary perspectives. With the help of an outside advisory committee (always a useful idea at academic institutions), I was able to convince the dean to let us try to make Food Studies work.

It worked, so much so that the food revolution has caught up with Food Studies. Food Studies is as much a part of today's food movement as are the organic, locavore, and small farm movements. Collectively, these movements feel like an avalanche, with Food Studies scholars racing to stay far enough ahead to make sense of it. I cannot keep count of the number of universities housing one or another food program offered by almost any conceivable discipline, many of these programs attached to flourishing organic gardens. I certainly cannot count the books. Our special collections library at NYU now houses fifty-five thousand cookbooks and other writings about food, all acquired within a period of just eight years. And we are by no means alone in taking food texts seriously.

Literature departments have been among the last academic disciplines to figure this out, often viewing food as too common, too populist, too quotidian, and, perhaps, too feminine to be worthy of serious study. Food Studies scholars all too frequently hear their research interests questioned—"Why would you want to study that?"—or dismissed summarily as "It's just food." Never mind that food constitutes a business generating more than a trillion dollars a year in the United States alone. Never mind that the most important public health problems affecting humanity have to do with the consumption of too little or too much food. And never mind the intense emotional and symbolic attachment that people of any culture and nationality feel about the food they consume and incorporate directly into their bodies.

Books That Cook brings the food revolution into the study of English literature—brilliantly, deftly, and with no apologies. No apologies are needed. As editors Jennifer Cognard-Black and Melissa A. Goldthwaite explain, Food Studies necessarily encompasses literature. Basic food texts—cookbooks and recipes—are as much a form of literature as are fiction, nonfiction, memoirs, and poetry. And why not? They tell stories. They convey myths. They are replete with drama, symbolic meaning, and psychological insight. Furthermore, they offer plenty to talk about: culture, religion, ethics, personal identity, and anything else that it means to be human. That food generates profound literary memories is famously known from what ensued after Marcel Proust dipped his madeleine in tea.

Writers of all times have used food memories to spark traditional literary texts. Today, we view cookbooks and recipes as equally worthy of literary analysis. Even recipes? As the editors explain,

> Like an instruction manual, the recipe is a how-to text, explaining the organization of a space (a kitchen), the acquisition of tools and materials (implements and ingredients), and the step-by-step process by which a reader (the cook) can synthesize these materials into a finished product (the dish). Yet the recipe is also intentionally collaborative. The text does not have full meaning until a reader puts the recipe in motion through cooking and then brings that food to a common table. . . . When a food is shared and eaten, the reader actually embodies the text.

In the selection from Alice B. Toklas's work in *Books That Cook,* she says—one hopes ironically—"As if a cookbook had anything to do with writing." As *Books That Cook* demonstrates, cookbooks and other quotidian writings about food have *everything* to do with the deeper meanings of expressed language, so much so that readers can interpret these selections on any number of levels: as English texts ripe for close textual analysis, as deeply moving fiction or memoir, as a way to learn about life, as suggestions for what to cook for dinner, or just as a pleasant way to pass time. You can even parse these writings as grammar, beginning with the declensions of the verb *to pie* given in the instructive selection from the *Anarchist Cookbook.* Food writing, as Kate Moses makes clear in her piece about Sylvia Plath, fiercely connects the life of the body to the life of the mind.

The pieces in *Books That Cook,* arranged as they are in menu sequence, have much to tell us about how and why what we eat as children so strongly influences our lives and how what we eat as adults cuts to our deepest emotions. The editors have selected riveting pieces by classic and contemporary writers who reflect more than the usual range of ethnicities, nationalities, and perspectives and whose work illustrates unique themes as well as those common to all.

The selections here point out the literary qualities—the poetry—in the most mundane aspects of food production and consumption, as well as their greater meaning. Bread is not just bread, as Sharon Olds tells us; it is "the having, the tasting, the giving of life." These writings collectively argue for the human hunger and passion for narrative as well as sustenance. We yearn for stories about what we are eating. Witness Sara Roahen's memoir of her post-Katrina exile from New Orleans: "Food without a narrative just tasted like food. . . . I was lost."

The editors suggest that you sample these writings as you might sample the dishes from a buffet or smorgasbord, taking them in small bites every now and then. But I, for one, could not put this book down. Never having thought about food writing in quite this way before, I was inspired by *Books That Cook*. My own scholarship, built on declarative sentences about the effects of industrial food systems on human health and welfare is, at first blush, far afield from the prose and poetry in this collection. But when I said that "our overabundant food system gives most of us the opportunity to make a political statement every time we eat—and to make a difference," I would now add writing to the list of interventions that food advocates can make.

Books That Cook propels the food movement and in doing so makes a political as well as a literary statement. It makes a difference. Read it. Savor the writings. Delight in them. Think about them. And if they inspire you to do your own writing about food, so much the better.

New York University, 1 May 2013

Marion Nestle

Paulette Goddard Professor of Nutrition,
Food Studies, and Public Health

ACKNOWLEDGMENTS

No book is possible without the assistance, care, diligence, and friendship of others. In particular, we would like to thank our editors, Eric Zinner and Alicia Nadkarni, at New York University Press as well as Dorothea Stillman Halliday (our managing editor), Andrew Katz (our copyeditor), and Charles Boyd Hames (our layout designer) for their good humor and hard work in bringing this project to fruition; Marilyn Moller and Heather Lundine for seeing the promise of this project in its early stages; Marion Nestle for her generosity of time and spirit; Sue Johnson for allowing us to use her whimsical culinary art; Anne Cognard and Beth Burke Davis for their typing prowess; and the anonymous reviewers, who provided thoughtful and enthusiastic reviews.

We are also grateful to English Department faculty and administrators of St. Mary's College of Maryland and Saint Joseph's University who have supported this project in a number of ways. We both received faculty development money, and Jennifer also received release time from teaching. Moreover, our department chairs make sure that our Books That Cook seminars are in regular rotation.

We appreciate Bill Kloefkorn, April Lindner, Michael S. Glaser, Karen Leona Anderson, Caroline M. Grant, Howard Dinin, Tenaya Darlington, Paul Hanstedt, Kathy Fagan, Caitlin Newcomer, and Cheryl Quimba for writing original pieces for this collection.

We also offer our deep thanks to friends and colleagues Carrie Patterson, Doug Toti, Christine Adams, Chuck Holden, Tom Barrett, Liisa Franzen, Adrianna Brodsky, Gail Savage, Alan and Sabine Dillingham, Kate Chandler, Ruth Feingold, Jeff Hammond, Karen Anderson, Jerry Gabriel, Ben Click, Robin and Julia Bates, Jennifer Tickle, Holly Blumner, Jackie and Alan Paskow, Betül Basaran, Sybol and Lane Anderson, Brandi Stanton, Libby Nutt Williams, Colby Caldwell, Gabriela Bulisova, Christine Bergmark, Brett Grohsgal, Lisa and Michael Kelley, Tucker Grube-O'Brien, Elina Snyder, Carole Greenwood, Elsa Walsh, Joan

Nathan, Joan and Alex Murray, Helen Jacobsen, Joanna Murray, Maureen Stanton, Michael Glaser, Rich Fusco, April Lindner, Kathy Akerley, and Jennifer Isherwood for their encouragement, advice, magnanimity, good food and large hearts.

We are additionally grateful to Andrea A. Lunsford for her indefatigable support and affection.

Our families have also contributed to this project, both directly and indirectly. Anne and Roger Cognard provided monetary, editorial, and (of greatest importance) spiritual support; Lora Black and Elizabeth and Craig MacLeod Walls gave personal contributions to help sustain this project, while Elizabeth also offered advice and pep talks over many a glass of wine. Ruth, Paul, Laura, Shawn, Emily, and Hannah Goldthwaite have been the life and laughter of numerous shared meals.

Finally, Jennifer is especially grateful to her spouse, Andrew, and daughter, Katharine Cognard-Black, for their daily acts of kindness and of love, especially Kate's delicious kitchen "creations" and the many cups of coffee that Andrew offered while Jennifer wrote. Melissa wishes to acknowledge her spouse, Howard Dinin, who cooks for her daily and nourishes her with delicious food, good company, and engaging conversation—and love to her sweet and constant canine companion, Artemis, who shares it all.

Cooking the Book

An Introduction to *Books That Cook*

JENNIFER COGNARD-BLACK AND MELISSA A. GOLDTHWAITE

> The act of reading is always a matter of a task begun as much as of a message understood, something that begins on a flat surface, counter or page, and then gets stirred and chopped and blended until what we make, in the end, is a dish, or story, all our own.
>
> —Adam Gopnik, "Cooked Books"

As a character from Peter Elbling's *The Food Taster* observes, "The joy of eating is like the joy of learning, for each feast is like a book. The dishes are words to be savored, enjoyed, and digested" (130).

The opposite, too, is true: the joy of learning is like eating, and words are dishes to be savored.

We have organized *Books That Cook* in the form of a cookbook, from an invocation to the final toast, from starters to desserts. As such, each section begins with part of an influential American cookbook, included chronologically to show the development of this genre. All literatures of food are indebted to the form and purpose of cookbooks, and, thus, the literary works within each section should be read as an extension of the cookbooks, while the cookbook excerpts should be understood as pieces of literature: as forms of storytelling and memory making all their own. Each section, too, includes an assortment of poetry, nonfiction, and fiction, with every selection offering at least one recipe. In our inclusions, we have sought to show the range of ways in which authors employ recipes, whether the recipe is in service of the story or the story serves to contextualize the recipe.

Why recipes? Why offer a collection of food writing that embeds bona fide recipes in each and every piece? Put simply, because recipes are far more than a set of instructions on how to make a dish. As Janet Floyd and Laurel Forster maintain in *The Recipe Reader*, "Food and cookery are crucial elements in all cultures. . . . The work of cooking and the texts that represent that work to us, situated as they are between the purchase of food and its consumption, can scarcely be less important to our sense of identity and shared values than food itself" (1). Recipes are culture keepers as well as culture makers. They both organize and express human memory.

Recipes as Cultural Texts

The word *recipe* comes from the Latin verb *recipere*, which means both "to give" and "to receive"; and, in fact, this dual function of giving and receiving is rooted in the form of the recipe itself. A recipe is almost always broken into three sections: an ingredient list, a set of instructions, and additional information on serving the dish. As a result, a recipe is both a handbook and a shared act of creation.

Like an instruction manual, the recipe is a how-to text, explaining the organization of a space (most often, a kitchen), the acquisition of tools and materials (implements and ingredients), and the step-by-step process by which a reader (the cook) can synthesize these materials into a finished product (the dish). Yet the recipe is also intentionally collaborative. The text does not have full meaning until a reader puts the recipe in motion through cooking and then brings that food to a common table. This act of sharing one's knowledge of cookery so that a reader may receive a certain dish does not simply pass through the written word. When a food is shared and eaten, the reader actually embodies the text. The reader consumes the author's culinary learning, incorporating this wisdom at the cellular level. In this way, it is not just a metaphor to say a recipe is "consumed," or read, by a reader, and it is significant that the reader's own body is altered as a result of reading and eating the text. In a very real sense, then, a recipe reader becomes that recipe: she breathes it, her heart beats it, and thus the text is known both by the mind and by the body.

In addition to changing the sum and substance of a reader, a recipe provides information beyond mere data. Whether written on notecards, published in cookbooks, or posted online, recipes contain food traditions, where culture and history are transmitted as well as transformed. Practices of sharing, preparing, and eating food create and convey human interaction. As a result, recipes reveal that food and foodways are both elastic and contradictory. For instance, a recipe can symbolize birth and/or death. Not only can it be a record of a cake made for a christening or potatoes prepared for a funeral; if the recipe itself was written by someone who is now dead, when the dish is prepared, the deceased author lives again in the food waiting on a descendant's plate. A recipe also can represent the natural as well as the artificial. Consider the difference between a homegrown and whole-food ingredient such as a peach versus the ingredient called for in many peach-pie recipes: one Michael Pollan has dubbed a "foodlike substance," that is, artificial vanilla extract made off the New Jersey turnpike by a flavorist in a commercial lab (1).

Indeed, a recipe can convey a host of cultural contradictions, from health and poison to war and peace, to surfeit and hunger, to art and commodity. Recipes are multifaceted in terms of their content, and yet they are also complex in their purpose. They reflect the intricacies of the cooks and eaters who exchange, use, and enjoy them.

Cookbooks as Literature

While we preserve personal recipes by recording them, sharing them, and eventually collecting them in containers such as a recipe box, even these measures will ultimately fail if the goal is to maintain the recipes for longer than one or two generations. In most cases, individual recipe cards and even community cookbooks are not consistently preserved in library archives. Inevitably, then, published cookbooks are the best way for culinary memory to be collected and retained, even after the authors are long dead.

In North America, the first published recipes appeared in cookbooks such as Eliza Smith's 1742 *Compleat Housewife*, believed to be the first cookbook printed in America, although it was written by an English author. The first cookbook written by an American was Amelia Simmons's *American Cookery*, published in 1796. Simmons, a domestic worker herself and so a woman who had firsthand knowledge of cookery, wanted to produce a book specifically for a Colonial audience, with attention paid to American tastes, ingredients, and necessities. Originally self-published,

Simmons's book was inexpensive, selling for only two shillings, three pence—a price that, as modern-day editor Mary Wilson points out, "justified its purchase even in homes where the family income would permit the buying of little printed matter besides the yearly almanac" (xi).

Simmons attempted to adapt recipes "to this Country"—including five "receipts" using Native American cornmeal, the inclusion of a "pompkin" pudding (or what we would now recognize as "pumpkin pie"), still another recipe for "brewing Spruce Beer," and the inclusion of the "Jerusalem artichoke" among the book's "Directions for . . . Procuring the Best Viands, Fish, &c."—a North American root vegetable that Julia Child eventually dedicated twelve pages to in *Mastering the Art of French Cooking* (Wilson xi–xiii).

Simmons's "receipts" do not look much like recipes we see in modern cookbooks, although they do have certain elements that define the genre and convey what is meant by eighteenth-century cookery. For instance, here is Simmons's recipe for Pompkin Pudding:

> Pompkin.
>
> No. 1. One quart stewed and strained, 3 pints cream, 9 beaten eggs, sugar, mace, nutmeg and ginger, laid into paste No. 7 or 3, and with a dough spur, cross and chequer it, and baked in dishes three quarters of an hour.
>
> No. 2. One quart of milk, 1 pint pompkin, 4 eggs, molasses, allspice and ginger in a crust, bake 1 hour.

This recipe is organized by offering two variations (labeled "No. 1" and "No. 2") and starts with a list of ingredients (notably an artery-clogging "9 beaten eggs"). Then, Simmons adds a few spare instructions on how to prepare said ingredients (by "crossing" and "chequering" the dough) and finishes with precise information on how to bake the pudding ("in dishes [for] three quarters of an hour"). This form reveals that Simmons's readers were Enlightenment thinkers: they appreciated both a rational approach and one that employed a specialized language ("stewing," "straining," "beating," "crossing," and "chequering"). As such, these choices distinguish this recipe as coming from a Colonial kitchen.

Yet beyond the form, this recipe also conveys traditional domesticity; relies on the idea that a pudding may be manufactured in precise and consistent ways, which suggests values instilled by the Industrial

Revolution; uses spices that reveal an imperial economy; and appropriates a Native American method for baking squashes into pielike breads. As a cultural symbol—specifically as a symbol of America, especially once pumpkin pie became a traditional part of Thanksgiving dinners—this brief eighteenth-century recipe conveys a tremendous amount of content and context. And even Simmons's short text is starting to sound a bit literary—part of a kind of culinary declaration of independence. In *Books That Cook*, the selection from Simmons demonstrates that her intended readers are literate women whom she imagines as national mothers raising the republic's future citizens. Her preface advises these women on how to cultivate and maintain a virtuous character while, in the words of cookbook historian Janet Theophano, "promot[ing] the egalitarian ideals of the new republic . . . [and enticing] her readers with an intimate glimpse of the good life by revealing upper-class culinary secrets" (233).

In addition to this beginning selection from Simmons, *Books That Cook* provides tidbits from other American cookbooks that mirror the changes in cooks and cookbook writers from the eighteenth century to the present day. With Lydia Maria Child's *American Frugal Housewife*, we move from the Colonial period to the early Victorian and see a new interest in working-class cooks. Dedicated to "those who are not ashamed of economy," the *Frugal Housewife* is built on a Franklinian sense of self-improvement as well as the abiding nineteenth-century interest in reform, offering penny-pinching advice ranging from conserving fire in bread baking to preparing and eating the heart, head, and neck of given animals. Lydia Maria Child charges her women readers to be thrifty cooks and housekeepers but also to serve as models of morality for their families, enjoining them to "prove, by the exertion of ingenuity and economy, that neatness, good taste, and gentility, are attainable without great expense."

At the end of the nineteenth century, when Fannie Merritt Farmer's *Boston Cooking-School Cook Book* was published, American cookery books changed once again, this time in favor of the new nutritionism. With a focus on the chemical makeup of the human body and the discovery of certain constituents of food such as calories, carbohydrates, and fat, nutritionism took hold of America at the same time that all kinds of national institutions became professionalized, from medicine to academe, the law, and cooking. In the section of Farmer's cookbook provided here, it is evident that she is interested in a scientific kind of precision, likening the kitchen to a laboratory and its products to fuel. With her mantra to adopt level measurements for all recipes, Farmer revolutionized the basic form of American cookbooks and popularized scientific cookery, in which a cook's job is to follow each recipe to the letter rather than engage in her own kind of kitchen magic.

In turn, Irma Rombauer's 1931 *Joy of Cooking* is an interesting fusion of scientific cookery and the earlier, chattier, reform-based American cookbooks by Simmons and Lydia Maria Child. In Rombauer's introduction, she writes, "In spite of the fact that the book is compiled with one eye on the family purse and the other on the bathroom scale, there are, of course, occasional lapses into indulgence" (n.p.). Note Rombauer's nod to Child's insistence on thrift, Farmer's devotion to measurement, and Simmons's conversational, even confessional, voice (admitting here to a delight in culinary indulgence). Rombauer's recipes, on the other hand, are mostly functional rather than conversational. The how-to of Farmer's scientific recipes is reflected in Rombauer's no-nonsense advice, which simultaneously empowers the reader to cook meticulous dishes while keeping the authority of authorship squarely with Rombauer herself.

In 1961, with the publication of *Mastering the Art of French Cooking*, American cookery became Frenchified. Not only that, but everyday cooking moved from the page to the stage, with Julia Child showing her viewers step-by-step how to cook Americanized French dishes through the wildly popular PBS television show *The French Chef*. Through these dual media, Child captivated middle-class Americans with the idea of *haute cuisine*, including a revived appreciation of fresh, whole foods. "The French are interested in vegetables as food rather than as purely nutrient objects," she explains in *Mastering*. Child continues, "The French objective is to produce a cooked green vegetable so green, fresh-tasting, and full of flavor that it really can be served as a separate course" (421). After two hundred episodes of *The French Chef* and sales of 1.4 million cookbooks by 1974, Child came to epitomize the chef celeb. With Julia Child, American food writing gave birth to the modern-day foodie: a middle-class American with a particular interest in food as a form of gastronomic poetry.

The final cookbook selection in *Books That Cook* is from Alice Waters's *Chez Panisse Menu Cookbook*, another innovative and best-selling cookbook that builds on Julia Child's insistence on using fresh, local, seasonal foods. When Waters opened her Berkeley restaurant Chez

Panisse in 1971, she did not realize the resonating effect it would have on American food politics. Crafting menus around local produce grown by California farmers and emphasizing dishes created out of seasonal, organic foods, Waters transformed American kitchens yet again. In the words of food historian Andrew F. Smith, Waters "joined fine cooking with community activism, supporting local farmers, organic food, sustainable agriculture, and other causes. Cooking is, in her view, a product of agriculture as well as a part of culture" (261). In 1996, Waters founded the Chez Panisse Foundation, which created, most notably, the Edible Schoolyard—a nationwide program where public-school children learn how to plant, harvest, cook, and eat their own food. With Waters, then, the cookbook selections of *Books That Cook* come full circle. In 1976, Waters stopped writing her Chez Panisse menus in French—thereby celebrating a specifically American cuisine as Simmons had two hundred years before. And Waters's belief that food is both political and nourishing echoes Lydia Maria Child's interest in sustaining the spiritual and everyday lives of women and their families as well as human bodies.

Menus for Reading

In *Chez Panisse Menu Cookbook,* Alice Waters writes, "Marrying the elements of a meal correctly so as to achieve that elusive equilibrium requires an understanding of each separate course and its importance within the overall structure of the menu" (9). *Books That Cook* is deliberately organized so that readers can achieve their own equilibrium between the individual selections and their overall experience of the collection. Both the structure of a menu cookbook and the inclusion of specific recipes within selections allow readers to dig in at any point in the book. Perhaps the title of a selection, such as Ellen Meloy's "Eat Your Pets," piques your interest, or perhaps Nora Ephron's "Potatoes and Love: Some Reflections" is more to your taste. You might choose a serving of poetry from each section, or perhaps you are hungry for eggs and decide to read that entire section from beginning to end. Individual taste in literature can be as idiosyncratic as one's taste in food, and *Books That Cook* allows readers to indulge such tastes with little concern for chronological sense making.

Yet this book also lends itself well to creating careful menus: literary meals to eat oneself or to serve to others, perhaps in a classroom. Menus, writes Sara Dickerman, "are a literature of control. Menu language, with its hyphens, quotation marks, and random outbursts of foreign words, serves less to describe food than to manage your expectations." We believe the structure of a menu speaks especially well to pedagogical aims—for like a recipe, a menu is also a cultural text. A menu has a structure that is immediately recognizable, one that links form to function. Yet a menu is not merely "functional," a way by which food may be organized in space and across time. It is also cultural. When an eater sits down to a meal and is handed a menu, he or she is handed a set of social assumptions (perhaps that meat precedes chocolate—i.e., that savory comes before sweet), an indication of ethnicity (in Europe, salads are often eaten after a meat or a fish course, while a cheese course is often included near the end of a meal), a class marker (is the menu in French?), and an expression of gender (depending on whether the menu is from a professional restaurant or an amateur kitchen), as well as a set of instructions on how the eater should imagine the meal.

Making selections in order to create a meal for yourself and others can be a personal process—one in which you decide what you are in the mood for or consider the tastes and dietary needs of your guests; yet in putting together this collection, we have taken into account several ways in which the readings might be organized to create a satisfying literary meal. You might, for example, read or assign each genre separately, charting the historical development of the cookbook genre; paying attention to metaphor, image, sound, and line breaks in poetry; understanding the ways food is used in fiction to develop character, setting, and plot; or considering speaker, tone, and the function of memory in nonfiction. You might analyze the readings rhetorically for voice, emotional and logical appeals, form, and style. You might also note connections between individual selections, such as the way in which Amelia Simmons's *American Cookery* has inspired Karen Leona Anderson's "Recipe: Gingerbread." In addition, several selections, including David Citino's "The Poet in the Kitchen" and Kate Moses's "Baking for Sylvia," demonstrate the mutually sustaining practices of cooking and writing.

Another way to sample these selections is to consider the ways in which readers are addressed or included: for instance, does the writer use the second person, talking to the reader directly as Ted Kooser does in "How to Make Rhubarb Wine"? Many of the pieces in *Books That Cook* guide readers through the process of actually cooking a dish. For a book club or in a class, then, these pieces might be compared and the recipes followed, the creations shared and consumed. In what way does a first-person speaker, such as Laurie Colwin in "Repulsive Dinners: A Memoir," invite identification? Do such personal memories evoke recollections for the reader as well? What is the effect of third-person narration, such as Fannie Flagg uses in the selection from *Fried Green Tomatoes at the Whistle Stop Cafe*?

Yet another way to approach *Books That Cook* is to do so topically or in terms of major themes. For example, one hallmark of American food writing is cultural diversity: immigration; the effects of travel and trade; the realities of living at a particular time in a particular place and ecosystem; gender, racial, ethnic, and cultural differences—all of these elements affect not only the foods we eat but our ways of understanding ourselves and our communities. Many of the selections here reflect the diversity evident in American food writing, even if that writing—such as Alice B. Toklas's "The Vegetable Gardens at Bilignin"—is set outside the literal boundaries of the nation itself.

What follows as a close to our introduction, then, is a series of sample reading menus for themed literary meals. These "menus" are not exhaustively representative of our selections but are meant just as a taste to whet your appetite.

Sample Reading Menus

Food and the Environment

"An Unspoken Hunger" by Terry Tempest Williams
"Eat Your Pets" by Ellen Meloy
"How to Make Stew in the Pinacate Desert: Recipe for Locke and Drum" by Gary Snyder
"Spirit-Fried No-Name River Brown Trout: A Recipe" by David James Duncan
"Summer Salad" by Melissa A. Goldthwaite

Cultural Critique

"All It Took Was a Road / Surprises of Urban Renewal" by Ntozake Shange
"American Liver Mush" by Ravi Shankar

"Eat Your Pets" by Ellen Meloy
"13/16" by Sherman Alexie
"Pie Throwing" by CrimethInc. Ex-Workers' Collective

Ethnic and Cultural Identity

"Puffballs: Finding the Inside" by Thomas Fox Averill
"Recipe: Gingerbread" by Karen Leona Anderson
"All It Took Was a Road / Surprises of Urban Renewal" by Ntozake Shange
"Turkey Bone Gumbo" by Sara Roahen
"Boiled Chicken Feet and Hundred-Year-Old Eggs" by Shirley Geok-Lin Lim
"13/16" by Sherman Alexie
"The Vegetable Gardens at Bilignin" by Alice B. Toklas
"Reception" by Kathy Fagan
"Repulsive Dinners: A Memoir" by Laurie Colwin
"The Demystification of Food" by Vertamae Smart-Grosvenor
"How to Cook Moong Dal, Bengali Style" by Deborah Thompson
"Food and Belonging: At 'Home' and in 'Alien Kitchens'" by Ketu H. Katrak
"Suman sa Ibos" by Cheryl Quimba

Love and Desire

"To Cèpe, with Love (or, The Alchemy of Longing)" by E. J. Levy
"An Unspoken Hunger" by Terry Tempest Williams
"Whistle Stop, Alabama" by Fannie Flagg
The Food Taster by Peter Elbling
"Reception" by Kathy Fagan
"Potatoes and Love: Some Reflections" by Nora Ephron
"Burn" by Jennifer Cognard-Black

How-To Poems

"Full Moon Soup with Snow" by April Lindner
"Coriander and Carrot" by Michael S. Glaser
"The Poem of Chicken Breast with Fettuccine" by David Citino
"How to Make Rhubarb Wine" by Ted Kooser

Living, Dying, and the Dead

"In Nancy's Kitchen" by Caroline M. Grant
"Making the Perfect Fried Egg Sandwich" by Howard Dinin
"Baking for Sylvia" by Kate Moses
"Pie" by Judith Moore
"Funeral Food" by Michael Lee West

Family Relationships

"Porkchop Gravy" by Bill Kloefkorn
Delights and Prejudices by James Beard
"Bread" by Sharon Olds
The Food Taster by Peter Elbling
"H Is for Happy" by M. F. K. Fisher
"Poison Egg" by Tenaya Darlington
"Half-Life" by Paul Hanstedt
"The Poet in the Kitchen" by David Citino
"A Good Roast Chicken" by Theresa Lust
"How to Cook Moong Dal, Bengali Style" by Deborah Thompson
"Food and Belonging: At 'Home' and in 'Alien Kitchens'" by Ketu H. Katrak
"All the Old Tales Are Tales of Hunger" by Caitlin Newcomer
"Suman sa Ibos" by Cheryl Quimba
"The Assurance of Caramel Cake" by Maya Angelou

Over four hundred years ago, Francis Bacon wrote, "Some books are to be tasted, others to be swallowed, and some few to be chewed and digested" (171). We invite you now to the table of *Books That Cook* in hopes that you will chew and digest this particular book that does, indeed, cook.

Eat. Savor. Enjoy. And as Julia Child would say, *Bon appétit*!

WORKS CITED

Bacon, Francis. "Of Studies." *The Essays or Counsels Civil and Moral*. 1597. London: Whittaker, 1851. 170–172.

Child, Julia. *Mastering the Art of French Cooking*. 1966. New York: Knopf, 2001.

Child, Lydia Maria. *The American Frugal Housewife*. 1832. Project Gutenberg. 18 September 2004. 10 October 2010. <http://www.gutenberg.org/dirs/1/3/4/9/13493/13493.txt>.

Dickerman, Sara. "Eat Your Words: A Guide to Menu English." *Slate* 29 April 2003. 5 January 2011. <http://www.slate.com/id/2082098/>.

Elbling, Peter. *The Food Taster*. New York: Plume, 2003.

Farmer, Fannie Merritt. *Boston Cooking-School Cookbook*. Boston: Little, Brown, 1896.

Floyd, Janet, and Laurel Forster. *The Recipe Reader: Narratives–Contexts–Traditions*. Aldershot, UK: Ashgate, 2003.

Gopnik, Adam. "Cooked Books: Real Food from Fictional Recipes." *New Yorker* 83.7 (9 April 2007): 80–85.

Pollan, Michael. *In Defense of Food: An Eater's Manifesto*. New York: Penguin, 2009.

Rombauer, Irma S. *The Joy of Cooking: A Compilation of Reliable Recipes with a Casual Culinary Chat*. 1931. New York: Scribner, 1998.

Simmons, Amelia. *American Cookery*. 1796. Project Gutenberg. 4 July 2004. 10 October 2012. <http://www.gutenberg.org/cache/epub/12815/pg12815.html>.

Smith, Andrew F. *Eating History: Thirty Turning Points in the Making of American Cuisine*. New York: Columbia University Press, 2009.

Theophano, Janet. *Eat My Words: Reading Women's Lives through the Cookbooks They Wrote*. New York: Palgrave, 2002.

Waters, Alice. *Chez Panisse Menu Cookbook*. New York: Random House, 1982.

Wilson, Mary Tolford. Introduction. *The First American Cookbook: A Facsimile of "American Cookery," 1796, by Amelia Simmons*. New York: Dover, 1984. vii–xiii.

Invocation

1

Porkchop Gravy

An Invocation

BILL KLOEFKORN

Not alone the blend of corn oil and flour and drippings,
and browned bits flaked from the chops, but
also the movement of the tablespoon in the hand

of your mother, movement and spoon and mother no less
ingredients than oil and flour, drippings and
bits, you beside her not yet a man but a boy tall enough

to watch the movement of the spoon, tall enough to see
the mixture in the black cast-iron skillet
blending, sizzling and blending, your mother with her

free hand feeding the fire with small sticks you gathered
this morning, not alone the sticks, but also
the elm and the walnut the dead limbs fell from, and

likewise the patience it takes for the blending, sizzle and
pop and your mother's thick hand moving
the spoon in a circle, mother in a sky-blue apron

not seeming to know you are there, or if knowing, not
minding, until it is time for the adding
of milk from a clear glass pitcher, not alone the milk

but also the udder from which the milk derived, milk-

white milk flowing slowly into the mixture
of oil and flour, drippings and bits and pieces, steam

rising aromatic and warm, small bubbles forming and
bursting, patience sustained until the milk
and the mixture begin to thicken, and your mother—

she's humming now, humming a tune you have heard
so many, many times, but can't remember
the name of—slows down the stirring, slows it and

slows it until she knows what the boy doesn't, that it's
time, precisely, for the delicate process
to end, time to give way to what the boy has been

waiting so long for: faces in a circle at the table,
the hesitation, the nod.
The beginning.

PART I

Starters

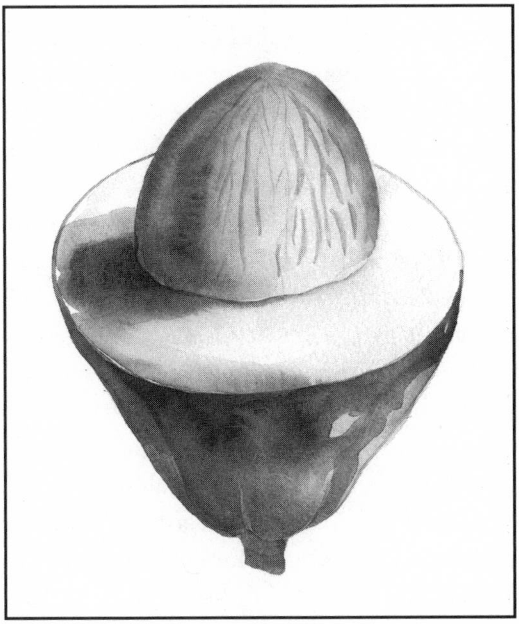

From the ancient Greeks serving bits of fish, cheese, and olives to stimulate diners' appetites to early twentieth-century hosts and hostesses offering bite-sized hors d'oeuvres along with drinks at cocktail parties, starters have long been a part of culinary history, and such traditions continue to this day. Nearly every culture has incorporated some kind of starter into its traditional diet—from Middle Eastern bowls of hummus and baba ghanoush to Italian plates of olives, cured meats, and grilled vegetables. Americans have adopted and adapted many of these traditions.

Hors d'oeuvres, however, have not always been just starters. From the seventeenth through mid-nineteenth centuries, especially in France but also in America, small plates of food remained on the table throughout the meal. For formal meals later in the nineteenth century, more elaborate hors d'oeuvres were often served either before or after the soup, though some foods—such as nuts and celery—continued to remain on the table.

Most American cookbooks from the eighteenth and nineteenth centuries, though they include recipes for soup, do not feature chapters on hors d'oeuvres. Amelia Simmons, whose 1796 book begins this section, starts out with many recipes for fish and meat rather than soups or other small tidbits—since animal flesh was deemed, by the first American settlers, the most important daily foodstuff other than bread. Fifty years later, however, Mary Randolph does begin her 1824 *Virginia Housewife, or, Methodical Cook* with soups. Jumping ahead to the end of the nineteenth century, most of the recommended menus at the end of Fannie Merritt Farmer's 1896 *Boston Cooking-School Cook Book* also begin with soup, and she provides a few menus for full-course dinners as well. For her sample twelve-course meal, for instance, she recommends starting with "Little Neck Clams or Bluepoints, with brown-bread sandwiches" before moving on to the soup, after which radishes, celery, almonds, or olives might be passed.[1] In other words, the Victorians were the ones to popularize the idea of small-plate or soup starters (though not salads), largely because the new middle class could afford to do so.

By the twentieth century, ideas for starters grew from traditional offerings of soups, clams, and oysters to more elaborate creations. In Irma Rombauer's first 1931 edition of *The Joy of Cooking,* she includes a whole chapter on hors d'oeuvres, offering various recipes for aspic salads, stuffed eggs, and oysters—a modest offering. Less than a decade later, in 1940, James Beard published his first book, *Hors d'Oeuvre and Canapés*—a collection completely devoted to cocktail-party fare, ranging from open-faced sandwiches to a variety of spreads. Later in the twentieth century, Martha Stewart took hors d'oeuvres to a whole other level, seeking to make them as attractive in appearance as they are delicious to eat. She recommended creating tiny cups from grapes, cherry tomatoes, and other fruits and vegetables; arranging edible flowers on the table; and being attentive to every imaginable detail. Her belief that hors d'oeuvres are like tiny jewels demonstrates the painstaking attention some of her recipes and presentations require. Just glancing through her books devoted to hors d'oeuvres, it is impossible not to notice an abundance of photographs of tables laden with elaborate, tiny portions of food.

Although "starters" can refer to appetizers, hors d'oeuvres, and soups (i.e., any first course of a meal), in this section we use this term and category more broadly to include the starting place for meal preparation (securing one's ingredients), as evidenced by the selection from Amelia Simmons's *American Cookery,* which provides meticulous guidance for choosing meat, poultry, and fish, and by the chapter from Thomas Fox Averill's novel, which provides a recipe for hunting puffballs, a kind of mushroom. Averill's fiction highlights real-life concerns: knowing the very basics about where food comes from and how to determine whether it is nutritious or poisonous are important starting places. E. J. Levy, too, writes of foraging mushrooms, and she links this practice to courtship, metaphorically tying the mushroom hunt to the risks and pleasures of new relationships: a different kind of "starter." And we see a similar theme—the risks of desire and relationships—in Terry Tempest Williams's "An Unspoken Hunger."

We also use "starters" to refer to memories of first foods. James Beard begins his memoir *Delights and Prejudices* by recalling the tastes of his childhood, especially razor clams and other seafood, which lead him to offer several recipes for clam chowder. He also recollects his earliest taste memory: when he was three, suffering from malaria, and his mother made him chicken jelly—a starting moment that was as pivotal for him as a Proustian madeleine, structuring and defining his life as a man who tastes food as well as one with good taste. As Beard writes, "The ability to recall a taste sensation, which I think of as 'taste memory,' is a God-given talent, akin to perfect pitch, which makes your life richer if you possess it. If you aren't born with it, you can never seem to acquire it."

Most of the recipes included in this section, though, are what modern cooks think of when they hear the word "starters": soups that can be served as a first course—such as Thomas Fox Averill's yucca soup; April Lindner's "full moon soup with snow," which illuminates the conditions under which it might be prepared; and Michael S. Glaser's coriander and carrot soup—or appetizers, such as Terry Tempest Williams's avocado with salsa and chilies or E. J. Levy's creamed morels on chive butter toast. Symbolically, all of these soups and appetizers signal beginnings: a coming-of-age for a young chef, the root vegetables of the old year brought into the new, or the start of a love affair. As such, we offer readers a number of options for how to begin to whet their literary appetite: some savory, some sweet; some more traditional and others quite experimental.

NOTE

1. Fannie Merritt Farmer, *Boston Cooking-School Cook Book* (Boston: Little, Brown, 1896), 520.

→ 2 ←

From *American Cookery*

AMELIA SIMMONS

Preface

As this treatise is calculated for the improvement of the rising generation of *Females* in America, the Lady of fashion and fortune will not be displeased, if many hints are suggested for the more general and universal knowledge of those females in this country, who by the loss of their parents, or other unfortunate circumstances, are reduced to the necessity of going into families in the line of domestics, or taking refuge with their friends or relations, and doing those things which are really essential to the perfecting them as good wives, and useful members of society.* The orphan, tho' left to the care of virtuous guardians, will find it essentially necessary to have an opinion and determination of her own. The world, and the fashion thereof, is so variable, that old people cannot accommodate themselves to the various changes and fashions which daily occur; *they* will adhere to the fashion of *their* day, and will not surrender their attachments to the *good old way*—while the young and the gay, bend and conform readily to the taste of the times, and fancy of the hour. By having an opinion and determination, I would not be understood to mean an obstinate perseverance in trifles, which borders on obstinacy—by no means, but only an adherence to those rules and maxims which have stood the test of ages, and will forever establish the *female character*, a virtuous character—altho' they conform to the ruling taste of the age in cookery, dress, language, manners, &c.

It must ever remain a check upon the poor solitary orphan, that while those females who have parents, or brothers, or riches, to defend their

* Nonstandard, eighteenth-century spelling within this selection has been left untouched.

indiscretions, that the orphan must depend solely upon *character*. How immensely important, therefore, that every action, every word, every thought, be regulated by the strictest purity, and that every movement meet the approbation of the good and wise.

The candor of the American Ladies is solicitously intreated by the Authoress, as she is circumscribed in her knowledge, this being an original work in this country. Should any future editions appear, she hopes to render it more valuable.

Directions for Catering, or the Procuring the Best Viands, Fish, &c.

How to Choose Flesh

Beef. The large stall fed ox beef is the best, it has a coarse open grain, and oily smoothness; dent it with your finger and it will immediately rise again; if old, it will be rough and spungy, and the dent remain.

Cow Beef is less boned, and generally more tender and juicy than the ox, in America, which is used to labor.

Of almost every species of Animals, Birds, and Fishes, the female is the tenderest, the richest flavour'd and among poultry the soonest fatened.

Mutton, grass-fed, is good two or three years old.

Lamb, if under six months is rich, and no danger of imposition; it may be known by its size, in distinguishing either.

Veal, is soon lost—great care therefore is necessary in purchasing. Veal bro't to market in panniers, or in carriages, is to be prefered to that bro't in bags, and flouncing on a sweaty horse.

Pork, is known by its size, and whether properly fattened by its appearance.

To Make the Best Bacon

To each ham put one ounce saltpetre, one pint bay salt, one pint molasses, shake together 6 or 8 weeks, or when a large quantity is together, bast[e] them with the liquor every day; when taken out to dry, smoke three weeks in cobs or malt fumes. To every ham may be added a cheek, if you stow away a barrel and not alter the composition, some add a shoulder. For transportation or exportation, double the period of smoaking.

Fish, How to Choose the Best in Market

Salmon, the noblest and richest fish taken in fresh water—the largest are the best. They are unlike almost every other fish, are ameliorated by being 3 or 4 days out of water, if kept from heat and the moon, which has much more injurious effect than the sun.

In all great fish-markets, great fish-mongers strictly examine the gills—if the bright redness is exchanged for a low brown, they are stale; but when live fish are bro't flouncing into market, you have only to elect the kind most agreeable to your palate and the season.

Shad, contrary to the generally received opinion are not so much richer flavored, as they are harder when first taken out of the water; opinions vary respecting them. I have tasted Shad thirty or forty miles from the place where caught, and really conceived that they had a richness of flavor, which did not appertain to those taken fresh and cooked immediately, and have proved both at the same table, and the truth may rest here, that a Shad 36 or 48 hours out of water, may not cook so hard and solid, and be esteemed so elegant, yet give a higher relished flavor to the taste.

Every species generally of *salt water Fish,* are best fresh from the water, tho' the *Hannah Hill, Black Fish, Lobster, Oyster, Flounder, Bass, Cod, Haddock,* and *Eel,* with many others, may be transported by land many miles, find a good market, and retain a good relish; but as generally, live ones are bought first, deceits are used to give them a freshness of appearance, such as peppering the gills, wetting the fins and tails, and even painting the gills, or wetting with animal blood. Experience and attention will dictate the choice of the best. Fresh gills, full bright eyes, moist fins and tails, are denotements of their being fresh caught; if they are soft, it[']s certain they are stale, but if deceits are used, your smell must approve or denounce them, and be your safest guide.

Of all fresh water fish, there are none that require, or so well afford haste in cookery, as the *Salmon Trout,* they are best when caught under a fall or cateract—from what philosophical circumstance is yet unsettled, yet true it is, that at the foot of a fall the waters are much colder than at the head; Trout choose those waters; if taken from them and hurried into dress, they are genuinely good; and take rank in point of superiority of flavor, of most other fish.

Perch and Roach, are noble pan fish. [T]he deeper the water from whence taken, the finer are their flavors; if taken from shallow water, with muddy bottoms, they are impregnated therewith, and are unsavory.

Eels, though taken from muddy bottoms, are best to jump in the pan.

Most white or soft fish are best bloated, which is done by salting, peppering, and drying in the sun, and in a chimney; after 30 or 40 hours drying, are best broiled, and moistened with butter, &c.

Poultry—How to Choose

Having before stated that the female in almost every instance, is preferable to the male, and peculiarly so in the *Peacock,* which, tho' beautifully plumaged, is tough, hard, stringy, and untasted, and even indelicious—while the *Pea Hen* is exactly otherwise, and the queen of all birds.

So also in a degree, *Turkey.*

Hen Turkey, is higher and richer flavor'd, easier fattened and plumper—they are no odds in market.

Dunghill Fowls, are from their frequent use, a tolerable proof of the former birds.

Chickens, of either kind are good, and the yellow leg'd the best, and their taste the sweetest.

Capons, if young are good, are known by short spurs and smooth legs.

All birds are known, whether fresh killed or stale, by a tight vent in the former, and a loose open vent if old or stale; their smell denotes their goodness; speckled rough legs denote age, while smooth legs and combs prove them young.

A Goose, if young, the bill will be yellow, and will have but few hairs, the bones will crack easily; but if old, the contrary, the bill will be red, and the pads still redder; the joints stiff and difficultly disjointed; if young, otherwise; choose one not very fleshy on the breast, but fat in the rump.

Ducks, are similar to geese.

Wild Ducks, have redder pads, and smaller than the tame ones, otherwise are like the goose or tame duck, or to be chosen by the same rules.

Wood Cocks, ought to be thick, fat and flesh firm, the nose dry, and throat clear.

Snipes, if young and fat, have full veins under the wing, and are small in the veins, otherwise like the Woodcock.

Partridges, if young, will have black bills, yellowish legs; if old, the legs look bluish; if old or stale, it may be perceived by smelling at their mouths.

Pigeons, young, have light red legs, and the flesh of a colour, and prick easily—old have red legs, blackish in parts, more hairs, plumper and loose vents—so also of grey or green Plover, Black Birds, Thrash, Lark, and wild Fowl in general.

Hares, are white flesh'd and flexible when new and fresh kill'd; if stale, their flesh will have a blackish hue, like old pigions, if the cleft in her lip spread much, is wide and ragged, she is old; the contrary when young.

Leveret, is like the Hare in every respect, that some are obliged to search for the knob or small bone on the fore leg or foot, to distinguish them.

Rabbits, the wild are the best, either are good and tender; if old there will be much yellowish fat about the kidneys, the claws long, wool rough, and mixed with grey hairs; if young the reverse. As to their being fresh, judge by the scent, they soon perish, if trap'd or shot, and left in pelt or undressed; their taint is quicker than veal, and the most sickish in nature; and will not, like beef or veal, be purged by fire.

The cultivation of Rabbits would be profitable in America, if the best methods were pursued—they are a very prolific and profitable animal—they are easily cultivated if properly attended, but not otherwise.—A Rabbit's borough, on which 3000 dollars may have been expended, might be very profitable; but on the small scale they would be well near market towns—easier bred, and more valuable.

Receipts

To Roast Beef

The general rules are, to have a brisk hot fire, to hang down rather than to spit, to baste with salt and water, and one quarter of an hour to every pound of beef, tho' tender beef will require less, while old tough beef will require more roasting; pricking with a fork will determine you whether done or not; rare done is the healthiest and the taste of this age.

Roast Mutton

If a breast let it be cauled, if a leg, stuffed or not, let it be done more gently than beef, and done more; the chine, saddle or leg require more fire and longer time than the breast, &c. Garnish with scraped horse radish, and serve with potatoes, beans, colliflow, water-cresses, or boiled onion, caper sauce, mashed turnip, or lettuce.

Roast Veal

As it is more tender than beef or mutton, and easily scorched, paper it, especially the fat parts, lay in some distance from the fire a while to heat gently, baste it well; a 15 pound piece requires one hour and a quarter roasting; garnish with green-parsley and sliced lemon.

Roast Lamb

Lay down to a clear good fire that will not want stirring or altering, baste with butter, dust on flour, baste with the dripping, and before you take it up, add more butter and sprinkle on a little salt and parsley shred fine; send to table with a nice sallad, green peas, fresh beans, or a colliflower, or asparagus.

To Stuff a Turkey

Grate a wheat loaf, one quarter of a pound butter, one quarter of a pound salt pork, finely chopped, 2 eggs, a little sweet marjoram, summer savory, parsley and sage, pepper and salt (if the pork be not sufficient,) fill the bird and sew up.

The same will answer for all Wild Fowl.

Water Fowls require onions.

The same ingredients stuff a *leg of Veal, fresh Pork* or a *loin of Veal.*

To Stuff and Roast a Turkey, or Fowl

One pound soft wheat bread, 3 ounces beef suet, 3 eggs, a little sweet thyme, sweet marjoram, pepper and salt, and some add a gill of wine; fill the bird therewith and sew up, hang down to a steady solid fire, basting frequently with salt and water, and roast until a steam emits from the breast, put one third of a pound of butter into the gravy, dust flour over the bird and baste with the gravy; serve up with boiled onions and cramberry-sauce, mangoes, pickles or celery.

Others omit the sweet herbs, and add parsley done with potatoes.

Boil and mash 3 pints potatoes, wet them with butter, add sweet herbs, pepper, salt, fill and roast as above.

To Stuff and Roast a Goslin

Boil the inwards tender, chop them fine, put double quantity of grated bread, 4 ounces butter, pepper, salt, (and sweet herbs if you like) 2 eggs moulded into the stuffing, parboil 4 onions and chop them into the stuffing, add wine, and roast the bird.

The above is a good stuffing for every kind of Water Fowl, which requires onion sauce.

To Smother a Fowl in Oysters.

Fill the bird with dry Oysters, and sew up and boil in water just sufficient to cover the bird, salt and season to your taste—when done tender, put into a deep dish and pour over it a pint of stewed oysters, well buttered and peppered, garnish a turkey with sprigs of parsley or leaves of cellery: a fowl is best with a parsley sauce.

To Stuff a Leg of Veal

Take one pound of veal, half pound pork (salted,) one pound grated bread, chop all very fine, with a handful of green parsley, pepper it, add 3 ounces butter and 3 eggs, (and sweet herbs if you like them,) cut the leg round like a ham and stab it full of holes, and fill in all the stuffing; then salt and pepper the leg and dust on some flour; if baked in an oven, put into a sauce pan with a little water, if potted, lay some scewers at the bottom of the pot, put in a little water and lay the leg on the scewers, with a gentle fire render it tender, (frequently adding water,) when done take out the leg, put butter in the pot and brown the leg, the gravy in a separate vessel must be thickened and buttered and a spoonful of ketchup added.

To Stuff a Leg of Pork to Bake or Roast

Corn the leg 48 hours and stuff with sausage meat and bake in a hot oven two hours and an half or roast.

To Alamode a Round of Beef

To a 14 or 16 pound round of beef, put one ounce salt-petre, 48 hours after stuff it with the following: one and half pound beef, one pound salt pork, two pound grated bread, chop all fine and rub in half pound butter, salt, pepper and cayenne, summer savory, thyme; lay it on scewers in a large pot, over 3 pints hot water (which it must occasionally be supplied with,) the steam of which in 4 or 5 hours will render the round tender if over a moderate fire; when tender, take away the gravy and thicken with flour and butter, and boil, brown the round with butter and flour, adding ketchup and wine to your taste.

To Alamode a Round

Take fat pork cut in slices or mince, season it with pepper, salt, sweet marjoram and thyme, cloves, mace and nutmeg, make holes in the beef and stuff it the night before cooked; put some bones across the bottom of the pot to keep from burning, put in one quart Claret wine, one quart water and one onion; lay the round on the bones, cover close and stop it round the top with dough; hang on in the morning and stew gently two hours; turn it, and stop tight and stew two hours more; when done tender, grate a crust of bread on the top and brown it before the fire; scum the gravy and serve in a butter boat, serve it with the residue of the gravy in the dish.

→ 3 ←

From *Delights and Prejudices*

JAMES BEARD

When Proust recollected the precise taste sensation of the little scalloped *Madeleine* cakes served at tea by his aunt, it led him into his monumental remembrance of things past. When I recollect the taste sensations of my childhood, they lead me to more cakes, more tastes: the great razor clams, the succulent Dungeness crab, the salmon, crawfish, mussels and trout of the Oregon coast; the black bottom pie served in a famous Portland restaurant; the Welsh rabbit of our Chinese cook, the white asparagus my mother canned, and the array of good dishes prepared by the two of them in that most memorable of kitchens.

The kitchen, reasonably enough, was the scene of my first gastronomic adventure. I was on all fours. I crawled into the vegetable bin, settled on a giant onion and ate it, skin and all. It must have marked me for life, for I have never ceased to love the hearty flavor of raw onions.

Another taste memory, my earliest, comes from the age of three. I lay abed with malaria and without much appetite, refusing all food except spoonfuls of the most superb chicken jelly that ever existed. For a time nothing counted in my life but chicken jelly. Either because it constituted my sole diet day after day or because it *was* magically good, chicken jelly and the flavor of perfectly prepared chicken have also remained a stimulant to my palate ever since.

This particular jelly was cooked slowly and carefully, beginning with two to three pounds of necks, gizzards, feet, heads, backbones, etc., covered with water to which an onion stuck with cloves, a piece of celery and a sprig of parsley were added. This was cooked slowly for an hour, then salted well. It was cooked again for two to three hours and strained. In this bouillon a good-sized fowl, cut into pieces, was cooked long and slowly until the meat fell from the bones. The whole was tasted, the seasoning corrected, and then it was strained and sometimes clarified. If clarified, the broth was poured through a linen napkin, then the white of an egg together with the shell was stirred in, and the broth was brought to the boiling point and strained again through a linen napkin. Finally it was cooled and then chilled. The resulting jelly had the true essence of chicken and a texture that was incredibly delightful.

I doubt if many people today want to eat chicken jelly unless they are ill or on a diet—the calorie count is low—but good chicken jelly has many uses in cooking. It gives a lift to vegetables cooked in it; it makes a fine Vichyssoise; and it provides the base for many excellent sauces. For a *chaud-froid* sauce it is incomparable.

Nowadays I find that a more practical approach to this delicacy can be achieved as follows:

SUPERB CHICKEN JELLY

Place 5 pounds backs and necks in 3 to 4 quarts water, together with 1 onion stuck with 2 cloves, a sprig of parsley, a bit of celery and a few peppercorns. Let this cook for about 3 hours—*à faible ébullition*. Then salt it well to taste. (I use coarse salt—Malden or kosher.) Now add 3 to 4 pounds chicken gizzards wrapped in a piece of cheesecloth after they have been washed. Add another quart of water and let them cook for 2 hours. Remove and save the gizzards. Then if you want a sensational dinner dish, add a good-sized capon or roasting chicken and poach it in this rich broth till it is just tender and cooked through. Be very careful not to overcook it! Serve with a little of the clarified broth and either rice or some crisp sautéed potatoes. Here you have superbly flavored chicken and so simply done. All it takes is the patience to watch the broth. If you have an electric oven, leave it at a low temperature with the automatic control on and forget about it.

If my earliest love in food was chicken jelly, my earliest hate was milk. I loathed milk, cold or hot. It simply couldn't be made attractive to me as a drink. And if occasionally a zealous adult with standard notions about growing children forced me to drink a glass, I promptly became sick. It has never failed to be an effective emetic for me, and I am still revolted when I see people drinking milk with a good meal. Eventually, though, I came to accept milk when it was combined with other ingredients and turned into a modest but delectable dish, clam soup. I grew to love this soup, served with great toasted soda crackers. (For dessert we often had more of the crackers spread with butter and good bitter marmalade.) Here are three different ways of preparing it.

CLAM SOUP

Razor clams are a must for this dish. You may purchase the minced clams from most good grocers, and if you care to write to Seaside, Oregon, you can get whole ones in tins. Heat 1 pint light cream and the juice from two 7-ounce cans minced clams to the boiling point. Add salt and pepper to taste, a dash of Tabasco sauce and 2 tablespoons butter. Now add the clams and just heat them through. Serve the soup at once with a dash of paprika or chopped parsley. This recipe will serve four lightly or two well.

CLAM SOUP II

In a blender, blend two 7-ounce cans whole razor clams in juice till the mixture is thick. Remove it to the top of a double boiler. Add 1 pint heavy cream, 2 tablespoons butter, and seasonings to taste. Heat the soup to the boiling point over hot water, and serve it with a dash of paprika.

CORN AND CLAM SOUP

In a blender, blend two 7-ounce cans whole razor clams and 1 cup whole-kernel corn (or one 12-ounce can) and place the mixture in the top of a double boiler over hot water. Add 1 cup light cream, ½ cup milk, 2 tablespoons butter and seasonings. Heat the soup to the boiling point, add ¼ cup bourbon, and serve it with a bit of chopped parsley.

While I'm on the subject of clams, I might as well produce the clam chowder recipe which my mother always prepared at the beach. It was very popular with our family and friends, and it resembles only faintly the chowders of other sections of the country.

CLAM CHOWDER

Cut 3 to 4 thick rashers lean bacon into rather small pieces and try out in a heavy skillet. Remove the bacon to absorbent paper and pour off all but 2 tablespoons of fat. Sauté 1 fairly large onion, coarsely chopped, in fat till it is just transparent. Add 4 smallish potatoes, peeled and diced, and enough clam broth, about 2 cups, to cover. Bring this to a boil. Cook until the potatoes are soft and almost disintegrated. Add salt and pepper to taste and a dash of Tabasco sauce. Heat 1 quart light cream and add potato-onion mixture, bacon bits and lastly 1½ cups chopped fresh or canned razor clams. Correct the seasoning. Add ¼ cup cognac, and when clams are just heated through, serve the chowder in hot cups with a dash of chopped parsley. This same chowder may be mixed in an electric blender and served cold with chopped chives and parsley.

The ability to recall a taste sensation, which I think of as "taste memory," is a God-given talent, akin to perfect pitch, which makes your life richer if you possess it. If you aren't born with it, you can never seem to acquire it. Great wine palates must depend on taste memory for the sureness of their judgment, and a Lichine or a Schoonmaker without this memory would never be able to perform the almost overpowering task of comparing vintages and selecting wines.

Cheese tasters, tea tasters, cognac tasters—all must depend for a living on the keenness of their taste memories. Great gastronomes also have a highly developed sense memory, or they would not make such a ceremony of tasting and enjoying food. And naturally good chefs and cooks must depend upon memory when they season or when they are combining subtle flavors to create a new sauce or a new dish.

Not all taste memory is accurate. Many people think of Mom's apple pie or Grandmother's dumplings as delicacies that cannot be equaled today. These memories are associated with happy times, and to the untrained palate the pie or the dumplings seemed delicious. If the same dishes were re-created and presented to a sophisticated palate, they would probably belie their reputations. Most of the home cooking one enjoyed in his youth was not as good as one remembers it.

I think I developed an accurate taste memory early in my life. I was not sentimentally attached to the cooking of any one person at home, and we ate in restaurants a good deal. I tried to be as objective as possible about taste and was somewhat precocious in appreciating the pleasure of blending satisfying flavors. While this meant that I learned to enjoy the delights of a good meal, it also meant that I soon grew intolerant of mediocre food. More than once, I'm afraid, my candid appraisals embarrassed a hostess or friends with whom we were sharing a meal. I often wonder why I didn't have a pie thrown at me!

4

Puffballs: Finding the Inside

From *Secrets of the Tsil Café*

THOMAS FOX AVERILL

I had written to my parents about the Edible Plants of New Mexico course, and the spring semester sequel as well. I did not write what Juan had told me about Domingo, about himself and Conseca, about my Hingler grandfather. But his telling had made things different for me: seeing one thing differently, I saw many things differently.

Maria Standing Tall and I began to cook together, everything from cattails to yucca cactus. We made teas from dandelions, mints, and rose hips. We gathered piñon* in the mountains, roasted them, shucked the thin shell of skin, and gorged ourselves.

Maria refused alcohol. She cooked for the pleasure of tasting food as it was, without beverage, sauce, spice, flavoring. I tasted with her, but I was enough the son of my father that I experimented, as well. One day I spent all afternoon creating a new soup.

YUCCA SOUP

1 quart turkey broth, finely strained

2 good-sized yucca† roots, and stalks, peeled and cubed

* Piñon (pine nuts): Nut pines found at elevations between 4,000 and 7,500 feet in the western mountains of North America, are short-trunked, small trees that yield their seeds/nuts in the fall and early winter. These seeds, rich in protein, have as many as 3,000 calories per pound. After harvesting them, Native Americans roasted them, then shelled them for eating or for longer storage.

† *Yucca (Yucca eleta, also* Soap tree, Our Lord's Candle, narrow leaf): *Native to the grasslands and deserts of the Southwest, from Texas to Arizona, and as far north as Kansas, and at elevations from 1,500 to 6,000 feet. Also known as palmilla yucca, it has a thick stem covered by yellowed, dry leaves. The leaves are spiny, thin, and grow in a crown-like cluster. The white, hanging-bell flowers bloom from spring to early summer. They, along with yucca stem (baked) and root, are prized as food among southwestern Native American tribes—Hopi, Tewa, Hano, Navajo, Ute, Apache, Zuni.*

Half a grocery bag full of yucca flowers, bitter centers removed
2 good-sized zucchini, cut into small cubes
4 tomatoes, sliced
1 tablespoon Chimayo chile powder
Salt to taste

Heat turkey broth and simmer yucca roots until softened. Meanwhile, boil yucca flowers for ten minutes and drain. Add flowers, zucchini, and tomatoes and cook just until zucchini is soft, but not clear. Dust with chile powder and adjust with salt.

I was more delighted than she was. When I pressed her, she said, "It's good. Not authentic, but good."

"You don't really like it," I said.

"My gift is in knowing foods," she said. "Your gift is in creating new things to do with food."

Maria Standing Tall reminded me of Juan: she used what she knew very directly. Once, after a late-summer rain, we gathered puffballs, a mushroom some people call stomach fungus. Puffballs are not poisonous. I was happily walking through a pine forest in the Jemez, gathering, even eating, an occasional find. Maria knew I had seen puffballs, so told me to pick generously and meet her at the stream we heard in the distance. After I'd filled my pack, I went toward the sound of rushing water. She sat on a rock, a long knife in her hand. "We'll check them now, to see which ones to keep," she said.

My stomach turned sour. "Check them?" I put my pack next to hers.

She cross-sectioned a puffball.

"I have a knife," I said. "What are we looking for?"

"See?" Three rejected mushrooms lay next to her on the rock. She picked one up. "This stuff looks like gelatin. That means it's a baby stinkhorn. I wouldn't want to eat one."

"Why not?" I asked, trying to remember if one of the mushrooms I'd eaten seemed gelatinous.

"They taste terrible," said Maria Standing Tall. She picked up another mushroom. "This yellow-green color means it's past its time. And look at this one." She showed me another puffball, again sliced on its longitude, this one full of holes. "Worms," she said.

I pulled out my pocketknife, sat down, and reached into my bag. "This one good?" I showed her a creamy white half.

"Perfect," she said.

I was relieved when the puffballs, one after the other, were fine, only two with holes and one past its prime.

"Uh-oh," she said, nearing the bottom of her bag. "This is why you cut them." She held up what looked like a puffball. "See this shape? Like a shadow of another mushroom inside?"

I nodded.

"It's a baby, of the *Amanita* mushroom. You never want to eat one. Highly poisonous. You can die."

"What are my chances?" I asked. "I ate two or three of these without checking them."

"Chances are good you're a fool," she said. "In the plant world, you have to know at what stage you find anything. Same with the human world." She stopped when she saw how frightened I was. "That was a half hour ago," she said. "You'd know by now."

Maria Standing Tall threw the poisonous mushroom as far as she could into the woods. Then she ate a perfect puffball. "In three weeks, we'll go to a corn dance."

Before the corn dance, Grandfather Hingler died of a heart attack. I drove to Santa Fe to meet my parents. Their trip had been hot and tiring. I'd seen my father angry at his father, but had never before seen him sad about him. I watched my father and Domingo mourn without letting the others who attended the viewing, the funeral, and the burial know about their separate but equal connection to their father. That was hard enough, and though they were friendly with each other, neither was able to get beyond the performance of the ritual. On my parents' last day in New Mexico, we all ate at *Domingo's,* and neither brother truly acknowledged the connection until we left to return to Grandmother Hingler's home for a last good-bye. Then, in an almost mocking show of emotion, Domingo saw my father to the door, hugged him and shouted, "*Hermano!*" And my father saw the convenience of the show, and broke from Domingo and shouted, "*Hermano, para siempre!*" The extravagance of their declarations made everyone in the restaurant think they were exaggerating a feeling, not revealing a bloodline.

After a last night with my grandmother, my parents left for home. They were going to take me back to Albuquerque first, so I could help deliver some furniture to Domingo. Just outside Santa Fe, my father pulled to the side of the road. "Damn," he said. He'd forgotten the envelope his mother had put on a table by her front door for him, the one that contained his father's and her wills. "There's a copy in there for Domingo, too. She wanted him to have it," he said. "She made a special trip to her safe deposit box."

"How could you forget it?" my mother asked him.

"You expect me to be thinking of her death so soon?"

"Can she mail it?" my mother asked.

"It's only twenty minutes back," he said.

We turned around. My father hit the steering wheel a couple of times and swore. Once, he parked on the side of the road again, his eyes too full of tears to drive. My mother patted his back and rubbed his neck. "It's okay," she said. I sat in the backseat and, to tell the truth, was happy to watch his heart do a little melting.

We pulled into the drive at *Agua Pura.* Juan was carrying a box across the courtyard, from his small house to the big one. He looked surprised. We piled out of the car, and he stood, expressionless. The box was full of personal odds and ends, his photographs, his toothpaste, the old clock he kept on his mantel. My father reached for the box. "You want some help with this?" he asked.

"Your mother," Juan said, "she says the house is too big to be in it all alone."

My father went inside for the large envelope. He said nothing to Juan about the box. When he came out the door, he called back over his shoulder. "Love," he said. "Love you both." My mother and I climbed back into the car. My father walked over to Juan's little house. He peered into the windows then came back. He started the car and we left.

"Well?" asked my mother.

"Nothing left in there but old furniture, and the bed where he used to sleep."

"They deserve some happiness," said my mother.

"They deserve whatever they deserve," said my father.

We delivered the furniture and the will, and then I said good-bye to my parents. I wasn't certain what to think of Juan and my grandmother, about all I'd learned and seen about the odd arrangements on *Agua Pura.*

In fact, by the time I attended the corn dance with Maria Standing Tall, I needed a ritual—something to make me see and feel and come to terms with who I was and what I might do. We went to one of the pueblos north of Albuquerque, along the broad river valleys that had made an agricultural habitat possible for the earliest Americans. We arrived "before the tourists," Maria said. She asked me to park my truck a respectful distance from where the ceremonial dancing would take place. The sky was that perfect blue known only to people who have lived in the Southwest, a land of both tremendous beauty and difficult sustenance. Difficulties were forgotten for the corn dance, and the peaceful sky was soon full of sound. Cars gunned for parking places, blaring their horns. Dogs barked, roosters crowed, children screamed, cried, laughed, shouted. Drums began what would be hours of steady rhythm. They were joined by the jangles, the beads, and the deep-throated humming of men.

Sound enriched what I observed. Homes, decorated with pine branches, wreaths and hanging ristras of red chiles, and totems offered to sun and wind. Small tents with hand-lettered signs offered tortillas and fry bread, skewers of beef, venison, and chicken. Some dancers were in full dress, beaded and feathered. Others, mostly children, wore primitive but proud imitations of their parents, and danced with pop-can tabs for necklaces, bottle caps for rattles.

The dancers, Maria told me, thanked the sun and the rain, beseeched the elements, too. I had no sense of the language, the music, of why people stood, sat, danced, gave voice to feeling. Maria Standing Tall was my interpreter. Nobody was allowed to photograph, so memory, she told me, must document what I saw, heard, and felt.

I didn't see, hear, and feel what she did: everything chaotic but purposeful, jangled and pure, patched together but smoothly run. One image stuck in my head: little corn-husk dolls, lined up in a booth, for sale, for children. Their heads, a loop of husk, had achiote seeds for eyes, a piece of blue corn for a nose, a straight strip of cayenne for a noncommittal mouth. Had my father ever seen a corn dance? Why had I never asked?

For six hours I stood next to Maria Standing Tall, watching her rhythmic swaying, aware of the humming and mutterings and catches in her throat. I did not know her.

I went home for Thanksgiving, the Anglo harvest ritual that consists of gorging the gut instead of communicating with ancestors and gods. In

New Mexico, I had harvested a bounty to bring to Kansas City. Great-grandmother Maria Tito had moved into my basement room, giving up her house after she'd fallen and broken her arm. My parents had put in an elevator chair, and she rode up and down with a delightful smile on her face. She'd lost just enough of her mind to be fun, not enough to be terribly difficult. Every time she saw me, she said, "You're Wes? So big." She'd lift her bushy eyebrows in mock disbelief. I slept on a couch my mother and I hauled into my old bed closet.

We had our usual gigantic Thanksgiving. Carson Flinn was there with Penelope, the young woman who had first helped him take notes after his stroke. "She spells better now," Carson told me when she was in the kitchen. "And she's even more beautiful."

I agreed. Her rusty hair had grown even longer, her eyes greener and more intense. She had square shoulders, graceful movements, a contagious giggle. I'd asked Cocoa to make sure I sat next to Penelope. I guessed she was just a year or two older than I was. "Last year of college," Carson Flinn confirmed.

Cocoa, though a guest for this dinner, still helped seat, water, and feed the others, like Ronald and his family. I'd brought everyone except Penelope a ristra as a gift. Ronald drank too much and draped his string of chiles around his neck. Carson Flinn, who had recovered some of his mobility and lost some weight, said the rusty pepper chain would have a place of honor in his kitchen. "Eat it, too," I reminded him.

Cocoa wondered when she'd find time to eat so many peppers. I gave her a possible recipe from a tent at the corn dance. "Nothing but four or five of these peppers—they're fairly mild—ground into beef, until it's about half pepper, half beef. Like grainy beef, and scooped up into tortillas. I'll make some tomorrow."

"Not tomorrow," said my father. "We're going on an expedition tomorrow."

"What about the restaurant?" I asked.

"Closed for pawpaws," he said. I thought he was making a joke, but I'd heard of pawpaws. "You may know your New Mexico edible plants, but you need to visit an oak-hickory forest instead of a pine one."

He roused me early. I wasn't sure which of us was more tired. He'd developed lumpy shadows under his eyes. He carried a carton of cigarettes and a thermos of coffee. I knew if he was tired, he'd at least be alert. We drove northwest out of Kansas City into the Missouri River bluffs. He parked the car off the road near a rusted iron bridge. We walked along a creek, into woods. I had no idea what to look for. We walked for half an hour, stepping around buckbrush, over wild grapevine, avoiding prickly gooseberry bushes and poison ivy. I was ready to give up. I had to urinate, and I sidled up to a hickory tree and unzipped my trousers. Just before I started my stream, my father yelled at me. He hurried over. "Our first find," he said.

Sure enough, just a few feet from the hickory tree grew what looked like its miniature. On the leaf-covered floor of the woods lay several pawpaws, and in the tree were three or four more. He picked one from the tree, wiped it on his pants, and ate it. I finished my business elsewhere, and he handed me my first pawpaw: slickly sweet, mango-like in texture, as soft as an overripe cantaloupe, a little pulpy around the hard buttons of seeds deposited randomly in its stubby banana shape, but rich throughout with a little nut taste from the skin.

PAWPAWS

One oak-hickory woods, preferably well watered
A diligent hour of search
A quick eye
An appetite
As many pawpaws as possible
A handkerchief

Search woods for an hour until you spot the small tree, broad leaves like a cross between hickory and catalpa. Look for the greenish plug of fruit, sometimes on the ground, if late in season, preferably on tree, just ready to fall. Eat immediately, and wipe hands on handkerchief when finished. Return to car without fruit in hand—the memory of gorging on pawpaws in the woods is better than trying to do anything with your harvest once in your kitchen.

"You like them?" my father asked.

"I like being here, eating, with you," I said.

"Everywhere in the New World," my father said, "are simple but completely rare foods, like these pawpaws. Few people have eaten them. I wish I could say I've eaten every one of those New World foods." He picked another of the soft fruits, another elongated, olive-colored pear, and put it in his mouth. He gave me one, too. When we finished the fruit from that tree, we found another, and another, until our appetites gave out.

Back at the car, my father turned to me. "By the way," he said, "some people say pawpaws give them the shits."

"Juan told me about Domingo," I said.

"About Domingo?" he asked. He was quiet for a time. "You mean about my father and Conseca," he said.

"That's what I mean. I wonder how that made you feel. Growing up."

We climbed into the car and drove for some time without saying anything. "Water under the bridge," he said. "Once, it really bothered me. Because nobody said anything. But it was always there inside the families, like we were different from what everybody thought we were. Domingo and I never talked about it. He went to Catholic school, I went to public. We handled it.

"Mostly, I just wanted things different for you. I mean, your mother and I have had our problems, but at least you know everything, right?"

"I didn't know about Domingo," I reminded him.

"When Juan told you, did it bother you?"

"Of course," I said. Then I was quiet for a long time. "I realized you'd always kept me from my grandparents. I got closer to them. Juan said I was too much like you," I said. "I wondered why I was in New Mexico, doing the things you did. Maybe I shouldn't be. Maybe I should be home."

"You want some Kansas City time? Because I could use you after your spring semester, for maybe a month or so. Just long enough to help me with something I have up my sleeve."

"I'm gardening there during the summers."

"There's a garden here," said my father.

"I don't even have a bedroom anymore," I reminded him.

"Wait'll you hear," he said. "It's a party. A big one. My fiftieth birthday. We're going to make it the biggest restaurant evening in the history of Kansas City. A meal like no other, ever. We'll eat things like pawpaws. Things that are local, or rare, or not usually done. We'll break all the taboos."

"Do you have a menu already?"

"A few things, because I want to say I've eaten them once in my life."

"Like?" I asked.

"Dog. And guinea pig. And insects."

"Dad, I thought When Available was just a joke."

"This isn't a joke. Will you help? It's a culmination, for me. And I'd like you there."

I thought about trying to live at home again. About leaving New Mexico and the garden Domingo would let me plant.

"Put your garden in," said my father. "Get your crops up. Then get some help watering and weeding and come up here June fifteenth. You'll be back in Albuquerque by July fifteenth, the day after my birthday. I'll pay you."

"I don't need pay," I said. "It'll be my birthday present to you."

"Tell your mother," he said.

"Does *she* like the idea of this big party?" I asked.

"Tell her you know about Domingo, so she'll know you do."

"She knows?"

"Everything I know."

The next day, I found my mother in her kitchen, drinking coffee and spreading bleu cheese over croissants. I began my day by saying, "Juan told me about Domingo."

"Oh, that," she said. "That was before I was married."

"Of course," I said. "Dad just told me I should tell you I know."

"He knows?" she asked.

"Sure he knows. He said to tell you, so you'd know that I know."

She was confused. In her confusion she looked around her kitchen, and then directly at the cabinet, the one with the hiding place. I knew she had something to hide, something about Domingo. "So Juan told you. *How* did he? Or *why*? I mean . . . you must have become very close."

"We gardened together. We talked. He wants to tell me about himself, and about Dad and about Domingo, and Grandfather Hingler. He's trying to grow me, like a plant."

She smiled. She was relieved, and her relief bothered me. "That's good," she said. "You always need information. That's what my grandmother Tito always gave me."

"And you'd do it for me?" I asked.

"Haven't I?" she asked.

"You haven't told me about you and Domingo," I said.

My mother was generous and expansive in her cooking. Carson Flinn once told me that my father served food with heat, my mother with warmth. But on that day she served her information cold, with no meat on the bones. Perhaps that's as it should have been.

When she and my father were courting, mostly by letter for those two years after their initial meeting and evenings tasting food and getting to know each other, my mother took one trip to New Mexico my father never knew about. She'd been struck by how alike the two of them were: Domingo a browner version of my father; Domingo a more relaxed and less intense version of my father; Domingo an already settled, already confident version of my father; Domingo, who offered her a different version of life.

"We were intimate on that trip. I'm not just talking about sex because when you get older you realize that's not everything. But we shared everything, as I had with your father."

"Did Domingo want to marry you?" I asked.

"I told him I couldn't. I corresponded with your father, and then I made the right decision. Your father and I married. That's all. Subject closed."

"Why didn't you marry Domingo, if he was like Dad without the problems?"

She smiled. "Your father and I were meant for each other. We like problems."

"Does he know? About Domingo?"

"It was my trip. Like research. Your father and I have kept our New World foods and Old World foods, the Tsil and Buen AppeTito, separate. We have a life together and separately. Domingo wouldn't have allowed that."

"He's too much like Juan? Too open?"

"You don't have to carry my secret," she said. "Tell your father about Domingo. Or I'll tell him, if you want."

"I'm coming back to help, next summer, for his fiftieth birthday," I said. "I'm just not sure about New Mexico."

"Good," she said. "I've missed you."

5

Full Moon Soup with Snow

APRIL LINDNER

When winter churns white over white
to freeze thyme and silence rosemary's last gasp,
when all the garden's dainty greens
have long wilted into memory,
when night edges in and the news
rasping through the radio
seems cruel, no matter:

In the kitchen's brisk fluorescence,
choose your sharpest knife.
Time to make do with roots,
knobby and pale as knuckles,
to pare and chop, sauté and wait.

First unsheathe the garlic
from white crackling paper. Whatever
the recipe calls for, triple it.
Set the shards dancing in warm olive oil.

Next, take the sleek and girlish leeks
with their thin, whiskery chins.
Loose their tight coiled rings
to free the crumbling earth hidden within.

Turnips. Pare away the wax
in shades of hyacinth and cream,
down to their densely packed
fragrant snowball hearts.

And the gnarly parsnips
with brown paperbaggy skins,
not much to the eye
but sweet underneath.

Chop everything bite size,
then boil in broth. Scatter
cracked black pepper and fennel seed.
Pour yourself a glass of ruby wine.
See how the full moon hangs on
pearly as an onion?

Pour the whole fragrant mishmash
steaming into the blender
to be whirled in a tornado
and turned to soup
made not from a stone

but the next step up: what sleeps
in cellars and keeps in jars.
Hardy remainders, not intended
for the eye. What lurks in the cellar
and refuses to perish.

6

To Cèpe, with Love (or, The Alchemy of Longing)

E. J. LEVY

I have hunted mushrooms with each of my last four lovers; I love the hunt and the hint of danger. The day after a good rain, we get into the car and drive into the high mountains that surround the valley of Taos, where I live, to a narrow one-lane dirt road that edges along steep cliffs, following switchbacks until we come to a gravel lot at the brink of the woods and park. From there we hike two miles into the mountains (sometimes holding hands, sometimes holding water bottles or pocket-sized guides to mycology) to forage in the underbrush of birch and aspen and piñon for wild mushrooms. We are looking for porcini (known to the French as cèpe) and chanterelles, the gourmet's delight, both of which—in the psychologically suggestive language of mushrooming—are known as "choice."

At first we follow the well-worn track through the woods to William's Lake, but I know soon enough we will diverge from this common course, lured away by a musky smell, or by the jaunty tilt of a plum-colored cap. We will crouch by a promising fungus and run a fingertip beneath its rim to feel for gills (which we'll reject, gilled mushrooms being mostly poisonous) or for the sponge layer that distinguishes boletus, the genus from which porcini come and which we seek.

I love the pursuit almost as much as I love the eating. There is always an element of risk. The possibility that when we reach the edge of the tree line and enter the lichen-patched boulder fields—where you find the frilled, bright-orange caps of chanterelles embedded in mossy pads between the last clumps of pine—that a sudden storm may come up and drench us or, worse yet, that lightning may strike. (It's a real possibility: New Mexico has the highest per capita incidence of death by lightning strike in the U.S.) But I enjoy the hint of danger, the slight possibility of poisoning. Risk is part of the pleasure, part of the reason I play this gustatory Russian roulette, gathering mushrooms, foraging in underbrush, following the scent of apricots that signals the presence of chanterelles, and the buttery, oak-inflected musk of porcini.

In food, as in love, I like to take my chances.

~

Throughout my twenties and much of my thirties, I fell in and out of love. I went through lovers rapidly—mistaking others' ardor for my own, mistaking mine for theirs—still trying (at the age my mother was when she bore me at thirty-five) to refine my romantic taste, sample all before I chose.

But if my love affairs have not been durable, my gustatory habits are. Each year (when the summer rains come to the high mountain peaks that surround the small town where I once lived in New Mexico), I hunt mushrooms. It is for me a rite of summer and of courtship.

~

Where I sought love, Vladimir Nabokov found a homeland: in his classic memoir *Speak, Memory*, Nabokov writes of hunting mushrooms in Russia before the revolution, of watching his mother emerge from the forest with the closed pleased look of the successful mushroom stalker.

"One of her greatest pleasures in summer was the very Russian sport of *hodit' po gribï* (looking for mushrooms). . . . Rainy weather would bring out these beautiful plants in profusion under the firs, birches and aspens in our park, especially in its older part, east of the carriage road that divided the park in two. Its shady recesses would then harbor that special boletic reek which makes a Russian's nostrils dilate—a dark, dank, satisfying blend of damp moss, rich earth, rotting leaves. . . .

"Near a white garden bench, on a round garden table of iron, she would lay out her boletes in concentric circles to count and sort them. . . . Before they were bundled away by a servant to a place she knew nothing about, to a doom that did not interest her, she would stand there admiring them, in a glow of quiet contentment. . . . The sun might cast a lurid gleam just before setting, and there, on the damp round table, her mushrooms would lie, very colorful, some bearing traces of extraneous vegetation—a grass blade sticking to a viscid fawn cap, or moss still clothing the bulbous base of a dark-stippled stem. And a tiny looper caterpillar would be there, too, measuring, like a child's finger and thumb, the rim of the table, and every now and then stretching upward to grope, in vain, for the shrub from which it had been dislodged."

(I love the finish here: Nabokov, like the caterpillar, groping to regain what has been lost—a homeland and past through memory.)

Like Nabokov, I am of Russian ancestry, part of that vast late nineteenth- / early twentieth-century migration, but his line is an aristocratic one and ours decidedly is not. Born of Russian peasant stock, I wonder if my penchant for hunting fungus in the underbrush has some genetic source, if it is some atavistic Russian instinct (as Nabokov suggests), for the smell of mushrooms on a summer evening is for me decidedly arousing, like certain women's perfume: I've been known to stop dead on a street to smell it, to sniff, smile, look around for the source, full of inchoate longing.

The first time I found an edible mushroom, I was looking for something else; or rather I was not looking for anything at all when I came on the king of mushrooms—*boletus edulis*—in a New Mexico mountain wood one August afternoon some fifteen years ago, a mushroom I would later learn is the mycological equivalent of filet mignon, smooth and meaty, buttery and rich, its smell a kind of cross between nuts and cream.

I had reached an enchanted age when I was discovering the world's pleasures for the first time, when each day seemed rich in unanticipated and unearned delight; in those days I wasn't looking for anything, because I felt, finally—at the age of twenty-six—that I'd found it all. I'd recently moved to New Mexico with a lanky wildlife biologist named Wendy, the first woman I'd fallen in love with; she was living in Las Vegas, New Mexico, when we met (unlike its famous raucous Nevada namesake, Las Vegas, New Mexico, is an utterly unglamorous town—a small Midwestern town on the edge of the Plains, nestled at the base of the Sangre de Christo mountains, which like the Rockies north of them demarcate the West); together we'd moved to Taos that spring.

I'd been raised with a middle-class wariness, the fear that what's been gained might be lost, and it was revelatory to discover with Wendy how easily one might live and how well, how numerous the pleasures of a quotidian existence might be. With her I forsook the wisdom of my upbringing—with its admonition to hard work and thrift, of application in hope of some better future, and learned instead the catechism of delight: I learned one needn't work endlessly to be worthy or virtuous, that there was abundant pleasure if only one lingered, paid attention to what was already here, all around us.

We discovered opalescent hot springs in canyons along the Rio Grande and hunted for the best breakfast burrito in the state; we made extravagant meals out of the novels we read, and attended to where the moon rose along the mountains and to the first blades of grass to come up in spring; we savored hot showers on frigid autumn mornings and the aching cold on the soles of our feet when we walked downstairs on a winter morning across *saltillo* tiles; the sweet smell of *piñon* smoke and the way that mist rose out of the gorge on chill mornings like a river of cloud or a vaporous snake; the sensual curve of adobe walls like flesh.

~

That first encounter with wild mushrooms happened—as so much of my life did then—as if governed by accident, happy chance. We'd been hiking in the mountains above Taos, taking one of the many foot trails that branch off from the narrow winding road that wends up from the high mesas of Taos to the ski valley at 9,000 feet, walking a narrow gravel track up a steep slope between trees along a cold mountain creek, when I noticed a bulbous shape, the color of a roasted bun—a brown hinting at red, plump as risen dough—poking up through pine duff at the base of a tree.

I crouched down and ran a finger beneath the cap, then pulled it from the pine needle bed above the creek. The underside was like no mushroom I'd seen before—not gilled, like the agarics I'd grown up eating sautéed in butter and wine; this had a spongy layer of yellow-white, as if it were fashioned from foam. Even Wendy, who knew the southwest well (having worked for years as an environmental consultant there), hadn't a clue what we were looking at.

The local paper had recently run an article about an Italian restaurateur in town who gathered wild mushrooms in the mountains to feed his clientele (he'd later be shut down for this rustic practice, having failed to obtain the proper license), and one or the other of us recalled it and thought how much our mushroom looked like his (though his was big as a hat, a small table lamp). Somehow we got our hands on a mycology guide and identified our find as the king of boletes—*boletus edulis*. We learned it was called *steinpilz* by the Germans, *porcini* in Italy, that the French called it *cèpe*. The book said it was edible and prized. Choice.

~

After that first find, woods were transformed. We'd pull over at the side of the road when driving past a particularly promising patch of forest after a rain, hop out, and find the pine needles pushed up by mushrooms plump as pears. Marvelous in wine and butter.

I had grown up with suburban lawns, where mushrooms were an ugly thing—sickly flat and flimsy, a gray and unlovely fungus, floppy as an ill-used felt hat. I hadn't imagined they could inspire delight. But we were thrilled by our finds. It amazed me to find after the caution of a suburban childhood that the world might provide such pleasures, that there was this abundance, if only one paid attention. And that too became a pleasure, learning to look, to see what had not been visible before.

For years afterwards the taste of boletes evoked for me the particular longing and anticipatory delight—close kin to nostalgia and unrequited love—that I'd first felt hunting mushrooms, just as it recalled Wendy, my partner then, an unprepossessing woman who seemed to me to have raised a lack of ambition to the level of a calling, hers a heroic disdain for common concerns of status and rank (though my family referred to this as a lack of focus). For years the sense of a world rich in possibilities if only we would stop and look was linked in my mind with her and the five years we lived happily together and with the patient undramatic attention of a mushroom hunt.

~

A few years after that first find, as I was hiking up to William's Lake one summer afternoon with a new beloved, we saw several people emerging from the pines, coming down from the steep alpine slopes, calling out to one another about their success, shouting it out, carrying fat paper bags which they held aloft as one might heft a felled bird or dead rabbit or a sack of gold. I asked what they were finding, and was told they were collecting chanterelles.

"Where?" I asked.

I knew this was not a question one should ask, like inquiring about finances and sexual habits; people jealously guard good mushroom fields.

To my surprise, the woman answered.

"All along here," she said. "They're all over."

We asked her if she'd show us how to identify them, not expecting that she would, but she didn't hesitate: she described the golden mushrooms, how they wedged close to the ground in the little mossy places or between the lichen-covered boulders that lay in a field at the edge of the tree line. I stared at the steeply inclined slope but saw nothing there. Or, rather, I saw what I'd always seen: pine needles and pine tree trunks and boughs and rocks and little tufts of grass.

But then she leaned down and pointed to a pad of moss by our feet, just at the edge of the dirt trail—*See?*—and I did. I saw a bright frill of neon orange, a wildly unnatural color, tucked into a bright green pad of moss. It seemed impossible ever to have missed it.

We thanked her and walked on, but soon we left the common path and stepped into a field that flanked the trail to the right—where enormous pink gneiss boulders were scabbed with pale green lichen and little clusters of pine sheltered pads of tender moss. There, among the boulders, we walked for a few minutes until suddenly we saw them—glowing like gold coins, like orange peels tossed off by some careless hiker, like dripped industrial paint—patches of radiant orange chanterelles. We crouched down to confirm the find: the smell of apricots was unmistakable, as were the veins beneath the caps in place of gills.

We filled our pockets, with delight.

~

Nabokov's elegant evocation aside, there's little mention of the lowly mushroom in the world's great literature. The English Romantic poet Percy Bysshe Shelley in his "Queen Mab: A Philosophical Poem" mentions mushrooms by way of measuring man's life, its span brief as that brief fruiting:

> Yon monarch, in his solitary pomp,
> Was but the mushroom of a summer day,
> That his light-wingèd footstep pressed to dust;
> Time was the king of earth; all things gave way. . . .

But Shakespeare grants the fungus only a passing nod in the stage directions of his *Midsummer Night's Dream,* and few others give fungus even a tip of the pen: John Galsworthy does in *A Man of Property II* and S. J. Perelman in *Westward Ha!*; Thomas Paine makes mention in the *Rights of Man,* and of course there's Alice's famous mushroom in Wonderland, which, like love and other hallucinogens, can make one taller or smaller.

But the mushroom's richly used in language, where it serves as adjective, verb, and noun. A quick glance at the *Oxford English Dictionary* reveals that the mushroom can be a thing we eat or hunt (a noun); it can be an adjective used to suggest sudden growth, as in the "mushrooming budget crisis"; it can be a verb—when speaking of a rapid expansion or a hunt for fungus (*let's go mushrooming!*). But such a summary obscures telling details.

Some 3,500 years ago there was a Neolithic mushroom cult in the highlands of Guatemala, whose stone effigies depict a mushroom cap perched atop a stout stem from which a human face stares out. It seems curious that the stone figures of the Neolithic mushroom cult, which look like a symbol of fertility (unmistakably phallic with their thick stems and bulging caps), are thought to have been part of a funerary rite. But it also seems apt. For perhaps the appeal of mushrooms derives precisely from this association with both fertility *and* death—the phallic-shaped form that grows out of decaying matter. Thanatos and Eros joined.

When I move to Washington DC to teach literature after graduate school (almost fifteen years after finding that first mushroom in the mountains above Taos), I am alone for the first time in decades; I left yet another lover (a wonderful writer I love and admire), and I begin to have doubts about myself. Despite having been lucky in love, I seem—like my philandering father perhaps—unable to settle down. The moment always comes when I wonder if there isn't more or better, a kinder love affair or a more stimulating one, a lover more inspiring or less demanding, or—if delighted with my partner—then a bigger world for us to share, another job or city we might prefer. I've loved being in love and have had faith that there would always be more up ahead, that—like mushrooms—there would be a perennial abundance. But at forty I begin to wonder if I have, in fact, used up my portion of love's harvest.

It is partly due to these doubts—partly due to my father's death—that I decide to take another path through the woods of love; for the first time in twenty years I get involved with a man.

As I child, I could not imagine sexual intercourse between men and women. I refused at age six to believe that my parents had done what Debbie Segal, a popular girl next door, reported was necessary to conceive a child. It was Debbie Segal who told me where babies came from and what blow jobs were. Afterwards, her younger sister, Patti, and I sat in the back seat of my parents' blue-and-white Pontiac and debated whether or not it was possible that our parents had ever done this *and enjoyed it* and decided they had not.

I will be past forty before I really change my mind about this.

My father will be dead, and I will, for the first time, go to bed with a man and actually take pleasure in it and understand the appeal of this intense intimacy, of making of two bodies one, a closeness that seems almost sickeningly intimate.

In sex, as in eating fungus, one must overcome disgust.

Disgust is a universal emotion evidently, though what disgusts us varies cross-culturally. Entomophagy (the eating of bugs) is popular throughout much of the world; Mexicans eat corn rot; the Japanese evidently find bleu cheese revolting, as we might scorpion soup or palm worms. Most kids find snot and feces fascinating, but are repelled by the thought of sex when they learn of it.

In English, the word *disgust* has its root in taste (from the Latin *gustare*, to taste), but in truth it's not bad taste that disgusts us but contamination we fear, according to William Ian Miller's *The Anatomy of Disgust*. Overcoming disgust—whether to eat a mushroom or make love—is to some extent to overcome fear of contamination. In sex we surmount disgust by making of it a pleasure, welcoming a trespass we would reject in another sphere. A beloved's tongue in one's mouth delights, while an uninvited stranger's would likely not. It is this welcome contamination of the policed borders of the self that characterizes desire, Miller argues; one mark of love our willingness to be polluted, to be altered, changed by the beloved. Willing submission to contamination then might be the secret of lust and love. A thing we perhaps practice when we dare to eat a mushroom.

~

The man I get involved with is a filmmaker—a kind, clever, independent guy past fifty with a boyish gait and the build of a jock. A Columbia dropout (he quit to be an actor) with good stories and an easygoing manner. A former restaurateur, he makes me wonderful dinners of rockfish and filet mignon, artichokes and Portobello mushrooms when I get home late at night from teaching; he builds us roaring fires, and makes me tea, and takes me to the theater and concerts and movies and little insider Washington parties stocked with *Times* reporters and former ambassadors (old Afghanistan hands, they say) and politicians I've seen on TV.

I give him Bruckner symphonies and Auden; he gives me pearls and Proust. We go to concerts, to movies, meditate and swim, make love for hours in front of countless roaring fires, but it's not his coterie or our charming diversions that compel me but the animal comfort he provides.

After my father's death, I begin to wake in a cold panic. Not every morning, not even every week, but once a month or so, on the anniversary of his death or near it, I wake early and terrified, heart pounding, sickened by fear—a pure, unadulterated terror. I am grateful beyond words when my lover takes me in his powerful arms and holds me against his chest, where I can hear that old brag of the heart and rest.

The last time this happens—six months into our love affair, eight months after my father's death, when the first waves of grief are beginning to subside—I wake before dawn disoriented, uncertain where I am, choked with dread (a reminder that the word *anxiety* derives from the Latin *angere,* to choke). My lover rises up like a *kouros* beside me, his outline visible in the dim predawn light, a blocky figure against the dark, and silently takes me in his arms and pulls me to him and holds me tightly, before letting me go again. I will love him for this with a fierce animal affection; love it's not worth trying to speak.

~

Death never seems far from the minds of my friends when I offer to prepare for them a meal of wild mushrooms—

I've strolled through woods in New England and come on trumpet chanterelles and held them up, delighted by my find, only to be peppered with stories of poisonings, false identification, death, questions about how I can *tell*. In the language of mushroom hunting, as in the language of romance, one speaks of the false and the true, as one might speak of love. But in the realm of fungi, if not in love, I'm confident of my ability to tell the difference.

When I came down from the mountain with my first bag of golden chanterelles, I proposed to make a dinner for my best friend and her fiancé—a pasta in chanterelle and white wine sauce. I was delighted with the bounty and wanted to share. My best friend balked at the offer. "I don't want Brian eating that," she said of her fiancé. "Are you *sure* they're *safe*?" Eventually I convinced them to dine with me, and Brian—an earthy Spaniard—seemed as pleased as I by all I'd found, this unexpected bounty. But even I lay awake that night after dinner and wondered, as I looked out the window up at stars, if I would survive the night, if Brian would, and our friendship. (All did.)

~

I wonder if what disturbs us about fungi (and appeals) is that they are such close kin to the dead. These things that grow from the earth, that feed on decaying matter, which eventually we all will be. (Mushrooms are a kind of distant kin to the living as well. Originally classified as plants, mushrooms are thought now to be more closely related to animals: taxonomically they are eukaryotic, since they—like us—do not photosynthesize their food but absorb it, as we ingest.)

I wonder if the curious appeal of the mushroom is that, in eating it, risk is redeemed. Even death is. In developing a taste for mushrooms, one cultivates a taste for decay, making the prospect tolerable, palatable even, learning that even loss has savor. A distinct, even a delicious, flavor.

~

In June, in Washington DC, it pours. Rain in Washington is unlike rain in the American west. In Taos, storms come across the mesa like curtains, or like gods dragging their skirts—delicate gray threads or tendrils drifting down from the clouds to touch the flat mesa tops that bracket the Rio Grande Gorge and stretch to the distant table top of Pedernal (which

O'Keeffe made famous with her paintings)—their hems drifting like a net across the distant horizon until you hear rain battering the windows and run to close them. There, the pueblo people describe two kinds of rain: male rain, which is hard and pelting, and a female rain, which falls gently, soaking the earth.

But here in DC, rain is nothing like that—in DC, rain is brutal, sudden; the sky can be clotted with romantic low gray-and-white clouds for hours (weather that always puts me in mind of Gilbert Stuart paintings, perhaps because of their creamy billows in the background from which our first president seems to emerge) when suddenly it pours; it is like a faucet turned on over your head. It is not a pelting; it's a deluge. Blinding. Like buckshot hammering the roofs of cars. (Spiders in a bathtub must feel this way when you turn on a faucet to wash them down.) Pedestrians' umbrellas sag and wilt, busted on one flank or another. It doesn't help that this summer's storm is an historic rain—when it's over, the IRS will be closed on account of flooding.

But in the wake of that epic storm, as I walk home from my lover's house on R Street, I smell fungi as I pass the well-coiffed hedges of embassies along Massachusetts Ave.

In the backyard of my apartment building, when I get home, a colony of pale gilled mushrooms have come up seemingly overnight, like tiny white umbrellas opened in the grass. I don't eat gilled mushrooms—agarics—which these will be; they are too likely to be toxic, too easy to mistake. But seeing them lets me know that others are around. Blooming. (Or in the parlance of mycology, fruiting.)

~

After torrential rains shut down the National Gallery and IRS, we drive out to my lover's country house in Virginia to hunt mushrooms. But it is the wrong season for mushrooms in Virginia, it seems; we are too late (or too early) for morels and perhaps for love—ours a May/September love affair. When he gets angry or afraid he bellows, *I'm too old to change*. And I silently think to myself that I am too young for a lover who bellows.

Though I crave the comfort of his arms, the enormous reassurance of his great good health (he's in better shape than I have ever been, than anyone I've ever known has been, save perhaps for my first boyfriend, who was—like this man—a jock), I don't want an ardor measured out in teaspoons.

When we fight, it is almost always after we have been making love, and I feel enormously close to him. Then he grows quiet, edgy, seemingly angry at me; he picks fights over small things until finally I lose my patience and fight too. Eventually, I worry that we have fought too much, that he no longer likes me, and we inevitably fight over this, my desire for reassurance. (Friends say he sounds more invested in this than I am, and it is true that he has spoken, as I've not thought to do, of "going the distance," feeling "ready to commit," thinking we're "made for each other," but he often retracts these claims almost as soon as he's made them.) And I begin to imagine not a future together but one without him.

It seems unlikely that our love affair will bear fruit.

~

On the third of July, he breaks up with me. He says he's finally come to see this relationship the way I have all along—as impermanent, as temporary; he no longer believes we have a future together. I can't disagree. I say he's right; I haven't thought we had a future, but I'd hoped we could have a summer love affair. He says he'd rather sleep alone than date for the sake of dating. And when he says this, as we prepare to go to dinner, I feel as if I have been struck in the face. I am heartbroken.

Three nights later, I decide to walk the two miles from my apartment to his house to tell him the things I have neglected to say—how much I like him, love him, admire him, how smart and funny he is, how I do not want this ever to end. I go to tell him what I should have said all along.

~

When I set out for his place at 7:45, it is one of those perfect summer evenings in this city—the light long and pale in the late day, illuminating the pine trees and the red brick and white trim of the small, two-story, Federal-style buildings that line my street in northwest DC. Neighbors next door are out on the front stoop chatting, on the lawn, smoking, playing with their massive dog (Alsatian? Burmese mountain dog?). The sky is high and pale blue, the clouds pink and organdy and amethyst. And as I walk, I am so happy. I bring a pint of fresh purple figs, their luscious pink insides sweet, and hope that we will reconcile.

I cross the street and watch the light, and as I walk, I catch the scent of mushrooms. I look over at the postage-stamp lawn in front of one of the duplexes and see there the unmistakable toasted-bun brown of a bolete. I reach down and feel beneath the cap and find it spongy, not gilled, and pluck it. (I find it's not one mushroom but two, a double stem, their two stalks joined at a base as one.) The mushrooms' caps are convex, like tiny tables, yellow pores radially arranged in the pattern known as boletinoid. When I press the yellow flesh under the cap, it doesn't bruise (bruising blue can signal toxins). I am elated. It seems a good sign that on the way to see the man I love as I've loved no other, I should find this prize.

But when he opens the door, I can see it is too late—he looks exhausted, as my high-school boyfriend did after our repeated breakups. He looks as if he hasn't slept in days. This vital man looks beat. We sit on the couch in a little pool of lamp light and talk, or rather I recite my litany of love, telling him all the things I love about him. He says he hadn't known those things, that he loves me too (reciting his own ardent litany), but he says, in a tone unmistakably truthful, that he hasn't the energy for this, and I can see in his face and in the curl of his shoulders that it's true. But when he kisses me goodbye, it is with such tenderness, such passion, that I do not feel bereft but hopeful.

~

What is the peculiar pleasure of hunting edible mushrooms? Whatever it is, it has for me the same quality as lust, the same myopic monomaniacal yearning as obsessive love.

After my father dies and I begin dating men, I will discover belatedly what all the fuss has been about. My best friend will note that men's parts are often compared to mushrooms—the head of the cock like a mushroom cap, the fungal taste of fluids—but such comparisons hold no interest for me, seem inapt. The desire I feel for my new lover's body is simpler than that—I like the satiny feel of his skin, the salty taste of him; free (for a time at least) of the *tristesse* that flavors mushrooms.

~

The next day, I go out to gather more mushrooms where I found the last; I round the same corner up the street from my place and pluck three more, but when I turn them over and press my nail against the foam-yellow underside, the flesh bruises an unmistakable blue, like spilled indigo ink—a sign of a toxic mushroom. I stand there with my bruised mushrooms, now bereft: how could I have mistaken the bad for the good, the toxic for the prized? What I'd taken for a good sign was no good at all. Or if it was a sign, it was a sign that I'd lost my touch, my powers of discrimination, that I'd mistaken the toxic for the beloved.

I'm ready to head home when it occurs to me that perhaps I'd picked a different mushroom the previous night, perhaps more than one kind grows here, side-by-side. I see another mushroom in the grass, like the one that I'd collected the night before. I lean down and pluck it. Press its flesh. It does not bruise. Its stem is apricot colored, sunk into the spongy yellow underside of the cap like a leg into a sock. Its cap—unlike the three I'd picked a moment before—is not concave but convex. They are as different as can be, only superficially similar. Here, in the same spot, the poisonous and the good. I am relieved; I am delighted. Perhaps after all I was not mistaken in my happiness last night, to think there might be something promising here.

I spend an hour on-line and with mycology guides trying to identify the little mushrooms, finally I settle on *gyroparus castaneus*, a choice edible among boletes, said to grow "gregariously." (I think it might be *boletus piperatus*, but the flesh does not bruise pink.) It is the tiny brown belly button in the center of the cap that gives it away, a little rise like the tip of a hand-turned wooden knob, a small distinctive bump.

I cut one open and find it wormy, decide to return it to its spot under the trees to propagate. But the other—the two mushrooms joined at the stem—I can't bear to cut open, to part them. It occurs to me to clean them for some later date with Rick, to have them ready, so when we're next together we can share the pleasure of this. But there is no guarantee that we will be together again.

The pleasure of mushroom hunting is like that of literary analysis—it teaches us to see. At first, on entering the woods, the ground is an undifferentiated mess of leaves and twigs and pine needles, a blur of browns and greens. But then, like stepping out into a summer's night from a well-lit house to look at stars, my eyes adjust and I see—there by the base of an oak—a small red cap spotted with white polka dots (*amanita muscaria*), or a beautiful sculptural lump of white, like a tiny Barbara Hepworth (or a miniature Henry Moore) done in ivory fungus flesh (*albatrellus ovinus*), or a luminous purple cap like gelatinous amethyst (*laccaria amethystea*), and as soon as I've seen these mushrooms, more appear. Like sprites that have been hiding, called forth by the alchemy of longing.

~

After Rick and I break up in July, I am surprised to find that I am grief stricken.

In truth, I hadn't thought our affair mattered that much. Though I've desired him intensely, ours has seemed an affair less of the heart than of the grave—a way of dodging grief in the wake of my father's death. Grief's escape hatch. Though he has occasionally talked about "going the distance," about feeling "ready to commit," though he has said at times that we seem made for each other, I've assumed this was merely romantic hyperbole, that he—as I—had not taken this to heart. (A hunch he often confirmed, saying that he loved me but was not in love, that he didn't fall in love anymore, that he always feared that we were temperamentally unsuited, that we could never have a future because we couldn't get a stable foundation.)

But in the wake of our breakup, I cannot stop crying; I feel anxious, sick at heart. The symptoms seem obvious—that the grief this affair has helped me to avoid is now emerging, and now I must weep for my father.

~

So I call a therapist I saw briefly after college when I was first "coming out" (a phrase that recalls the push of mushroom caps through duff, lifting the weight of layers of accumulated forest litter from old trees), a woman who is gentle and reminds me of grass, the wide-open fields of the Midwest (it's something about her gentleness), who with a single question years ago released me to love women when that had seemed impossible till then (I'd said I thought I might be attracted to women. "So what would that mean?" she'd asked, turning a key in that low locked door).

When I tell her about Rick and me now, how we cannot seem to settle down, how sad I am that we've broken up again, I expect her to say that this is displaced grief, that we should talk about my dead father, but she says, a little impatiently it seems, "You need to *choose* him. He has chosen you, but you haven't chosen him. You need to let him know that you choose him."

I am frankly shocked by her response.

"Why are you afraid to choose," she asks, "to let him know that you want him?"

"Because it will hurt if he doesn't want me back," I say, as if it were obvious, ridiculous to ask, but this seems lame even as I say it, inadequate.

In my whole life, I have rarely chosen anything or anyone; I've let others' choices shape me, afraid of an arduous ardor perhaps. Of choice. Of being found wanting.

~

In the psychologically significant language of the mushroom hunt, the best mushrooms are known as "choice," a fact that will go unremarked by me until I am heartbroken over Rick. Then it will occur to me that perhaps all along what I've been hunting through these woods is decision itself, that my repetitive quest these many years with many lovers has been less for an elusive and delectable quarry (the jaunty porcini with its burnt-sienna glow, the neon orange of a frilled chanterelle) than for choice itself. To make one.

~

"To love with all one's soul and leave the rest to fate, was the simple rule she heeded," Nabokov wrote of his mother (lost to him by then, as his homeland was). "'*Vot zapomni* [now remember]' she would say in conspiratorial tones as she drew my attention to this or that loved thing in Vyra. . . ."

~

Two weeks after we split up, I dream that I have missed a boat (*missed the boat*!), and I fear that perhaps I have. I decide to call him to tell him that I miss him, that I'd like to skip the breakup part and go straight to being friends, but I do not really mean this. The truth is, I miss him like a limb and want very much to get back together.

I get his answering machine and leave my message, dreading that he may not call me back, but it seems best to lay myself open and love (even though this brings with it the possibility of loss and rejection). To my amazement, he calls back within minutes; says he was just about to call me; tells me he has hand-washed the bathing suit I'd left at his country house when we went out there seeking mushrooms. (I know, of course, that he might have simply mailed the suit to me, so the fact that he was going to call me heartens, gives me hope.)

We agree to meet the following Thursday, and I am briefly elated, but when I get to his doorstep a few days later and knock, I am nervous, wondering what I'll say and how we'll be. When I walk in, he takes me in his arms and kisses me passionately, and in that moment it seems it will all be okay.

But there's no guarantee, no sure thing. I am sure only of this: that for now this kind, strange, passionate, reticent man is the one I want, the one out of six billion I choose.

Later in the apartment where I live alone, I take a dried bag of mushrooms that I brought with me from New Mexico, labeled in an old Sharpie pen from the days when my lover and I hiked into the mountains above Taos and gathered these like happiness, abundant as our joy was then, from the pillows of green moss and the massive, lichen-covered boulders beside the foot path.

I take a good red wine and reconstitute the desiccated mushroom caps, which look like wood chips or dried leaves, and which taste a little like dirt, like smoke, the taste I imagine loss would have were it a food, the taste history itself might have—meaty and sustaining, with the faint tang of blood and earth—like a great and sorrowful joy. (I imagine that the Germans must have a word for this flavor and this feeling, but I find to my delight that it's the Russians who do, my landsman and Nabokov's, and that that word is *umilenie*, which describes a heartbreak joy, a complex mixture of sorrow and tenderness, rapture and grief.) I eat my heart out.

Epilogue

We survived that breakup, and later that summer we dined together, sharing the feast of spring: morels, prepared using my favorite recipe: Morels in Cream on Chive Toast. It's quick (thirty minutes) and fabulous.

Ingredients: ½ pound morel mushrooms, ends trimmed; 2 tablespoons unsalted butter; 3 small shallots, chopped; 2 tablespoons dry white wine or white vermouth; ¼ cup crème fraiche; Celtic sea salt or Kosher salt and freshly ground black pepper; 4 slices good white bread, crusts trimmed; 1 tablespoon fresh chopped chives.

1. Brush excess dirt from mushrooms (do not soak or rinse with water). Slice mushrooms in half lengthwise; chop into ¼-inch pieces.
2. Melt butter in a large skillet over medium-high heat. Add shallots and sauté until very limp, about 3 minutes. Add mushrooms and cook, stirring, for 5 minutes. Add wine, reduce heat to medium, cover, and cook for 5 minutes more.
3. Uncover pot and continue cooking, stirring occasionally, until most of the liquid has evaporated, about 3 minutes. Stir in crème fraiche; simmer until slightly thickened, 2 minutes longer. Season with salt and pepper to taste.
4. Toast bread and spread with butter. Cut each slice in half diagonally and sprinkle lightly with chives. Top each toast triangle with some mushroom mixture. Sprinkle with additional chives, garnish with sea salt, and serve.

You will want to eat this all yourself, but like many things, it is more delectable shared by two.

→ 7 ←

Coriander and Carrot

MICHAEL S. GLASER

On the third consecutive
rainy day,
the soup should be made.

Carrots peeled and cooked until soft,
a blurp of good olive oil,
a dollop of coriander
a clove of garlic
a pinch of sea-salt, pepper,

and then the blender,
where blades turn the mixture
to mush.

Taste.

Add whatever is needed:
More salt,
Perhaps some basil or leek,
some milk or cream,
until it is just right.

Then beat, heat and serve
with homemade granary bread
and sweet creamery butter.

Tell yourself that in the old days
the gods must have eaten like this.

Imagine them happy.

8

An Unspoken Hunger

From *An Unspoken Hunger: Stories from the Field*

TERRY TEMPEST WILLIAMS

It is an unspoken hunger we deflect with knives—one avocado between us, cut neatly in half, twisted then separated from the large wooden pit. With the green fleshy boats in hand, we slice vertical strips from one end to the other. Vegetable planks. We smother the avocado with salsa, hot chilies at noon in the desert. We look at each other and smile, eating avocados with sharp silver blades, risking the blood of our tongues repeatedly.

PART II

Bread, Polenta, and Pasta

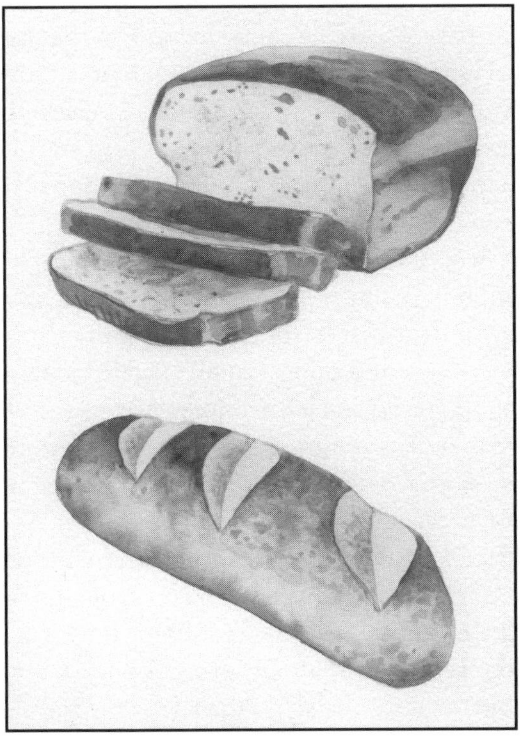

Bread

From the bread made from corn and cooked on heated rocks and then buried in hot ashes by Native Americans to home bakers such as Lydia Maria Child paying attention to the temperature of her home, water, and oven as well as considering different leavening methods, across time and region, bread has been an essential and basic part of American cookery. With the influence and traditions of many other culinary cultures, most of which include the "staff of life"[1] in one form or another, bread choice in the United States has evolved far beyond the johnnycake and Boston brown bread of early America to include croissants and baguettes originating from France; pumpernickel loafs introduced by German immigrants; bagels, bialys, and challah from eastern Europe; pita from the Mediterranean; tortillas from Mexico; naan and roti from South Asia; and focaccia from Italy.

Other breads have American roots. In 1849, San Francisco's Boudin Bakery began selling San Francisco sourdough bread. In the 1870s, the Parker House Hotel in Boston developed Parker House rolls. And Wonder Bread, first developed in the 1920s and sold sliced starting in 1930, was the first commercially sliced bread distributed nationally—a symbol of American industrialization.

By the 1960s, with the rise of environmentalism and a backlash against overly refined foods, Wonder Bread became, for many people, less a symbol of progress than a target for criticism. By the 1970s and early '80s, with vegetarian, vegan, and other California-cuisine-based cookbooks being published nationally—such as Mollie Katzen's *Enchanted Broccoli Forest*—many Americans returned to baking their own bread at home, especially breads with whole grains, often constructing their experiences in the exuberant, exaggerated language of hippie poets. As Katzen herself says, "It is difficult to talk about bread-baking without lapsing into sentimentality. One is tempted to go on and on about how exhilarated and connected to the universe one feels, about how the kitchen atmosphere acquires sublime soulfulness, about how born-again bread-makers are magical, charismatic individuals."[2] In the late 1980s and early '90s, home bread-making machines became all the rage, allowing individuals to have fresh-baked bread without intensive labor. Such appliances, though, began to wane in popularity in the late '90s and into the early 2000s, when low-carb diets, such as the Atkins Diet, came into vogue. Today—as, yet again, food fads change and low-carb diets are losing their appeal over regimens focusing on eating moderate amounts of a variety of foods, including breads—both commercial bakeries such as Panera as well as artisanal patisseries now cater to a range of tastes and dietary dicta.

Although different kinds of breads have risen and fallen in popularity, in many ways the concerns of bread makers have remained that same: in 1828, Lydia Maria Child considered the effects of the weather on her baking; nearly 180 years later, Alice Waters, in *The Art of Simple Food*, observes that weather affects bread, that "humidity, heat, and cold each exert their influence" and that "this makes baking ever-changing and forever fascinating."[3] The forever fascinating process of bread baking—and the ways it both evolves and remains the same—is evident in Karen Leona Anderson's contemporary poem "Recipe: Gingerbread," in which she draws from Amelia Simmons's 1796 *American Cookery*, even as she alludes to more modern baking practices.

In addition to bread's place as a food staple in most homes, it has also entered our language as a powerful metaphor. A person who supports a family economically is referred to as a "breadwinner," and "bread and butter" is a phrase that refers to a person's source of regular income. Anderson's poem considers Simmons's method of supporting herself by writing a cookbook, and the first selection from Lydia Maria Child's *The American Frugal Housewife* provides tips for how to use that "bread and butter" economically, arguing that every family member "should be employed either in earning or saving money." And, although Child does not employ the phrase the "best thing since sliced bread," she certainly relies on maxims and does praise the kind of innovation and industry that this expression implies.

In turn, Sharon Olds, in her poem "Bread," creates a different kind of metaphor, simultaneously showing a preadolescent girl baking bread and contemplating the young girl's physical development, the way the girl—like the bread she bakes—is "shaped, glazed, and at any moment goes / into the oven, to turn to that porous / warm substance, and then under the / knife to be sliced for the having, the tasting, and the /giving of life." Although the idea of a girl-turned-woman being "sliced for the having" may at first seem violent and disturbing, Olds ends on a hopeful note, suggesting the life-giving potential of women and women's bodies.

Although Olds's metaphor—comparing a developing girl's body to baking bread—may seem unorthodox, comparing bread to a body is not. Bread, especially for Christians, has religious significance. The Lord's Prayer includes the line "give us our daily bread," a plea that God will provide necessities, and—at the Last Supper—Jesus compared the bread to his body, a comparison still made in practices of Communion and the Eucharist. Although the selections in this chapter are not overtly religious, we do see within them how the sharing of bread is a kind of communion, especially in the selection from Fannie Flagg's novel *Fried Green Tomatoes at the Whistle Stop Cafe*. In this piece, Idgie and Ruth share buttermilk biscuits and the honey that Idgie—at great personal risk—has harvested for Ruth. Idgie admits that she would kill for Ruth if anyone hurt her. Ruth, however, says that there is no good reason to kill. The two then engage in the following conversation, which makes a connection between self-sacrifice and love:

> "All right, then, I'd die for you. How about that? Don't you think somebody could die for love?"
>
> "No."
>
> "The Bible says Jesus Christ did."
>
> "That's different."
>
> "No it isn't. I could die right now, and I wouldn't mind. I'd be the only corpse with a smile on my face."

From this first moment, Flagg develops the love between Idgie and Ruth—from Idgie's young infatuation to an enduring commitment between the two—showing the loyalty possible even in life's most severe trials, a loyalty that is symbolized by their shared bread.

Polenta and Pasta

Although polenta and pasta are not breads, we include them in this chapter as examples of other grain-based foods that, like bread, are seen by many people as both staples and comfort foods. The main ingredients of such dishes—either corn or wheat—hark back to those used by Native Americans and Colonial settlers, yet these dishes further emphasize the ways other cultures and their food traditions—in this case Italian—have influenced both American food and literature.

Caroline M. Grant shows both communion and comfort in her essay "In Nancy's Kitchen," which considers her mother-in-law's legacy and the relationship they shared. Of Nancy, Grant explains, "Food was her religion and her culture." She writes of sumptuous shared meals around a well-worn monastery table secured in Italy by her in-laws, and we see how the abundance and simplicity of Italian foodways have shaped their family. Grant ends with two recipes, one sweet and one savory, that call for the use of the common Italian grain polenta. (Nancy was known to put a roll of polenta in a stocking as a Christmas gift.)

Peter Elbling, too, highlights Italian culinary culture in his historical novel *The Food Taster*, though his version of sixteenth-century Italy and the adventures of a food taster for the reviled Duke Federico are far from the loving family meals that Grant describes. Yet Elbling's narrator, like Flagg's focal characters, considers what might be worth killing and dying for, and he also contemplates the nature of love—both familial and romantic—as well as of comfort: themes that are, in many ways, the staples or "the bread" of literature.

NOTES

1. "And when I have broken the staff of your bread, ten women shall bake your bread in one oven, and they shall deliver you your bread again by weight: and ye shall eat, and not be satisfied" (The King James Bible, Leviticus 26:26).
2. Mollie Katzen, *The Enchanted Broccoli Forest . . . and Other Timeless Delicacies* (Berkeley, CA: Ten Speed, 1982), 85.
3. Alice Waters, *The Art of Simple Food* (New York: Clarkson Potter, 2007), 59.

9

From *The American Frugal Housewife*

LYDIA MARIA CHILD

The true economy of housekeeping is simply the art of gathering up all the fragments, so that nothing be lost.* I mean fragments of *time*, as well as *materials*. Nothing should be thrown away so long as it is possible to make any use of it, however trifling that use may be; and whatever be the size of a family, every member should be employed either in earning or saving money.

"Time is money." For this reason, cheap as stockings are, it is good economy to knit them. Cotton and woollen yarn are both cheap; hose that are knit wear twice as long as woven ones; and they can be done at odd minutes of time, which would not be otherwise employed. Where there are children, or aged people, it is sufficient to recommend knitting, that it is an *employment*.

In this point of view, patchwork is good economy. It is indeed a foolish waste of time to tear cloth into bits for the sake of arranging it anew in fantastic figures; but a large family may be kept out of idleness, and a few shillings saved, by thus using scraps of gowns, curtains, &c.

In the country, where grain is raised, it is a good plan to teach children to prepare and braid straw for their own bonnets, and their brothers' hats.

Where turkeys and geese are kept, handsome feather fans may as well be made by the younger members of a family, as to be bought. The sooner children are taught to turn their faculties to some account, the better for them and for their parents.

In this country, we are apt to let children romp away their existence, till they get to be thirteen or fourteen. This is not well. It is not well for the

* Nonstandard, eighteenth-century spelling within this selection has been left untouched.

purses and patience of parents; and it has a still worse effect on the morals and habits of the children. *Begin early* is the great maxim for everything in education. A child of six years old can be made useful; and should be taught to consider every day lost in which some little thing has not been done to assist others.

Children can very early be taught to take all the care of their own clothes.

They can knit garters, suspenders, and stockings; they can make patchwork and braid straw; they can make mats for the table, and mats for the floor; they can weed the garden, and pick cranberries from the meadow, to be carried to market.

Provided brothers and sisters go together, and are not allowed to go with bad children, it is a great deal better for the boys and girls on a farm to be picking blackberries at six cents a quart, than to be wearing out their clothes in useless play. They enjoy themselves just as well; and they are earning something to buy clothes, at the same time they are tearing them.

It is wise to keep an exact account of all you expend—even of a paper of pins. This answers two purposes; it makes you more careful in spending money, and it enables your husband to judge precisely whether his family live within his income. No false pride, or foolish ambition to appear as well as others, should ever induce a person to live one cent beyond the income of which he is certain. If you have two dollars a day, let nothing but sickness induce you to spend more than nine shillings; if you have one dollar a day, do not spend but seventy-five cents; if you have half a dollar a day, be satisfied to spend forty cents.

To associate with influential and genteel people with an appearance of equality, unquestionably has its advantages; particularly where there is a family of sons and daughters just coming upon the theatre of life; but, like all other external advantages, these have their proper price, and may be bought too dearly. They who never reserve a cent of their income, with which to meet any unforeseen calamity, "pay too dear for the whistle," whatever temporary benefits they may derive from society. Self-denial, in proportion to the narrowness of your income, will eventually be the happiest and most respectable course for you and yours. If you are prosperous, perseverance and industry will not fail to place you in such a situation as your ambition covets; and if you are not prosperous, it will be well for your children that they have not been educated to higher hopes than they will ever realize.

If you are about to furnish a house, do not spend all your money, be it much or little. Do not let the beauty of this thing, and the cheapness of that, tempt you to buy unnecessary articles. Doctor Franklin's maxim was a wise one, "Nothing is cheap that we do not want." Buy merely enough to get along with at first. It is only by experience that you can tell what will be the wants of your family. If you spend all your money, you will find you have purchased many things you do not want, and have no means left to get many things which you do want. If you have enough, and more than enough, to get everything suitable to your situation, do not think you must spend it all, merely because you happen to have it. Begin humbly. As riches increase, it is easy and pleasant to increase in hospitality and splendour; but it is always painful and inconvenient to decrease. After all, these things are viewed in their proper light by the truly judicious and respectable. Neatness, tastefulness, and good sense, may be shown in the management of a small household, and the arrangement of a little furniture, as well as upon a larger scale; and these qualities are always praised, and always treated with respect and attention. The consideration which many purchase by living beyond their income, and of course living upon others, is not worth the trouble it costs. The glare there is about this false and wicked parade is deceptive; it does not in fact procure a man valuable friends, or extensive influence. More than that, it is wrong—morally wrong, so far as the individual is concerned; and injurious beyond calculation to the interests of our country. To what are the increasing beggary and discouraged exertions of the present period owing? A multitude of causes have no doubt tended to increase the evil; but the root of the whole matter is the extravagance of all classes of people. We never shall be prosperous till we make pride and vanity yield to the dictates of honesty and prudence! We never shall be free from embarrassment until we cease to be ashamed of industry and economy. Let women do their share towards reformation—Let their fathers and husbands see them happy without finery; and if their husbands and fathers have (as is often the case) a foolish pride in seeing them decorated, let them gently and gradually check this feeling, by showing that they have better and surer means of commanding respect—Let them prove, by the exertion of ingenuity and economy, that neatness, good taste, and gentility, are attainable without great expense.

The writer has no apology to offer for this cheap little book of economical hints, except her deep conviction that such a book is needed. In this case, renown is out of the question, and ridicule is a matter of indifference.

The information conveyed is of a common kind; but it is such as the majority of young housekeepers do not possess, and such as they cannot obtain from cookery books. Books of this kind have usually been written for the wealthy: I have written for the poor. I have said nothing about *rich* cooking; those who can afford to be epicures will find the best of information in the "Seventy-five Receipts." I have attempted to teach how money can be *saved*, not how it can be *enjoyed*. If any persons think some of the maxims too rigidly economical, let them inquire how the largest fortunes among us have been made. They will find thousands and millions have been accumulated by a scrupulous attention to sums "infinitely more minute than sixty cents."

In early childhood, you lay the foundation of poverty or riches, in the habits you give your children. Teach them to save everything,—not for their *own* use, for that would make them selfish—but for *some* use. Teach them to *share* everything with their playmates; but never allow them to *destroy* anything.

I once visited a family where the most exact economy was observed; yet nothing was mean or uncomfortable. It is the character of true economy to be as comfortable and genteel with a little, as others can be with much. In this family, when the father brought home a package, the older children would, of their own accord, put away the paper and twine neatly, instead of throwing them in the fire, or tearing them to pieces. If the little ones wanted a piece of twine to play scratch-cradle, or spin a top, there it was, in readiness; and when they threw it upon the floor, the older children had no need to be told to put it again in its place.

The other day, I heard a mechanic say, "I have a wife and two little children; we live in a very small house; but, to save my life, I cannot spend less than twelve hundred a year." Another replied, "You are not economical; I spend but eight hundred." I thought to myself,—"Neither of you pick up your twine and paper." A third one, who was present, was silent; but after they were gone, he said, "I keep house, and comfortably too, with a wife and children, for six hundred a year; but I suppose they would have thought me mean, if I had told them so." I did not think him mean; it merely occurred to me that his wife and children were in the habit of picking up paper and twine.

Economy is generally despised as a low virtue, tending to make people ungenerous and selfish. This is true of avarice; but it is not so of economy. The man who is economical, is laying up for himself the permanent power of being useful and generous. He who thoughtlessly gives away ten dollars, when he owes a hundred more than he can pay, deserves no praise,—he obeys a sudden impulse, more like instinct than reason: it would be real charity to check this feeling; because the good he does may be doubtful, while the injury he does his family and creditors is certain. True economy is a careful treasurer in the service of benevolence; and where they are united respectability, prosperity and peace will follow.

Bread, Yeast &c.

It is more difficult to give rules for making bread than for anything else; it depends so much on judgment and experience. In summer, bread should be mixed with cold water; during a chilly, damp spell, the water should be slightly warm; in severe cold weather, it should be mixed quite warm, and set in a warm place during the night. If your yeast is new and lively, a small quantity will make the bread rise; if it be old and heavy, it will take more. In these things I believe wisdom must be gained by a few mistakes.

Six quarts of meal will make two good sized loaves of *Brown Bread*. Some like to have it half Indian meal and half rye meal; others prefer it one third Indian, and two thirds rye. Many mix their brown bread over night; but there is no need of it; and it is more likely to sour, particularly in summer. If you do mix it the night before you bake it, you must not put in more than half the yeast I am about to mention, unless the weather is intensely cold. The meal should be sifted separately. Put the Indian in your bread-pan, sprinkle a little salt among it, and wet it thoroughly with scalding water. Stir it up while you are scalding it. Be sure and have hot water enough; for Indian absorbs a great deal of water. When it is cool, pour in your rye; add two gills of lively yeast, and mix it with water as stiff as you can knead it. Let it stand an hour and a half, in a cool place in summer, on the hearth in winter. It should be put into a very hot oven, and baked three or four hours. It is all the better for remaining in the oven over night.

Flour Bread should have a sponge set the night before. The sponge should be soft enough to pour; mixed with water, warm or cold, according to the temperature of the weather. One gill of lively yeast is enough to put into sponge for two loaves. I should judge about three pints of sponge would be right for two loaves. The warmth of the place in which the sponge is set, should be determined by the coldness of the weather. If your sponge looks frothy in the morning, it is a sign your bread will be good; if it does not rise, stir in a little more emptings; if it rises too much, taste of it, to see if it has any acid taste; if so, put in a tea-spoonful of pearlash when you mould in your flour; be sure the pearlash is well dissolved in water; if there are little lumps, your bread will be full of bitter spots. About an hour before your oven is ready, stir in flour into your sponge till it is stiff enough to lay on a well floured board or table. Knead it up pretty stiff, and put it into well greased pans, and let it stand in a cool or warm place, according to the weather. If the oven is ready, put them in fifteen or twenty minutes after the dough begins to rise up and crack; if the oven is not ready, move the pans to a cooler spot, to prevent the dough from becoming sour by too much rising. Common sized loaves will bake in three quarters of an hour. If they slip easily in the pans, it is a sign they are done. Some people do not set a soft sponge for flour bread; they knead it up all ready to put in the pans the night before, and leave it to rise. White bread and pies should not be set in the oven until the brown bread and beans have been in half an hour. If the oven be too hot, it will bind the crust so suddenly that the bread cannot rise; if it be too cold, the bread will fall. Flour bread should not be too stiff.

Some people like one third Indian in their flour. Others like one third rye; and some think the nicest of all bread is one third Indian, one third rye, and one third flour, made according to the directions for flour bread. When Indian is used, it should be salted, and scalded, before the other meal is put in. A mixture of other grains is economical when flour is high.

Dyspepsia Bread.—The American Farmer publishes the following receipt for making bread, which has proved highly salutary to persons afflicted with that complaint, viz.:—Three quarts unbolted wheat meal; one quart soft water, warm, but not hot; one gill of fresh yeast; one gill of molasses, or not, as may suit the taste; one tea-spoonful of saleratus.

To make Rice Bread.—Boil a pint of rice soft; add a pint of leaven; then, three quarts of the flour; put it to rise in a tin or earthen vessel until it has risen sufficiently; divide it into three parts; then bake it as other bread, and you will have three large loaves.

Heating ovens must be regulated by experience and observation. There is a difference in wood in giving out heat; there is a great difference in the construction of ovens; and when an oven is extremely cold, either on account of the weather, or want of use, it must be heated more. Economical people heat ovens with pine wood, fagots, brush, and such light stuff. If you have none but hard wood, you must remember that it makes very hot coals, and therefore less of it will answer. A smart fire for an hour and a half is a general rule for common sized family ovens, provided brown bread and beans are to be baked. An hour is long enough to heat an oven for flour bread. Pies bear about as much heat as flour bread: pumpkin pies will bear more. If you are afraid your oven is too hot, throw in a little flour and shut it up for a minute. If it scorches black immediately, the heat is too furious; if it merely browns, it is right. Some people wet an old broom two or three times, and turn it round near the top of the oven till it dries; this prevents pies and cake from scorching on the top. When you go into a new house, heat your oven two or three times, to get it seasoned, before you use it. After the wood is burned, rake the coals over the bottom of the oven, and let them lie a few minutes.

Those who make their own bread should make yeast too. When bread is nearly out, always think whether yeast is in readiness; for it takes a day and night to prepare it. One handful of hops, with two or three handsful of malt and rye bran, should be boiled fifteen or twenty minutes, in two quarts of water, then strained, hung on to boil again, and thickened with half a pint of rye and water stirred up quite thick, and a little molasses; boil it a minute or two, and then take it off to cool. When just about lukewarm, put in a cupful of good lively yeast, and set it in a cool place in summer, and warm place in winter. If it is too warm when you put in the old yeast, all the spirit will be killed.

In summer, yeast sours easily; therefore, make but little at a time. Bottle it when it gets well a working; it keeps better when the air is corked out. If you find it acid, but still spirited, put a little pearlash to it, as you use it; but by no means put it into your bread unless it foams up bright and lively as soon as the pearlash mixes with it. Never keep yeast in tin; it destroys its life.

There is another method of making yeast, which is much easier, and I think quite as good. Stir rye and cold water, till you make a stiff thickening. Then pour in boiling water, and stir it all the time, till you make it as thin as the yeast you buy; three or four table spoons heaping full are enough for a quart of water. When it gets about cold, put in half a pint of lively yeast. When it works well, bottle it; but if very lively, do not cork your bottle *very* tight, for fear it will burst. Always think to make new yeast before the old is gone; so that you may have some to work with. Always wash and scald your bottle clean after it has contained sour yeast. Beware of freezing yeast.

Milk yeast is made quicker than any other. A pint of new milk with a tea-spoonful of salt, and a large spoon of flour stirred in, set by the fire to keep lukewarm, will make yeast fit for use in an hour. Twice the quantity of common yeast is necessary, and unless used soon is good for nothing. Bread made of this yeast dries sooner. It is convenient in summer, when one wants to make biscuits suddenly.

A species of leaven may be made that will keep any length of time. Three ounces of hops in a pail of water boiled down to a quart; strain it, and stir in a quart of rye meal while boiling hot. Cool it and add half a pint of good yeast; after it has risen a few hours, thicken it with Indian meal stiff enough to roll out upon a board; then put it in the sun and air a few days to dry. A piece of this cake two inches square, dissolved in warm water, and thickened with a little flour will make a large loaf of bread.

Potatoes make a very good yeast. Mash three large potatoes fine; pour a pint of boiling water over them; when almost cold, stir in two spoonfuls of flour, two of molasses, and a cup of good yeast. This yeast should be used while new.

→ 10 ←

Recipe: Gingerbread

KAREN LEONA ANDERSON

after Amelia Simmons's American Cookery (1796)

Three pounds flour—breathes America's
orphan, pearl-complexioned,

a sweetheart but in need of a living—
a grated nutmeg, two ounces ginger,

one pound sugar. Spice: she has
for us a powder: something

bitter: *three small spoons*
pearl ash dissolved in cream;

a new chemical leavening
from the burnt down trees

of Albany. So nice,
so not yeast. So—

one pound butter,
four eggs—laborless:

not eighteen whites beaten
to a raging foam: not fat

to rub into nine pounds of flour,
no sticky miscarriage, no

mother, no child. No need.
Just *knead the dough stiff* and

shape it to your fancy; lady,
orphan, knows how to feed

herself; the rag paper

cheap; the page gone quick
—*bake 15 minutes*—

with ink—

11

Whistle Stop, Alabama

From *Fried Green Tomatoes at the Whistle Stop Cafe*

FANNIE FLAGG

July 18, 1924

Ruth had been in Whistle Stop for about two months, and this Saturday morning, someone knocked at her bedroom window at 6 A.M. Ruth opened her eyes and saw Idgie sitting in the chinaberry tree and motioning for her to open the window.

Ruth got up, half asleep. "What are you up so early for?"

"You promised we could go on a picnic today."

"I know, but does it have to be this early? It's Saturday."

"Please. You promised you would. If you don't come right now, I'll jump off the roof and kill myself. Then what would you do?"

Ruth laughed. "Well, what about Patsy Ruth and Mildred and Essie Rue, aren't they going to come with us?"

"No."

"Don't you think we should ask them?"

"No. Please, I want you to myself. Please. I want to show you something."

"Idgie, I don't want to hurt their feelings."

"Oh, you won't hurt their feelings. They don't want to come anyhow. I asked them already, and they want to stay home in case their old stupid boyfriends come by."

"Are you sure?"

"Sure I'm sure," she lied.

"What about Ninny and Julian?"

"They said they've got things to do today. Come on, Ruth, Sipsey's already made us a lunch, just for the two of us. If you don't come, I'll jump and then you'll have my death on your hands. I'll be dead in my grave and you'll wish you'd have come to just one little picnic."

"Well, all right. Let me get dressed, at least."

"Hurry up! Don't get all dressed up, just come on out—I'll meet you in the car."

"Are we going in the car?"

"Sure. Why not?"

"Okay."

Idgie had failed to mention that she had sneaked into Julian's room at 5 A.M. and had stolen the keys to his Model T out of his pants pockets, and it was extremely important to get going before he woke up.

They drove way out to this place that Idgie had found years ago, by Double Springs Lake, where there was a waterfall that flowed into this crystal clear stream that was filled with beautiful brown and gray stones, as round and smooth as eggs.

Idgie spread the blanket out and got the basket out of the car. She was being very mysterious.

Finally, she said, "Ruth, if I show you something, do you swear that you will never tell another living soul?"

"Show me what? What is it?"

"Do you swear? You won't tell?"

"I swear. What is it?"

"I'll show you."

Idgie reached into the picnic basket and got out an empty glass jar, said, "Let's go," and they walked about a mile back up into the woods.

Idgie pointed to a tree and said, "There it is!"

"There is what?"

"That big oak tree over there."

"Oh."

She took Ruth by the hand and walked her over to the left, about one hundred feet away, behind a tree, and said, "Now, Ruth, you stay right here, and no matter what happens, don't move."

"What are you going to do?"

"Never mind, you just watch me, all right? And be quiet. Don't make any noise, whatever you do."

Idgie, who was barefoot, started walking over to the big oak tree and about halfway there, turned to see if Ruth was watching. When she got about ten feet from the tree, she made sure again that Ruth was still watching. Then she did the most amazing thing. She very slowly tiptoed up to it, humming very softly, and stuck her hand with the jar in it, right in the hole in the middle of the oak.

All of a sudden, Ruth heard a sound like a buzz saw, and the sky went black as hordes of angry bees swarmed out of the hole.

In seconds, Idgie was covered from head to foot with thousands of bees. Idgie just stood there, and in a minute, carefully pulled her hand out of the tree and started walking slowly back toward Ruth, still humming. By the time she had gotten back, almost all the bees had flown away and what had been a completely black figure was now Idgie, standing there, grinning from ear to ear, with a jar of wild honey.

She held it up, offering the jar to Ruth. "Here you are, madame, this is for you."

Ruth, who had been scared out of her wits, slid down the tree onto the ground, and burst into tears. "I thought you were dead! Why did you do that? You could have been killed!"

Idgie said, "Oh, don't cry. I'm sorry. Here, don't you want the honey? I got it just for you . . . please don't cry. It's all right, I do it all the time. I never get stung. Honest. Here, let me help you up, you're getting yourself all dirty."

She handed Ruth the old blue bandanna she had in her overalls pocket. Ruth was still shaky, but she got up and blew her nose and wiped off her dress.

Idgie tried to cheer her up. "Just think, Ruth, I never did it for anybody else before. Now nobody in the whole world knows I can do that but you. I just wanted for us to have a secret together, that's all."

Ruth didn't respond.

"I'm sorry, Ruth, please don't be mad at me."

"Mad?" Ruth put her arms around Idgie and said, "Oh Idgie, I'm not mad at you. It's just that I don't know what I'd do if anything ever happened to you. I really don't."

Idgie's heart started pounding so hard it almost knocked her over.

After they had eaten the chicken and potato salad and all the biscuits and most of the honey, Ruth leaned back against the tree and Idgie put her head in her lap. "You know, Ruth, I'd kill for you. Anybody that would ever hurt you, I'd kill them in a minute and never think twice about it."

"Oh Idgie, that's a terrible thing to say."

"No it isn't. I'd rather kill for love than kill for hate. Wouldn't you?"

"Well, I don't think we should ever kill for any reason."

"All right, then, I'd die for you. How about that? Don't you think somebody could die for love?"

"No."

"The Bible says Jesus Christ did."

"That's different."

"No it isn't. I could die right now, and I wouldn't mind. I'd be the only corpse with a smile on my face."

"Don't be silly."

"I could have been killed today, couldn't I have?"

Ruth took her hand and smiled down at her. "My Idgie's a bee charmer."

"Is that what I am?"

"That's what you are. I've heard there were people who could do it, but I'd never seen one before today."

"Is it bad?"

"Nooo. It's wonderful. Don't you know that?"

"Naw, I thought it was crazy or something."

"No—it a wonderful thing to be."

Ruth leaned down and whispered in her ear. "You're an old bee charmer, Idgie Threadgoode, that's what you are. . . ."

Idgie smiled back at her and looked up into the clear blue sky that reflected in her eyes, and she was as happy as anybody who is in love in the summer time can be.

Sipsey's Recipes

Compliments of Evelyn Couch

BUTTERMILK BISCUITS

- 2 cups flour
- 2 teaspoons baking powder
- 2 teaspoons salt
- ¼ teaspoon soda
- ½ cup Crisco
- 1 cup buttermilk

Sift dry ingredients together. Add Crisco and blend well until like fine meal. Add buttermilk and mix. Roll out thin and cut into desired size biscuit. Bake in greased pan at 450 degrees until golden brown.

12

Bread

SHARON OLDS

When my daughter makes bread, a cloud of flour
hangs in the air like pollen. She sifts and
sifts again, the salt and sugar
close as the grain of her skin. She heats the
water to body temperature
with the sausage lard, fragrant as her scalp
the day before hair-wash, and works them together on a
floured board. Her broad palms
bend the paste toward her and the heel of her hand
presses it away, until the dough
begins to snap, glossy and elastic as the
torso bending over it,
this ten-year-old girl, random specks of
yeast in her flesh beginning to heat,
her volume doubling every month now, but still
raw and hard. She slaps the dough and it
crackles under her palm, sleek and
ferocious and still leashed, like her body, no
breasts rising like bubbles of air toward the
surface of the loaf. She greases the pan, she is
shaped, glazed, and at any moment goes
into the oven, to turn to that porous
warm substance, and then under the
knife to be sliced for the having, the tasting, and the
giving of life.

13

In Nancy's Kitchen

CAROLINE M. GRANT

In Nancy's kitchen, we found nineteen pounds of pasta, three bottles of clam juice, six jars of chutney, and seven different types of olive paste. In Nancy's kitchen, three packages of ice cream cones stood next to two bags of chips and one box of matzo meal. In Nancy's kitchen, you could open any cupboard and find the fixings for a complete meal, but you might search for an hour before finding a measuring cup (there was one, behind the ramekins, next to the olive oil, in the cupboard over the stove). In Nancy's kitchen, crystal wineglasses clinked shoulders with French country pottery, and a tin of white truffles threatened to fall over onto a twisted, half-spent tube of sweetened vanilla chestnut puree. We found enough rustic burlap bags of Arborio to sandbag the house in a flood. My mother-in-law had cans of soup for emergencies and a box of Kraft macaroni and cheese because her niece and nephews didn't really like what Jim, her late husband, made them from scratch. They've grown past the mac-and-cheese stage, but a box remained, just in case.

My husband Tony, our one-year-old son Ben, and I were staying with Tony's mom Nancy because she was bedridden with leg pain. We thought it was a result of overly ambitious physical therapy after a back injury, just a temporary inconvenience. We thought she just needed company and a couple warm meals until she was back on her feet and back to her morning routine: the paper and a bowl of polenta with cracked pepper at the Depot downtown, then home for a spell before heading over the hill to Larkspur, where she would sit at her regular table in the Italian café with a cappuccino and the *New York Times* crossword puzzle.

The first weekend we were all out of sorts. Ben didn't sleep well in the unfamiliar portacrib; Tony and I didn't sleep well in the overheated guest room; Nancy didn't sleep well for concern about us. We didn't bring enough clothing; we didn't bring enough toys to distract Ben from his Nonna's unbabyproofed cupboards. But the second weekend, though fighting a rising tide of worry (why is she still in such crying pain?), we were ready. We loaded the car as if for a trip cross-country, not just across the bridge, and settled in.

At first we kept Ben's high chair in the dining room and excused ourselves from Nancy to feed him. But Ben's a good eater, and we soon realized his meals could highlight our days. We rolled his high chair into her bedroom, and three times a day his meals were a show, the day's entertainment. He flapped his arms, impatient at how slowly we shoveled spoonfuls into his eager mouth, then flapped again to demand the sippy cup. Working on finger food, he carefully picked up each piece, head bent low with concentration, his fingers awkward tweezers, then held it aloft like a trophy: "Ta-da! Apple chunk!" we'd narrate. "Ta-da! Green pea!"

Nancy, her glasses temporarily lost somewhere in her bed's chaos of newspapers, telephone, and remote control, would ask what Ben was eating and would be particularly pleased if it was something she enjoyed, too—Cheerios held her interest somewhat less, for instance, than pasta. "What kind of pasta is he eating? Fusilli, really? With sauce? What kind? Has he had ravioli yet? Oh, tortellini? Mmmm." Invariably, Ben's dinner would inspire a reminiscence of some past meal, maybe one long ago, when she and her husband lived in Rome, or perhaps one we'd all shared at a restaurant just weeks before.

I met Nancy the summer that Tony and I started dating, when he brought me to spend the weekend at his parents' house in Stinson Beach. Tony's relationship with his mother was easy, companionable, maybe because she'd had a whole life—twenty years of marriage, full of travel and music and art—before having kids. She'd been surprised by motherhood and viewed it always as a gift to celebrate. (The night she went into labor with Tony, she liked to remember, she'd enjoyed a shrimp curry and a dry martini.) She treated him with the same delight she'd met him with thirty years before; he treated her like a queen; they both made plenty of room in the sun for me.

That weekend, she greeted me warmly and took us out for dinner at The Sand Dollar, the local seafood place where everyone knew her family so well that our dinner was frequently interrupted by friends stopping by to say hello. Friday was lobster night, and since Tony is a vegetarian, she was delighted that I would keep her company with the messy meal. After dinner, and for the rest of the weekend, she made herself scarce. I woke Saturday morning to find a variety of sweet rolls and three different kinds of peppermint tea laid out for me on the rough wooden kitchen table; Tony had given her an idea of what I liked to eat for breakfast, and she characteristically, as I would learn, bought a generous assortment to cover all possibilities. Tony sometimes hesitated to tell his mom he liked some food, knowing from long experience that she would lay in abundant supply for his visits; she would literally buy stock in the company if that would keep a favorite product on the shelves.

I was delighted to find in her a kindred spirit. Like me, she was as interested in talking and reading about food as she was in cooking and eating it. Food was her religion and her culture: she ate corned beef and cabbage for St. Patrick's Day, latkes for Passover, and steamed pork buns for the Lunar New Year; she filled the family's Christmas stockings with chocolates and oranges, of course, but also bottles of hot sauce and jars of chutney, and someone always found a roll of polenta. The next year, when Tony and I planned a trip to Italy, we coordinated our itinerary to overlap with Nancy's holiday in Venice and Florence. My friends were amazed, asking, "You're meeting Tony's *mom* on your romantic Italian vacation?" And I just nodded and smiled, knowing that meeting up with Nancy always meant meeting up with good food, interesting people, memorable experiences. We arrived in Venice, a few days after Nancy, and found a message to meet her in the Piazza San Marco. We showered quickly to wash off the long journey, then headed out. I spotted her from across the piazza, sitting at a small metal table, her smile growing broader as we walked across the stones. I was bleary-eyed from jetlag and everything looked hazy to me in the late afternoon sun, but I could see tears spring to Nancy's eyes as we reached her, so glad to introduce us now to this country she loved.

She had her own plans for the trip, personal reunions mapped out with a particular list of churches and museums. But starting that first afternoon in Venice, and each day following, we would rendezvous at her hotel around five to share details of the day's explorations over a bottle of Prosecco and a bowl of salted almonds, a ritual we dubbed "Nancy Hour." We mark it with our friends to this day.

Her delight in a good meal shared with close friends never diminished, even as her ability to host them did. Before she was widowed, she and her husband Jim would gather friends regularly for sumptuous meals at the beach house. They would start in the kitchen with drinks and salty snacks, and always at some point Nancy would turn from what she was doing and ask, "Jim, would you chop some parsley for me?" (One year for their anniversary she gave him a knife inscribed with those words.) Then they would all carry their drinks into the dining room and sit around the monastery table Nancy and Jim had carried home from their life in Italy. The table is long but very narrow, so everybody feels close. Its dark walnut top is scarred with knife marks and burns from hot dishes that lost their trivets, water rings and even some glitter from the boys' elementary school art projects. It's a table to linger over, so they did, talking and feasting for hours—bouillabaisse and paella, roasts and pastas— enjoying the food for longer, even, than it took to cook.

After Jim died, Nancy sold the Stinson Beach house, put the monastery table into storage, and moved to a small place in Mill Valley. She needed to be less isolated, wanted to be closer to friends and family. She no longer entertained the way she once had; the gatherings were smaller, mostly just family, and she wasn't too proud to buy a dish or two ready-made from the nice market in town, or to laugh at her cooking misfires. She made us a beautiful, complicated vegetarian jambalaya once (how do you make vegetarian jambalaya? I still do not know) but didn't manage to get all the plastic off the veggie sausage, so we fished the glossy bits out of our mouths and set them, like so many shrimp tails, on the edge of our plates. Her friends still gave her the ingredients for the generous feasts she used to make before her hands became too knotted up by arthritis to mince garlic easily. The generosity that inspired the lavish food gifts never abated; that's why she had three different kinds of lemon-flavored oils (olive, hazelnut, and grape seed) in three different cupboards.

We fell into a tradition of renting a house in Stinson for Thanksgiving. Nancy packed old cardboard wine boxes with the rolling pin, the food processor, extra mixing bowls, and sharp knives. We couldn't help teasing her a little for bringing most of her kitchen with her on vacation, but we used it all. The rental kitchens were always too small for more than one cook at a time, but we were used to that in Mill Valley; she and I cooked in turns, like children engaged in parallel play, talking about each other's dishes but not involving ourselves in them. We didn't share the intimacy of tasting and adding to each other's food; instead, the conversation about recipes or ingredients, articles in *Gourmet* or *Saveur*, breakfasts at the Depot or Rulli's—this soundtrack to our cooking—was always a bit more important than the cooking process itself. Sometimes the food conversation moved into the living room, where we would play Scrabble to determine what dish would get the tiny oven first, the turkey or the vegetarian shepherd's pie. Over the course of the week, she made at least three trips to Mill Valley for forgotten ingredients and fresh provisions. We accused her jokingly of sneaking over the hill for her polenta fix, and she laughed but didn't correct us.

After Tony and I married, we found a house with a dining room just the right size for the old monastery table. I don't know who was more pleased, Nancy or I, when we took it out of storage, dusted it off, and set it up. Just a few weeks later, the 9/11 attacks occurred; I was pregnant with Ben and feeling particularly vulnerable, so we gathered friends around the table for the first time. We made comfort food: Tony's mushroom ravioli with brown butter and fried sage leaves; salad with pears sautéed in red wine and spiced walnuts; my chocolate bread pudding.

To no one's surprise, Nancy was an even more doting grandmother than mother, and we made sure she saw a lot of Ben. Sometimes Tony would take him out to Mill Valley before work to surprise Nancy at the Depot and share some polenta. More often, we met up for weekend lunches, first with Ben nursing quietly in my arms or, when he was older, gnawing away at a sourdough crust. No one was happier than Nancy when Ben started eating table food, and she established a fancy high chair in her dining room so that he could easily participate in the family meals.

But the familiar space became suddenly fraught when Nancy fell sick. We were anxious about her, and newly anxious about Ben, too, who was just starting to walk. Her house seemed a minefield of disaster for a curious toddler. And no room held greater appeal—because it was the place we all spent so much time—or greater potential for harm than her fabulous, messy, disorganized kitchen.

~

Her kitchen was my dream come true. To call it well stocked was an understatement. Name an ingredient, she had it on hand, and had the talent to turn it into a delicious dish. Name a cuisine, you'd find the ingredients to make a full meal.

But her kitchen was also my worst nightmare. Nesting bowls lived apart from their mates, stacked awkwardly with plates and pots; measuring cups sat far from any ingredients needing measuring (the breakfast cereal?) while a bag of rice, bottle of brandy, and tins of ground cinnamon shared a crowded shelf with a corkscrew and two silver platters. (I imagined the cooking show her kitchen would inspire: You have one hour to make a meal from the materials found in one cupboard. Go!) A black plastic trash bag sat slumped on the floor (I never understood why she wouldn't use a trash can), and good luck finding a free surface to set a dish. One year, Nancy cleared off the kitchen table, put a red bow on it, and "gave" it to her husband for Christmas (he was thrilled, though of course it didn't last).

I always steered clear of Nancy in action in her kitchen. The room's cramped L didn't allow for multiple cooks, but we would have stepped on each other's toes in less literal ways, anyway. Like me, she'd start any menu plan with cookbook research, pulling several off the shelf and consulting their grease-stained and dog-eared pages while she assembled a grocery list. But once back from the market, our approaches diverged. I'd prep my ingredients, chopping, measuring, and methodically assembling my *mise-en-place*. She'd pull ingredients out of cupboards, shopping bags, and refrigerator shelves as she needed them, measuring (or not) on the fly, and leave the open tins, sagging packages, and half-chopped bunches of herbs, still bundled at the stem, jumbled on the counter in her wake. A soggy stew of potato peels, eggshells, and dirty pans simmered in the sink.

When Nancy was cooking, none of this mess mattered—she certainly never seemed to notice it, let alone apologize for it—because somehow it never interfered with the generous feasts that would emerge from her kitchen. But now that she was bedridden, the kitchen mess was just that: a sad mess. And with Ben suddenly able to walk in, open any low cupboard, and help himself to a snack of dish soap and hot sauce poured over food-processor blades, the mess mattered.

So before I could cook for Nancy in her kitchen, I had to make it a tiny bit more like my own. I had to tidy up. It was an act of faith. Every box of stale crackers that I threw away, every can of tomato paste that I wiped off and reshelved, was assurance that Nancy would come back to the kitchen and mess it up all over again. It is my father's side of me that counted what I found, my mother's side that rearranged and organized it. And it was a gift I received from Nancy that turned it all into a game to distract her from her pain.

It started one morning, while she and Ben were both napping. I wandered into the kitchen (figuring that while moving the hazards out of Ben's reach, I could find something to fix for lunch) and was temporarily paralyzed—always my first reaction—by the clutter. I took a deep breath, opened a cabinet, and started unloading the contents onto a tray. I made a list of it all, then moved on to the next cabinet with another tray (there was no shortage of trays). Lunch forgotten, I continued my project, digging into the scrapbook of her kitchen. A messy kitchen doesn't keep secrets, after all, and if you know how to read the signs, you can learn about a person from the packages on the shelves. I dusted off labels, laughed at the bag of raspberry-flavored licorice (a gift from a well-meaning friend who knew she loved the flavors and mistakenly assumed the combination would be even better), and lost myself happily in reminiscences of meals past.

After a while, Tony appeared in the doorway, took in the scene (me, sitting on the floor surrounded by towers of tuna cans, stacks of crackers, and piles of pasta), and announced he would go pick up sandwiches.

That afternoon, while Tony and Ben sat playing in Nancy's room, I began making periodic reports of my findings.

"Nancy, guess how many pounds of pasta you have?"

"Oh, my, well . . . maybe, four?" She laughed, embarrassed, knowing it was likely more.

"Nineteen!" I called out.

"Mom!" Tony laughed. "You could start a restaurant."

"Well," she answered thoughtfully, "maybe I should. Maybe I should."

We played "Guess How Much Is in Your Kitchen?" for hours over the following days, until eventually I typed up the list and presented it to her. Over the next few weeks, I often overheard Nancy on the phone with friends, distracting them from the bad news of her diagnosis (lung cancer, metastasized to her bones) by reading passages from the list and marveling over her own excess.

We fell into a routine that spring and summer, trying to care for Nancy without disrupting ourselves too much, as that would have upset her. Weekends were easy to spend together with her; during the week, Tony would rise early and drive to work before Ben was awake, so that he could get home in the late afternoon and eat dinner with us. After dinner, I'd put Ben to bed and Tony would drive out to Mill Valley to spend the evening with his mom.

She was hospitalized briefly for treatment, and I was determined to bring her a proper Easter dinner. I spent hours trying to figure out a meal I could cook ahead, transport easily, and serve at room temperature. I pored over cookbooks, hunting for ideas and comparing recipes. I was so pleased with my eventual menu: poached salmon with dill sauce, steamed green beans with lemon zest and slivered almonds, lemon tart. I'd never poached a salmon before, and Nancy was delighted, so proud of me.

But otherwise, I didn't cook much for Nancy during her illness. Her appetite diminished, her sense of taste deteriorated. One shop's chicken soup still tasted good to her, sometimes a little toast. She didn't want us to go to the trouble of stirring polenta just for her and didn't want us to eat something just because she did. Besides, it was rare now that I cooked anything healthy. Tony and I were settling into separate kitchen roles: he cooked with the stove; I used the oven. I was reverting to what I had first learned as my own mother's sous chef; she'd hand me the butter wrappers to grease the cookie sheets, show me how to sift flour onto a piece of waxed paper. I absorbed, through hours of baking at her side, the feel of kneading bread or rolling out biscuits. But, also, stove-top dinner making now seemed to me, to the mother of a curious toddler, all sharp knives and high heat. The oven felt safer. I could make bread or cookie dough in stages, prepping ingredients while Ben sat on the kitchen floor banging away with his bowl and spoon, and then leave it all to settle him for a nap. After a break, we could roll out and cut cookies together, or he could knead his own lump of dough. He'd sit and play for an hour with the (unplugged) stand mixer, pushing in and swapping out the whisk, the dough hook, and then the flat paddle, one by one. So I happily ceded dinner making to Tony, who, like his mother before him, was graceful and easy with stovetop improvisation. For me, caught between the needs of an unpredictably declining mother-in-law and a clamorously insistent toddler, the steady rhythms and predictably satisfying outcomes of baking were a balm.

She came home from the hospital in time for her birthday, just a few weeks before she passed away. Tony steamed tender green beans and dressed them with butter and lemon zest, grilled baby zucchini, and made pasta with homemade pesto; I baked a chocolate torte topped with a scattering of raspberries for dessert. We opened a bottle of Prosecco and toasted her, and although she brought the glass to her lips, I don't think she tasted her wine. I don't think she ate more than a bite of anything. It took all her strength to come to the table (she insisted on coming to the table). She sat very quietly, pleased with our effort, happy that we were celebrating her birthday with such a meal.

Nancy's been gone almost seven years now. Ben doesn't remember her, and our younger son, Eli, never knew her. I show them pictures and tell them about the meals we shared. I tell them about the steak she ordered in Florence, covered with a bed of the brightest green spinach we'd ever seen, or the chocolate tower that was a regular part of our dinners in a local Italian restaurant; she'd tap the bottom with her fork to release a stream of chocolate. I tell them how happy she was when In-N-Out Burger, a fixture of her LA childhood, finally opened in Northern California, or about the meal at the raw-food restaurant that left her so hungry she went out for a second dinner afterward. We make wishes, as she did, on the first peach of summer. We talk while we cook, and I tell them stories of their Nonna.

SIMPLE POLENTA

Combine 3 cups of water and 1 teaspoon of sea salt in a large pot. Bring to a rolling boil over high heat and then, while stirring, slowly add 1 cup of coarsely ground cornmeal, pouring it into the water in a steady stream. Once the mixture returns to a boil, turn it down to simmer and continue to stir constantly until the polenta has thickened and started to pull away from the edges of the pot, about 15–30 minutes. For soft polenta, pour into bowls and serve with butter, salt, and pepper to taste. Or pour the polenta into a roasting pan and let cool until set. Slice into wedges and then grill or fry with olive oil.

LEMON POLENTA COOKIES

½ pound (2 sticks) unsalted butter, at room temperature
1 cup granulated sugar, whirred in a food processor for 30 seconds, or superfine sugar
½ teaspoon salt
1 large egg plus 1 egg yolk
1 teaspoon finely grated lemon zest
2 teaspoons vanilla
1½ cups all-purpose flour
1 cup cornmeal

In a large bowl, beat the butter and sugar together until fluffy. Add the egg yolk and beat until well blended. Then add the egg, vanilla, and lemon zest and beat until well combined. Gradually stir in the flour and cornmeal, mixing just until combined.

Divide the dough in half, wrap in plastic, and chill until firm, at least an hour and up to two days.

To bake, preheat oven to 375°. Working with one piece of dough at a time (keeping the rest chilled), either scoop dough into tablespoon-sized balls, put on parchment-lined cookie sheets, spaced about 2 inches apart, and flatten to about ⅛-inch thick with the bottom of a flour-coated glass or measuring cup. Or roll the dough out on a flour-coated surface and cut into desired shapes with cookie cutters.

Bake 6–8 minutes, until evenly browned. Immediately transfer the cookies to racks to cool.

→ 14 ←

From *The Food Taster*

PETER ELBLING

Going on a journey with Federico was like going to war. Lists were drawn up of who should go and who should stay, then more lists were made of what to take. These lists changed every day, sometimes from hour to hour. Cecchi hardly slept for months and those parts of his beard which were gray turned white and those which were white fell out.

To begin with, there were to be no more than forty of us, but then three boys were required to look after the horses, and the cart master said he needed at least three servants and so did Federico's dressers. The number grew to eighty. The whole palace wanted to leave, but since few monasteries or palaces could house that number, carpenters, laborers, and sewers were added to build tents wherever we stayed. We were now a hundred. When Federico saw how much this would cost, he threatened to castrate Cecchi, burn his body, and then behead him. Cecchi reduced the number to sixty. By now Federico had grown so fat, and his gout so painful, that a special cart had to be built to carry him. It was lined with silken cushions and sheets, and pictures of jousting knights were painted on the sides. Federico tested it twice a day to make sure it was comfortable.

Since Miranda and Tommaso were not going to Milano, they paid little attention to the preparations. Besides, they were too much in love to care. Although Miranda had not been with child, I feared that could happen while I was away and since she often spoke of marrying Tommaso I was tempted to tell her of the pact I had made with him. In truth, I was surprised he had not mentioned it, but I guessed this was because he now loved her and wanted to respect me. This changed my feelings toward him and in this mood I went to the kitchen intending to say that although the four years were not yet up I would be happy to announce their marriage.

Tommaso was placing pieces of spit-roasted thrushes onto slices of toast. He had mixed up some spices, which by smelling the bowl I could tell included fennel, pepper, cinnamon, nutmeg, egg yolks, and vinegar. He poured the mix over the birds, placed the slices of toast in a pan, and put them over the flames. I told him it was fit for a duke and there was no doubt that he would one day be cooking for the pope.

"I could be a chef in Roma or Firenze right now if I wanted to," he boasted. He told me about new recipes he had invented, of special foods and spices from India he wanted to try, even ways of improving the kitchen. Never once did he mention Miranda. The longer I listened, the more uneasy I became. I thought—he has grown tired of Miranda, but does not know it yet. So I said nothing about the marriage contract.

Miranda spoke of him with as much love as ever and wandered about the kitchen wanting to be close to him, but where they had once walked side-by-side, now Tommaso walked a little ahead. He no longer brought her ribbons or combs and looked away when she spoke to him. He yawned when she sang and once when I was watching from the window, I saw her lead his hand to her breast. Laughing, he pulled away and strode off.

Septivus told me that Miranda had missed her lessons and had been seen weeping in Emilia's garden. I looked for her there and in the stables, but could not find her. I sought out her friends, asking them if they knew the cause of Miranda's distress.

"Tommaso," they answered, as if the whole world knew. "We warned her his word was not to be trusted."

I found Miranda in our room tearing at her hair, beating herself about the breast, and scratching her face like the shrieking harpies in Dante's *Inferno*. "He no longer loves me," she wept.

"No. It cannot be true."

"It is!" she screamed. "He told me. He told me!"

I sliced a mandrake root into tiny pieces, fed her a little, and she fell into a restless sleep. Then I sharpened my knife and went looking for Tommaso.

He was putting on a tight-fitting, green velvet jacket over some deep red silk hose. Rings twinkled on his fingers and the chains around his wrist glinted in the moonlight. I asked him where he was going at this late hour.

"What is it to you?" He pulled on a pair of black boots.

"You have upset my daughter."

"Your daughter." He shook his curls so that they sprayed out across his neck. "Your prisoner. She cannot pee without you watching over her."

"That is because I do not want her to become a whore like the girl you are going to see."

"I am not going to see a whore," he said hotly.

"You told me you loved her."

"I did not tell her of our betrothal so I did not break my promise to her."

"In the Bible, Jacob waited for Rachel for fourteen years."

"That was the Bible." He adjusted the feather in his hat. "This is Corsoli. My name is Tommaso, not Jacob. And tonight I am going to hunt the hare."

"What happened to your love?"

He shrugged as if he had lost a cheap coin. I threw myself at him, grasped his throat, and slammed him into the wall. I pulled my dagger and pressed the point into the crevice of his neck bone.

"I will teach you to taste the peach before you buy it." I drove my knee into his stomach. "You think I will carefully cut your face like Miranda did?" I pierced the skin and could feel his flesh quivering around the point of the knife. Blood spurted over the blade. "Tell me, what happened to your love?"

"I do not know," he begged, "I do not know."

"You do not know?" I pulled the knife across his neck. I wanted him to feel as much pain as Miranda felt.

"Who knows where love goes?" he gasped in bewilderment.

I was about to drive the knife into Tommaso's throat when a voice said, "No, Babbo!" with such power that I stopped.

Miranda was standing behind me, her head lifted high, her face as white as chalk. "He is not worth dying for."

"But he—"

"If you kill him and are hanged, what will happen to me?"

I lowered my knife. Tommaso pointed to Miranda and cried, "If you believe this will put me in your debt, then kill me now."

Miranda replied. "It is I who owe you. For you have closed my heart and opened my eyes." She reached her hand out to me. "Babbo, come. Anger shortens our lives and we have much to be grateful for."

I told her to come to Milano with me. "You will see wonderful palaces. There will be balls and parties and many fine young men."

"I do not want many fine young men."

I asked if there was any way I could be of comfort to her.

She said, "I am comforted by God. It is Tommaso who is restless. He always has been and always will be. That is his nature. That is why he needs me."

"You still love him? After what he has done to you?"

"Does the shepherd stop loving the lamb who strays? I am his balm, Babbo. Without me he is lost."

Then she lay down on her bed and in a few moments was sleeping the sleep of the dead, while I stared out at the hillside wondering if I would ever be as wise as she.

~

Federico wanted to leave at the end of Lent, but Nero was sick and we had to wait three days. Then Federico would not leave on the seventh of the month, so it was not until the following Tuesday that the bishop blessed the journey and wished Federico "*buona ventura*" in his desire to find a wife.

As we emerged from the Duomo Santa Caterina into the bright spring morning, the bell rang joyfully and the most beautiful rainbow I had ever seen embraced the heavens, each color so clear and vibrant that we knew God was watching over us.

Twenty knights dressed in full armor climbed upon their horses, their red and white banners waving from their lances. Then came Federico's cart (pulled by eight horses), twenty more knights, carts containing Federico's clothing, and another cart bearing gifts. After that were the falconers, chamberlains, grooms, clerks, kitchen staff, dressers, whores, and more carts containing everything else.

Miranda watched from our window as we gathered in the courtyard. The night before I had urged her to practice her lyre, fulfill her duties cheerfully, and promise to take several drops of a potion for her humors before she went to bed. In truth, it was the juice of apple mixed with the powder of a dead frog and it dulled all feelings of romance. Although Tommaso was no longer in love with her, I feared that because she was a woman she might fall in love with someone else just to show him she no longer cared.

"Women are different than men," I counseled her. "They are weaker in the face of love, yet they are braver in their pursuit of it and I do not want you to get with child."

"Nor do I," she had yawned.

Now she suddenly ran out of the palace and threw herself into my arms. I held her close and whispered I was sorry she was not coming and that I would miss her. She said she was sorry for her rudeness and, putting on a brave smile, said that I had no need to worry on her behalf; she would discharge all of her duties faithfully and with good cheer.

There was a fanfare of trumpets, Federico's carriage stirred, and then we were moving out of the courtyard toward the Weeping Steps like a long colorful snake. All of Corsoli watched us leave. Federico threw a few gold coins to the cheering crowds though I swear the cheering became even louder after we passed through the city gates.

A brisk wind chased the puffy white clouds across the bright blue sky. The green hills were dotted with patches of yellow violas and blue lupines. Everywhere the sound of running water accompanied us, dripping from trees, spilling over rocks and rushing in little streams underfoot to the bottom of the valley. I felt the same as I did when I first left home: this journey would change my life!

Halfway down the valley, Federico's cart bounced over a boulder, the back left wheel snapped off, and the cart crashed to the ground. Federico emerged like a mad bull, tangled up in sheets and blankets, red in the face. "Who built this piece of shit?" he screamed.

Cecchi said they were Frenchmen who had been hired for the task, but who had since left Corsoli.

"Then we declare war on France," Federico shouted.

"Is that before or after the cart is fixed?" I muttered. A chamberlain next to me laughed. Federico ordered him killed. Instead, he was taken back to the palace and thrown into the dungeon. Cecchi said he knew some Italian workmen who could fix the cart and while Federico was carried back to the palace, Cecchi sent for the men who had built it—they were from Corsoli—and warned them if they did not repair the cart correctly they would be hanged. Two days later the procession started again. This time no one watched us leave.

The second day Federico complained that the path was too bumpy and any rock or stone larger than a ducat had to be removed before we could continue. Every servant, soldier, and minister—even Cecchi—had to get down on their hands and knees and clear them all away. By the end of the morning the road was so smooth you could have rolled an egg on it. Cecchi said at this rate it would take five years to get to Milano. Federico cursed and ordered all the geese from the nearby farms killed, and their feathers stuffed into his cushions. From then on many farmers drove their livestock into hiding when they heard we were coming. The abbeys were not so lucky.

At the bottom of the valley, we stopped at the abbey of Abbot Tottorini, the same one who had turned Miranda and Tommaso away during the plague. I remembered that he made his own wine and cheese and thought it only right to tell Federico how wonderful they were. Federico agreed with me. Indeed, he liked them so much we stayed for a whole week.

On the fifth day, I rode to my father's farm. Although my last visit had been a bitter one, I hoped that time had softened his heart toward me. I wanted him to see what I had made of myself. His house looked as if the slightest wind would blow it down. I looked about but could not see him, so I called out his name.

"In here," he cried out.

I no longer remembered if the house had always stunk like that or if it was because I was now used to the perfumes of the palace, but I could not enter and stood in the doorway. At last, my father's shrunken frame limped out of the darkness. He was bent over almost double now and he smelled of decay and death. He squinted at my new leather jerkin and brightly colored hose, but although I said my name I was not sure if he knew who I was. I put my arms around him and offered him a few coins. He could not open his hands properly so I pushed the coins into the spaces between his fingers. I told him I was accompanying Duke Federico to Milano and asked if he wanted to see the procession.

"What for?" he croaked.

"The knights, the duke's carriage. They are magnificent."

"Magnificent? Spain! Spain is magnificent."

"Spain? What do you know about Spain? You have never been out of the valley!"

"Vittore tells me," he said. "Spain is magnificent."

"Oh, so Vittore has fled to Spain."

"He is commanding a ship!"

"Yes, and I am the king of France."

He waved a finger at me. "Jealous," he shouted. "You are jealous. Jealous!"

"And you are a fool!" I said, climbing on my horse. "And I was a fool to come here."

He tried to throw the coins at me, but his hands could not let go of them.

The abbot Tottorini was waiting for me when I returned, his fat face sagging around his jowls. He hissed that all his wine had been drunk, and his cheese and fruit eaten. He said he prayed that all my children grew tails, my blood would boil, and that I caught the French disease. I told him he should wait until we had left before he insulted me or I would tell Federico about some of the tricks he liked to perform with the nuns. Then I made sure that whatever wine and cheese we had not drunk or eaten, we took with us.

I almost forgot! Just before we reached the abbey, we passed a peasant standing in his field. His skinny body was lost inside his shift and his naked legs protruded into the stony soil like sticks of wood which had been left out in the sun. When some of the soldiers laughed at him, the peasant ran alongside Federico's carriage, screaming that he had lost his children in the famine while Federico ate like a pig. He ran between the horses and before anyone could stop him, leaped onto Federico's cart just as Federico stuck his head out to discover the cause of the yelling.

Oi me! I do not know who was more surprised, the peasant or Federico. Before the peasant could harm Federico, the knights slashed him to pieces with their swords and he fell onto the ground where the knights continued to lance and slice him long after his soul had left the earth.

Federico was eager to reach Firenze and stay with Bento Verana, a wealthy wool merchant who traded with Corsoli. Most of the servants remained on Verana's estate in the country, but a few of us stayed in his palazzo overlooking the Arno. Verana was a thin-faced, stern-looking man who dressed as a priest and regarded his wealth as something to be hoarded and not enjoyed. But because he treated everyone with dignity and was said to be honest in his business dealings, he had no need of a food taster. He said at our first meal that since he considered Federico a friend he would be offended if Federico used a food taster in his house.

Federico licked his lips, not knowing what to say. I said, "My Lord, it is not that Duke Federico fears being poisoned. He has a tender digestion and as mine is the same as his; by tasting his food I am able to spare him any discomfort before it arises."

Federico nodded and said that was exactly so. Unfortunately, I could not soothe the other discomforts so easily. The Firenzani ate differently than we in Corsoli did. They liked more vegetables—pumpkins, leeks, broad beans—and less meat. They ate spinach with anchovies, baked fruit into their ravioli, and made desserts in the shapes of emblems. They used less seasoning and considered the uses of spices a gaudy display of wealth, employed squares of cloth called napkins to wipe their mouths, ate from gold plates instead of trenchers, and covered their mouths when they belched.

"There are so many things to remember," Federico complained at dinner. "I cannot enjoy the food!"

"But conversation is the real food, is it not?" Verana answered. "Too much food leads to gluttony, and gluttony slows the brain just as too much drink dulls the senses. Because the body is forced to expend energy to digest the meal, conversation is forgotten and the diners are reduced to animals who gorge themselves in silence. In my house, conversation is first on the menu."

Septivus chimed in. "The joy of eating is like the joy of learning, for each feast is like a book. The dishes are words to be savored, enjoyed, and digested. As Petrarch said, 'I ate in the morning what I would digest in the evening. I swallowed as a boy what I would ponder as a man!'"

"Indeed," cried Verana. "To be a slave to the stomach instead of acquiring knowledge at the table is, in my reckoning, to fail as a man." Verana must have seen Federico's face, for even from where I was standing I could see that Federico's bottom lip was now lower than his chin. "But come, let us eat. Forget the seasoning, Federico. Truly the best seasoning is the company of good friends."

O my soul! I prayed for his sake that Septivus would not say another word, for as surely as there are stars in the sky, one of Federico's black moods was coming on. So when Verana recommended a thin pancake stuffed with liver called *fegatelli,* I took a small bite and suggested Federico not eat it because his stomach was too delicate. Federico loved that.

"Did you see Verana's face?" he roared afterward. "Well done, Ugo." I hoped he would instruct Cecchi to give me a gold coin but he did not.

Verana said much of what he learned came from a book by a Dutchman called Erasmus, which had just been translated into Italian, and after dinner he presented a copy to Federico. No one had ever given Federico a book before and he held it in his hand as if he did not know what to do with it. When he returned to his room, he threw the book at Cecchi and told him to burn it. We left Verana's palazzo soon after because Federico said he would starve if he stayed another day.

I was sorry to leave Firenze. While it is true the Firenzani have "sharp eyes and bad tongues," they live in a beautiful city! I saw the blessed Duomo and the statues in the Piazza della Signoria and best of all, the stupendous David by Michelangelo next to City Hall. I wanted to kiss that magnificent sculptor's hands and kneel at his feet, but his servant said that unfortunately he had left for Roma that very morning. I saw many fine palaces built by wealthy princes and merchants, but the ones I liked best belonged to the guilds. As we journeyed on to Bologna, I could not stop thinking about them and soon an idea began forming in my head. I had never had an idea such as this one before and it thrilled and excited me. The hills on either side of us were covered in a rich tapestry of red, blue, and yellow flowers. I was sure that God Himself must live here since harmony and beauty are the truest aspects of His soul and my idea was in keeping with these surroundings. Thus I was sure my idea had been blessed by God. It was as follows:

Of all the servants, be they chamberlains, grooms, scribes, cooks or so on, surely the food taster is the bravest of all. What other servant risks his life not once, but two or three times a day just in the service of his work? In truth, we are as brave as the bravest knight, for if a knight is outnumbered in battle he runs away—I have known many that fled before the battle even started—but does a food taster run away? No! Every day he does battle and every day he stays until the battle is ended. Why then, if there are guilds for goldsmiths, lawyers, spinners, weavers, bakers, and tailors, should there not be a guild for food tasters? Are we not as important as they? The very existence of our princes depends on us! Of course a food tasters' guild would be smaller, sometimes only one person to a city, but we could still meet, discuss new foods, poisons, antidotes, even assassins.

Thinking about this helped pass the hours of travel. Even as I was hunting for boar I was planning our initiation rites. I thought they should not only be severe, but useful. I listed them as follows:

1. An apprentice food taster should be starved for three days, after which he should be blindfolded and made to taste tiny amounts of poison which would be increased until he identified them correctly. If he survived, he would have proven his ability. If he died, then he was obviously not suited for the task.
2. To make sure his heart was strong, he should be told after eating a meal that there was poison in it. If he immediately clutched an amulet and began praying to God, he should be thrown out the window, for if there had been poison in the meal, he would soon be dead anyway. But if he immediately found a woman and made sport with her, then he should be admitted with full honors. For a food taster must remain calm at all times: calmness will save a life, whereas a man who dabbles in superstition will act on the first thing that comes to his mind, which is usually wrong!
3. Most importantly, the examinations must be held in summer and in the open air since the emetics would cause such a foul odor in an enclosed room as to make a pig sick.

Having made these rules, I looked forward to meeting other food tasters to discuss my ideas with them.

But I met very few tasters on the way to Milano. A clown who claimed that he had faked his death was too stupid to change his story even after I told him who I was and so did not deserve to be in my guild. I also met a thin, nervous man with white hair, a pronounced nose, and thick lips. He sat in a chair in the sun and did not answer my questions, but every so often licked his lips with his tongue. When I asked him why, he said he was not aware he did so. Later, I saw other tasters do the same thing. They said they had been doing it ever since they could remember and were of the opinion that wet lips could better detect poisons.

In Piacenza, I met a taster who was convinced Federico had told me to fake my death; since *he*, the taster, was not capable of such cunning, how could *I* have done so?

Federico had planned to arrive in Milano in time for the feast of San Pietro. The guests included princes, merchants from Liguria, Genoa, and Savoy, as well as cardinals and an ambassador of the emperor. These many men of importance would ensure that many women would be there, too. However, we had traveled so slowly that the feast was already in progress the night we arrived. Federico was in a bad mood. Outside Parma, the cart had lurched unexpectedly while one of his whores was sitting on top of him. She had hit her head on a wooden beam, her eyes had become glassy, and she had muttered strange things. Fearing he would catch her madness, Federico left her on the side of the road. His gout had also been plaguing him badly. The gatekeepers allowed him and a few servants, including me, into the *castello*. The others were to follow in the morning.

I must say something in praise of Milano. If a finer city exists, then they must invent new words to describe it. To begin with, the roads in the center of the city are not only as straight as gun barrels but also paved too, so that the carriages, of which there are many, may have a smoother ride! Is that not a miracle? And the castle! If a more magnificent one exists, I have not seen it. It is almost as big as Corsoli itself and has an enormous moat around it. They told me the pig-swilling French stole many of its treasures, but *potta!* Everywhere I looked I saw the most beautiful paintings and the most exquisite sculptures! I remember a painting of Mary Magdalene by Il Giampietrino, which was so beautiful and tender it was no wonder Our Lord had reached out to her. By now I could write well enough to record things like this.

One staircase, designed by Leonardo da Vinci, was so magnificent I walked up and down it several times because it made me feel like a prince. Bold, colorful carpets of Oriental designs lined the hallways. A hundred scenes were painted on the ceilings and from the center of each room hung a chandelier with a thousand candles. Servants scurried to and fro, beautiful women entertained themselves, and from every room came the sound of laughter and music. If one is going to die in the service of a prince, I said to myself, then let it be for Duke Sforza.

Then I found the kitchen! Oh, what better sanctuary is there for a weary traveler than the hiss of boiling pots, the sight of steam curling up from the oven, and the warm smell of pies cooking? And what a kitchen! Compared to this, the kitchen in Corsoli was like a mouse-hole. There were three times as many ovens, five times the number of cauldrons, and more knives than in the Turkish army. I ate quickly because I wanted to visit the servants' quarters, for I was sure that such a magnificent prince would have extended his generosity to those who worked for him. I should have known better.

Just as in Corsoli, the servants' rooms were smaller and uncared for. Since French and Swiss soldiers had recently lived here, the stench was almost unbearable. As I wandered the hallways, my disappointment increasing with each step, the sound of voices pulled me to an open door. I peered in.

Six or seven men sat drinking and playing cards. One, a dandy with a careless attitude, wore a large feather in his hat and lounged with one leg over the arm of his chair. Another was a man with a bulbous onionlike face whose right eyelid was half closed from a knife wound. He was arguing with a fat man who looked as if he might have been a monk. "But if he sides with Venezia, then what?" the onion-faced man said fiercely.

The Fat One shrugged. "It depends on the pope."

The onion-faced man spat. "The pope changes sides more often than the weather."

"Who does not?" said the Fat One. "Besides I heard—" He saw me in the doorway. "What do you want?" he said brusquely.

"I have just arrived with Duke Federico Basillione DiVincelli," I said. "I am his food taster."

The others stopped their conversation to look at me. "Welcome," said the dandy in a smooth high voice. "We are all tasters here."

"Yes, come in," they cried.

At long last, I was home.

RAFIOLI COMMUN DE HERBE VANZATI (MINT AND SPINACH RAVIOLI)

This is plain old spinach ravioli, but with exotic flavorings. The pinches of spice at the end are important. From the fourteenth-century anonymous work *Libro per Cuoco*.

1 (10-ounce) bag spinach leaves, chopped, about 6 cups, loosely packed
¼ cup chopped fresh mint
¼ cup chopped parsley
2 tablespoons olive oil

1 egg, lightly beaten
½ cup shredded mozzarella cheese
Ground cinnamon
Ground ginger
Ground cumin
Salt, pepper
Ravioli dough
Boiling salted water
Parmesan cheese, grated

Sauté spinach, mint, and parsley in olive oil until spinach is wilted. Let cool. Stir in egg, mozzarella, ⅛ teaspoon cinnamon, ⅛ teaspoon ginger, and ⅛ teaspoon cumin, and salt and pepper to taste.

Divide ravioli dough into 8 portions. Roll each piece through a pasta machine on successively finer settings into thin sheets, about 4 inches wide and 16 to 18 inches long. Spread 1 pasta sheet on floured work surface. Place filling by teaspoons at 8 regular intervals about 2 inches apart, 1 inch from the right-hand long edge of sheet. Lightly moisten pasta around fillings. Fold left half of pasta over filling, carefully squeezing out all air pockets. Seal between fillings by pressing firmly with sides of hands. Cut into 8 (2-inch) squares with filling in center of each. Transfer to floured cloth. Repeat with remaining sheets of dough.

Cook ravioli in boiling salted water until they float to surface, about 5 minutes. Remove with slotted spoon and drain in colander. Serve sprinkled with cinnamon, ginger, cumin, and grated Parmesan cheese to taste. Makes 8 servings.

RAVIOLI DOUGH

2 cups unbleached flour
2 extra-large eggs
1 tablespoon olive oil

Place flour in food-processor bowl fitted with metal blade. Beat eggs and olive oil in small bowl until blended, then add to food processor with motor running. Process until dough forms a ball and is very smooth. Turn dough out onto lightly floured work surface. Knead well, adding small amounts of flour as needed to keep from sticking to hands and surface, until dough is smooth and very elastic. Let dough stand 20 to 30 minutes before rolling out.

PART III

Eggs

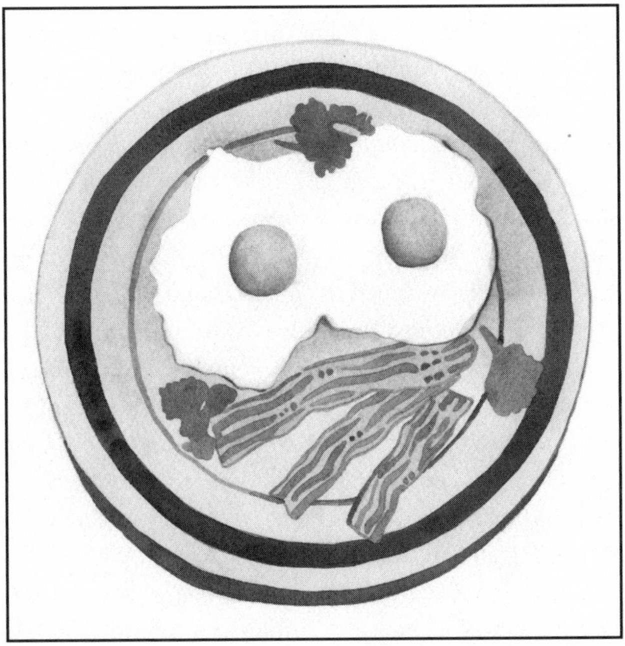

Although colonists from Europe brought laying hens to America, poultry breeding did not become popular until the nineteenth century, particularly during the latter half, when chickens could be found on most farms. By late century, commercial hatcheries were in place, and by the twentieth century, egg commercialization had increased, with artificial lighting used to help boost egg-laying productivity and machines for washing and packing the eggs. Such industrialization has—over time—resulted in debates over methods of mass production and concerns over sanitation (and the possibility of salmonella poisoning) as well as the treatment of animals. These concerns have led to some producers seeking certifications, such as "certified humane" and "certified organic," to indicate more responsible practices.

A versatile food, eggs can be prepared for any meal or snack—not to mention their importance in baking. In the section of Fannie Merritt Farmer's 1896 *Boston Cooking-School Cook Book* included in this chapter, she offers more than two-dozen recipes for eggs, and the other authors represented here show not only different methods of preparation—from fried-egg sandwiches (Fisher and Dinin) to soft-boiled eggs and omelets (Darlington)—but also the possibility of using eggs of different and distinct origin: chicken, turtle, and quail.

Eggs have long been valued for their nutrition and versatility. Farmer notes the nutritive value of eggs, claiming that "they contain all the elements, in the right proportion, necessary for the support of the body" and pointing out that they can be a valuable substitute for meat—also urging that fresh eggs be used when available. Although eggs have continued to be a part of most Americans' diets, in the 1980s and into the '90s, their popularity waned because of concerns about their cholesterol content and cholesterol's link to heart disease. Over the past decade, however, medical studies have largely decreased fears about moderate egg consumption, although conflicting studies still exist. Reports of the health benefits of eggs, though, are just as often in the news. One could say that the reputation of eggs is, at best, scrambled.

Even in literature, we see mixed responses as well as cautions related to egg dishes. M. F. K. Fisher, for example, in remembering the fried-egg sandwiches given to her by a neighbor, writes that her mother "shuddered at the thought of such greasebound proteins," though the shudder, perhaps, came more from the drippings used in cooking than the eggs themselves. Fisher's title, though, shows her own joyous response to the egg sandwiches: "H Is for Happy." After Ntozake Shange shares a recipe for raw turtle eggs and spices, which she praises as a "very sexy little dish," she warns in a parenthetical, "Please be aware that raw eggs may contain salmonella bacteria." The notion that eggs can be toxic is also evident in Tenaya Darlington's short story "Poison Egg," in which the narrator plans to poison herself with a soft-boiled egg—one her father made her for breakfast—after her father reveals he has a boyfriend. And yet it is ultimately eggs—two quail eggs, made into a tiny omelet—that symbolize the narrator's eventual acceptance and affection for her father and his partner.

Eggs are often used as symbols in literature—most often to suggest life and the promise of rebirth. As Howard Dinin, in "Perfect Fried Egg Sandwich," observes, the egg is:

> Life itself
> and contained in that
> a death.
> Not a paradox:
> a meal, even for the dying.

In this poem, the egg as a symbol of life is especially poignant since the speaker makes the egg sandwich for a loved one who is dying, offering life-giving sustenance despite the reality of impending death. Thus, we see the complexity of eggs not only in diets but also in writing: they represent fear and joy, health and illness, life and death.

15

From *Boston Cooking-School Cook Book*

FANNIE MERRITT FARMER

Food.

Food is anything which nourishes the body. Thirteen elements enter into the composition of the body: oxygen, 62½%; carbon, 21½%; hydrogen, 10%; nitrogen, 3%; calcium, phosphorus, potassium, sulphur, chlorine, sodium, magnesium, iron, and fluorine the remaining 3%. Others are found occasionally, but, as their uses are unknown, will not be considered.

Food is necessary for growth, repair, and energy; therefore the elements composing the body must be found in the food. The thirteen elements named are formed into chemical compounds by the vegetable and animal kingdoms to support the highest order of being, man. All food must undergo chemical change after being taken into the body, before it can be utilized by the body; this is the office of the digestive system.

Food is classified as follows:—

I. Organic
1. Proteid (nitrogenous or albuminous).
2. Carbohydrates (sugar and starch).
3. Fats and oils.
II. Inorganic
1. Mineral matter.
2. Water.

The chief office of proteids is to build and repair tissues. They can furnish energy, but at greater cost than carbohydrates, fats, and oils. They contain nitrogen, carbon, oxygen, hydrogen, and sulphur or phosphorus, and include all forms of animal foods (excepting fats and glycogen) and some vegetable foods. Examples: milk, cheese, eggs, meat, fish, cereals, peas, beans, and lentils. The principal constituent of proteid food is albumen. Albumen as found in food takes different names, but has the same chemical composition; as, *albumen* in eggs, *fibrin* in meat, *casein* in milk and cheese, *vegetable casein* or *legumen* in peas, beans, and lentils; and *gluten* in wheat. To this same class belongs gelatine.

The chief office of the carbohydrates is to furnish energy and maintain heat. They contain carbon, hydrogen, and oxygen, and include foods containing starch and sugar. Examples: vegetables, fruits, cereals, sugars, and gums.

The chief office of fats and oils is to store energy and heat to be used as needed, and constitute the adipose tissues of the body. Examples: butter, cream, fat of meat, fish, cereals, nuts, and the berry of the olive-tree.

The chief office of mineral matter is to furnish the necessary salts which are found in all animal and vegetable foods. Examples: sodium chloride (common salt); carbonates, sulphates and phosphates of sodium, potassium, and magnesium; besides calcium phosphates and iron.

Water constitutes about two-thirds the weight of the body, and is in all tissues and fluids; therefore its abundant use is necessary. One of the greatest errors in diet is neglect to take enough water; while it is found in all animal and vegetable food, the amount is insufficient.

Correct Proportions of Food.

Age, sex, occupation, climate, and season must determine the diet of a person in normal condition.

Liquid food (milk or milk in preparation with the various prepared foods on the market) should constitute the diet of a child for the first eighteen months. After the teeth appear, by which time ferments have been developed for the digestion of starchy foods, entire wheat bread, baked potatoes, cereals, meat broths, and occasionally boiled eggs may be given. If mothers would use Dr. Johnson's Educators in place of the various sweet crackers, children would be as well pleased and better nourished; with a glass of milk they form a supper suited to the needs of little ones, and experience has shown children seldom tire of them. The diet should be gradually increased by the addition of cooked fruits, vegetables, and simple desserts; the third or fourth year fish and meat may be introduced, if given sparingly. Always avoid salted meats, coarse vegetables (beets, carrots, and turnips), cheese, fried food, pastry, rich desserts, confections, condiments, tea, coffee, and iced water. For school children the diet should be varied and abundant, constantly bearing in mind that this is a period of great mental and physical growth. Where children have broken down, supposedly from over-work, the cause has often been traced to impoverished diet. It must not be forgotten that digestive processes go on so rapidly that the stomach is soon emptied. Thanks to the institutor of the school luncheon-counter!

The daily average ratio of an adult requires

3½ oz. proteid.	10 oz. starch.
3 oz. fat.	1 oz. salt.
5 pints water.	

About one-third of the water is taken in our food, the remainder as a beverage. To keep in health and do the best mental and physical work, authorities agree that a mixed diet is suited for temperate climates, although sound arguments appear from the vegetarian. Women, even though they do the same amount of work as men, as a rule require less food. Brain workers should take their proteid in a form easily digested. In consideration of this fact, fish and eggs form desirable substitutes for meat. The working man needs quantity as well as quality, that the stomach may have something to act upon. Corned beef, cabbage, brown-bread, and pastry will not overtax his digestion. In old age the digestive organs lessen in activity, and diet should be almost as simple as that of a child, increasing the amount of carbohydrates and decreasing the amount of proteids and fat.

Eggs.

Composition.

Proteid, 14.9%.	Mineral matter, 1%.
Fat, 10.6%.	Water, 73.5%.

Eggs, like milk, form a typical food, inasmuch as they contain all the elements, in the right proportion, necessary for support of the body. Their highly concentrated, nutritive value renders it necessary to use them in combination with other foods, rich in starch (bread, potatoes, etc.). In order that the stomach may have enough to act upon, a certain amount of bulk must be furnished.

A pound of eggs (nine) is equivalent in nutritive value to a pound of beef. From this it may be seen that eggs, at even twenty-five cents per dozen, should not be freely used by the strict economist. Eggs being rich in proteid, serve as a valuable substitute for meat. In most families, their use in the making of cake, custard, puddings, etc., renders them almost indispensable. It is surprising how many intelligent women, who look well to the affairs of the kitchen, are satisfied to use what are termed "cooking eggs"; this shows poor judgment from an economical standpoint. Strictly fresh eggs should always be used, if obtainable. An egg after the first twenty-four hours steadily deteriorates. If exposed to air, owing to the porous structure of the shell, there is an evaporation of water, air rushes in, and decomposition takes place.

White of egg contains albumen in its purest form. Albumen coagulates at a temperature of from 134° to 160°F. Herein lies the importance of cooking eggs at a low temperature, thus rendering them easy of digestion. Eggs cooked in boiling water are tough and horny, difficult of digestion, and should never be served.

When eggs come from the market, they should be washed, and put away in a cold place.

Ways of Determining Freshness of Eggs.

I. Hold in front of candle flame in dark room, and the centre should look clear.
II. Place in basin of cold water, and they should sink.
III. Place large end to the cheek, and a warmth should be felt.

Ways of Keeping Eggs.

I. Pack in sawdust, small end down.
II. Keep in lime water.
III. From July to September a large number of eggs are packed, small ends down, in cases having compartments, one for each egg, and kept in cold storage. Eggs are often kept in cold storage six months, and then sold as cooking eggs.

Boiled Eggs.

Have ready a saucepan containing boiling water. Carefully put in with a spoon the number of eggs desired, covering them with water. Remove saucepan to back of range, where water will not boil. Cook from six to eight minutes if liked "soft boiled," forty to forty-five if liked "hard boiled." Eggs may be cooked by placing in cold water and allowing water to heat gradually until the boiling point is reached, when they will be "soft boiled." In using hard-boiled eggs for making other dishes, when taken from the hot water they should be plunged into cold water to prevent, if possible, discoloration of yolks.

Eggs perfectly cooked should be placed and kept in water at a uniform temperature of 175°F.

Dropped Eggs (Poached).

Have ready a shallow pan two-thirds full of boiling salted water, allowing one-half tablespoon salt to one quart of water. Put two or three buttered muffin rings in the water. Break each egg separately into a cup, and carefully slip into a muffin ring. The water should cover the eggs. When there is a film over the top, and the white is firm, carefully remove with a buttered skimmer to circular pieces of buttered toast, and let each person season his own egg with butter, salt, and pepper. If cooked for an invalid, garnish with four toast-points and a bit of parsley. An egg-poacher may be used instead of muffin rings.

Eggs à la Finnoise.

Dropped Eggs, served with Tomato Sauce

Eggs à la Suisse.

4 eggs.
½ cup cream.
1 tablespoon butter.
Salt.
Pepper.
Cayenne.
2 tablespoons grated cheese.

Heat a small omelet pan, put in butter, and when melted, add cream. Slip in the eggs one at a time, sprinkle with salt, pepper, and a few grains of cayenne. When whites are nearly firm, sprinkle with cheese. Finish cooking, and serve on buttered toast. Strain cream over the toast.

Baked or Shirred Eggs.

Butter an egg-shirrer. Cover bottom and sides with fine cracker crumbs. Break an egg into a cup, and carefully slip into shirrer. Cover with seasoned buttered crumbs, and bake in moderate oven until white is firm and crumbs brown. The shirrers should be placed on a tin plate, that they may be easily removed from the oven.

Eggs may be baked in small tomatoes. Cut a slice from stem end of tomato, scoop out the pulp, slip in an egg, sprinkle with salt and pepper, cover with buttered crumbs, and bake.

Scrambled Eggs.

5 eggs.
½ cup milk.
½ teaspoon salt.
⅛ teaspoon pepper.
2 tablespoons butter.

Beat eggs slightly with silver fork; add salt, pepper, and milk. Heat omelet pan, put in butter, and when melted, turn in the mixture. Cook until of creamy consistency, stirring and scraping from bottom of the pan.

Scrambled Eggs with Tomato Sauce.

6 eggs.
1¾ cups tomatoes.
2 teaspoons sugar.
4 tablespoons butter.
1 slice onion.
½ teaspoon salt.
⅛ teaspoon pepper.

Simmer tomatoes and sugar five minutes; fry butter and onion three minutes; remove onion, and add tomatoes, seasonings, and eggs slightly beaten. Cook as Scrambled Eggs. Serve with entire wheat bread or brown bread toast.

Scrambled Eggs with Anchovy Toast.
Spread thin slices of buttered toast with Anchovy Paste. Arrange on patter, and cover with scrambled eggs.

Eggs à la Buckingham.
Make five slices milk toast, and arrange on platter. Use recipe for Scrambled Eggs, having the eggs slightly under done. Pour eggs over toast, sprinkle with four tablespoons grated mild cheese. Put in oven to melt cheese, and finish cooking eggs.

Buttered Eggs.
Heat omelet pan. Put in one tablespoon butter; when melted, slip in an egg, and cook until the white is firm. Turn it over once while cooking. Add more butter as needed, using just enough to keep egg from sticking.

Buttered Eggs with Tomatoes.
Cut tomatoes in one-third inch slices. Sprinkle with salt and pepper, dredge with flour, and sauté in butter. Serve a buttered egg on each slice of tomato.

Fried Eggs.
Fried eggs are cooked as Buttered Eggs, without being turned. In this case the fat is taken by spoonfuls and poured over the eggs. Lard, pork, ham, or bacon fat, are usually employed,—a considerable amount being used.

Eggs à la Goldenrod.

3 hard boiled eggs.
1 tablespoon butter.
1 tablespoon flour.
1 cup milk.
½ teaspoon salt.
⅛ teaspoon pepper.
5 slices toast.
Parsley.

Make a thin white sauce with butter, flour, milk, and seasonings. Separate yolks from whites of eggs. Chop whites finely, and add them to the sauce.

Cut four slices of toast in halves lengthwise. Arrange on platter, and pour over the sauce. Force the yolks through a potato ricer or strainer, sprinkling over the top. Garnish with parsley and remaining toast, cut in points.

Eggs au Gratin.

Arrange Dropped Eggs on a shallow buttered dish. Sprinkle with grated Parmesan cheese. Pour over eggs one pint Yellow Béchamel Sauce. Cover with stale bread crumbs, and sprinkle with grated cheese. Brown in oven. Tomato or White Sauce may be used.

Eggs in Batter.

1 egg.
1½ tablespoons thick cream.
2 tablespoons fine stale bread crumbs.
¼ teaspoon salt.

Mix cream, bread crumbs, and salt. Put one-half tablespoon of mixture in egg-shirrer. Slip in egg, and cover with remaining mixture. Bake six minutes in moderate oven.

Curried Eggs.

3 hard boiled eggs.
2 tablespoons butter.
2 tablespoons flour.
¼ teaspoon salt.
½ teaspoon curry powder.
⅛ teaspoon pepper.
1 cup hot milk.

Melt butter, add flour and seasonings, and gradually hot milk. Cut eggs in eighths lengthwise, and re-heat in sauce.

Scalloped Eggs.

6 hard boiled eggs.
1 pint White Sauce
¾ cup chopped cold meat.
¾ cup buttered cracker crumbs.

Chop eggs finely. Sprinkle bottom of a buttered baking dish with crumbs, cover with one-half the eggs, eggs with sauce, and sauce with meat; repeat. Cover with remaining crumbs. Place in oven on centre grate, and bake until brown. Ham is the best meat to use for this dish. Chicken, veal, or fish may be used.

Stuffed Eggs in a Nest.
Cut hard boiled eggs in halves, lengthwise. Remove yolks, and put whites aside in pairs. Mash yolks, and add half the amount of devilled ham and enough melted butter to make of consistency to shape. Make in balls size of original yolks, and refill whites. Form remainder of mixture into a nest. Arrange eggs in the nest, and pour over one cup White Sauce. Sprinkle with buttered crumbs, and bake until crumbs are brown.

Egg Farci.
Cut hard boiled eggs in halves, crosswise. Remove yolks, and put whites aside in pairs. Mash yolks, and add equal amounts of cold cooked chicken or veal, finely chopped. Moisten with melted butter or Mayonnaise. Season to taste with salt, pepper, lemon juice, mustard, and cayenne. Shape, and refill whites.

Omelets.
For omelets select large eggs, allowing one egg for each person, and one tablespoon liquid for each egg. Keep an omelet pan especially for omelets, and see that it is kept clean and smooth. A frying-pan may be used in place of omelet pan.

Plain Omelet.

4 eggs.
½ teaspoon salt.
Few grains pepper.
4 tablespoons hot water.
1 tablespoon butter.
1½ cups Thin White Sauce.

Separate yolks from whites. Beat yolks until thick and lemon colored; add salt, pepper, and hot water. Beat whites until stiff and dry, cutting and folding them into first mixture until they have taken up mixture. Heat omelet pan, and butter sides and bottom. Turn in mixture, spread evenly, place on range where it will cook slowly, occasionally turning the pan that omelet may brown evenly. When well "puffed" and delicately browned underneath, place pan on centre grate of oven to finish cooking the top. The omelet is cooked if it is firm to the touch when pressed by the finger. If it clings to the finger like the beaten white of egg, it needs longer cooking. Fold and turn on hot platter, and pour around one and one-half cups Thin White Sauce.

Milk is sometimes used in place of hot water, but hot water makes a more tender omelet.

To Fold and Turn an Omelet.

Hold omelet pan by handle with the left hand. With a case knife make two one-half inch incisions opposite each other at right angles to handle. Place knife under the part of omelet nearest handle, tip pan to nearly a vertical position; by carefully coaxing the omelet with knife it will fold and turn without breaking.

Omelet with Meat or Vegetables.

Mix and cook Plain Omelet. Fold in remnants of finely chopped cooked chicken, veal, or ham. Remnants of fish may be flaked and added to White Sauce; or cooked peas, asparagus, or cauliflower may be added.

Oyster Omelet.

Mix and cook Plain Omelet. Fold in one pint oysters, parboiled, drained from their liquor, and cut in halves. Turn on platter, and pour around Thin White Sauce.

Orange Omelet.

3 eggs.
2 tablespoons powdered sugar.
Few grains salt.
1 teaspoon lemon juice.
2 oranges.
½ tablespoon butter.
2½ tablespoons orange juice.

Follow directions for Plain Omelet. Remove skin from oranges and cut in slices, lengthwise. Fold in one-third of the slices of orange, well sprinkled with powdered sugar; put remaining slices around omelet, and sprinkle with sugar.

Jelly Omelet.

Mix and cook Plain Omelet, omitting pepper and one-half the salt, and adding one tablespoon sugar. Spread before folding with jam, jelly, or marmalade. Fold, turn, and sprinkle with sugar.

Bread Omelet.

4 eggs.
½ cup milk.
½ cup stale bread crumbs.
¾ teaspoon salt.
⅛ teaspoon pepper.
1 tablespoon butter.

Soak bread crumbs fifteen minutes in milk, add beaten yolks and seasonings, fold in whites. Cook and serve as Plain Omelet.

French Omelet.

4 eggs.
4 tablespoons milk.
½ teaspoon salt.
⅛ teaspoon pepper.
2 tablespoons butter.

Beat eggs slightly, just enough to blend yolks and whites, add the milk and seasonings. Put butter in hot omelet pan; when melted, turn in the mixture; as it cooks, prick and pick up with a fork until the whole is of creamy consistency. Place on hotter part of range that it may brown quickly underneath. Fold and turn on hot platter.

Spanish Omelet.

Mix and cook a French Omelet. Serve with Tomato Sauce in the centre and around omelet.

Tomato Sauce. Cook two tablespoons of butter with one tablespoon of finely chopped onion, until yellow. Add one and three-fourths cups tomatoes, and cook until moisture has nearly evaporated. Add one tablespoon sliced mushrooms, one-fourth teaspoon salt, and few grains cayenne. This is improved by a small piece of red or green pepper, finely chopped, cooked with butter and onion.

16

H Is for Happy

From *An Alphabet for Gourmets*

M. F. K. FISHER

. . . and for what kind of dinner is most often just that evanescent, unpredictable, and purely heaven-sent thing.

In general, I think, human beings are happiest at table when they are very young, very much in love, or very lone. It is rare to be happy in a group: a man can be merry, gay, keenly excited, but not happy in the sense of being free—free from life's cluttering and clutching.

When I was a child my Aunt Gwen (who was not an aunt at all but a large-boned and enormous-hearted woman who, thank God, lived next door to us) used to walk my little sister Anne and me up into the hills at sundown. She insisted on pockets. We had to have at least two apiece when we were with her. In one of them, on these twilight promenades, would be some cookies. In the other, oh, deep sensuous delight! Would be a fried egg sandwich!

Nobody but Aunt Gwen ever made fried egg sandwiches for us. Grandmother was carefully protected from the fact that we had ever even heard of them, and as for Mother, preoccupied with a second set of children, she shuddered at the thought of such greasebound proteins with a thoroughness which should have made us chary but instead succeeded only in satisfying our human need for secrets.

The three of us, Aunt Gwen weighing a good four times what Anne and I did put together, would sneak out of the family ken whenever we could, into the blue-ing air, our pockets sagging and our spirits spiraling in a kind of intoxication of freedom, breathlessness, fatigue, and delicious anticipation. We would climb high above other mortals, onto a far rock or a fallen eucalyptus tree, and sit there, sometimes close as burrs and sometimes apart, singing straight through *Pinafore* and the Episcopal Hymn Book (Aunt Gwen was British and everything from contralto to basso profundo in the Whittier church choir), and biting voluptuously into our tough, soggy, indigestive and luscious suppers. We flourished on them, both physically and in our tenacious spirits.

Lone meals, which can be happy too, are perhaps the hardest to put on paper, with a drop of cyanide on their noses and a pin through their guts. They are the fleetingest of the gastronomical butterflies. I have known some. We all have. They are compounded in almost equal parts of peace, nostalgia, and good digestion, with sometimes an amenable touch of alcohol thrown in.

As for dining-in-love, I think of a lunch at the Lafayette in New York, in the front café with the glass pushed back and the May air flowing almost visibly over the marble tabletops, and the waiter named Pons, and a bottle of Louis Martini's Folle Blanche and moules more-or-less marinières but delicious, and then a walk in new black-heeled shoes with white stitching on them beside a man I had just met and a week later was to marry, in spite of my obdurate resolve never to marry again and my cynical recognition of his super-salesmanship. Anyone in the world could dream as well . . . being blessed . . .

Group happiness is another thing. Few of us can think with honesty of a time when we were indeed happy at table with more than our own selves or one another. And if we succeed in it, our thinking is dictated no matter how mysteriously by the wind, the wine, and the wish of that particular moment.

Now, for no reason that I consciously know of, I remember a lunch at the Casino at Berne, in Switzerland. I was with my father and mother, my husband, and a friend deep in his own murky moods but still attainable socially. We had driven there from Vevey, and we sat in the glass-enclosed bourgeois sparkle of a main dining-room with a fine combination of tired bones and bottoms, thirst, hunger, and the effect of altitude.

I do not recall that we drank anything stronger than sherry before lunch, but we may have; my father, a forthright man who had edited a paper in the hard-liquor days when his Midwest village had fifteen saloons and three churches or thereabouts, may have downed a drink or two of Scotch, or the Bernese play on words, *ein Gift*, aptly called "poison" and made of half sweet vermouth and half any alcohol from vodka to gin.

Then, and this is the part I best remember, we had carafes of a rosé wine that was believed to be at its peak, its consummateness, in Berne, and indeed in that very room. Zizerser it was called. It came in the open café pitchers with the Federal mark at the top, naming the liquid content. It was a gay, frivolous color. It was poured into fine glasses (they were one of the many good things about that casino) from a height of two feet or so, and miracle! It foamed! It bubbled! It was full of magic gas, that wine, which melted out of it with every inch of altitude it lost, so that when I took down a case of it and proudly poured it lake-side, in Vevey, it was merely a pink pretty drink, flat as flat. In Berne it was champagne. We drank deep.

So did our driver, François, and later when a frenzied-looking mountaineer waved back our car, we drove on with nonchalance along a cliff road above fabulous gorges, singing "Covered all over with Sweet Violets" and "Fir Heimat" (ensemble) and "Rover Was Blind but Brave" (my mother), until finally a rock about half as big as our enormous old Daimler sailed lazily down in front of us and settled a few feet from the engine.

We stopped in time.

Another mountaineer, with tiny stars of gold in his ear lobes to make him hear better, dropped into sight from the pine forest. Go back, go back, he cried. We are blasting a new road. You might have been killed. All right, all right, we said.

He lingered, under the obvious spell of our happiness. We talked. My father introduced my mother as the sweetest singer in Onawaiowa, which she once was. My husband breathed deeply, as if in sleep. My friend looked out over the plumy treetops and sighed for a lost love. François blinked in a surfeit of content. We all sat about, on felled branches and running boards, and drank some superlative cognac from an unlabeled bottle, which my father had bought secretly from a Vevey wine merchant and brought along for just this important moment.

A couple more boulders drifted down and settled, dustily and noisily but without active danger, within a few feet of us.

The mountaineer sang three or four songs of his canton. Then, because of the Zizerser and mostly and mainly because we were for that one moment in all time a group of truly happy people, we began to yodel. My father, as a small-town editor, had the edge on us: he had practiced for years at the more unbridled of the local service-club luncheons and banquets. My mother found herself shooting off only too easily into *Aida* and the more probable sections of *Parsifal.* My husband and even my friend hummed and buzzed, and I too buzzed and hummed. And François? He really yodeled, right along with the man from the mountains.

It was a fine thing. Whatever we had eaten at lunch, trout I think, went properly with the Zizerser, and we were full and we were happy, beyond the wine and the brandy, beyond the immediate danger of blasted boulders and cascading slides, beyond any feeling of foolishness. If we had lunched on milk and pap, that noontime in the Casino, we still would have felt the outer-world bliss that was ours, winy and full, on the Oberland mountainside that summer day.

It happened more than ten years ago, but if I should live a hundred and ten more I would still feel the freedom of it.

AUNT GWEN'S FRIED EGG SANDWICHES

Ingredients (Physical)

½ to 1 cup drippings
6 fresh eggs
12 slices of bread
waxed paper

The drippings are very English, the kind poured off an unidentified succession of beef, mutton, and bacon pans, melted gradually into one dark puddle of thick unappetizing grease, which immediately upon being dabbed into a thick hot iron skillet sends out rendingly appetizing smells.

The eggs must be fresh, preferably brown ones, best of all freckled brown ones.

The bread must be good bread, no puffy, blanched, uniform blotters from a paper cocoon.

The waxed paper must be of honest quality, since at the corners where it will leak a little some of it will stick to the sandwich and in a way merge with it and be eaten.

Ingredients (Spiritual)

These have been amply indicated in the text, and their prime requisite—Aunt Gwen herself would be the first to cry no to any further exposition of them. Suffice it that they were equal parts of hunger and happiness.

Method

Heat the drippings in a wide flat-bottomed skillet until they spit and smoke. Break in the eggs, which will immediately bubble around the edges, making them crisp and indigestible, and break their yolks with a fork and swirl them around, so that they are scattered fairly evenly through the whites. This will cook very quickly, and the eggs should be tough as leather.

Either push them to one side of the pan or remove them, and fry bread in the drippings for each sandwich, two slices to an egg. It too will send off a blue smoke. Fry it on one side only, so that when the sandwiches are slapped together their insides will turn soggy at once. Add to this sogginess by pressing them firmly together. Wrap them well in the waxed paper, where they will steam comfortably.

These sandwiches, if properly made and wrapped, are guaranteed, if properly carried in sweater or pinafore pockets, to make large oily stains around them.

Seasoning depends on the state of the drippings. As I remember Aunt Gwen's they were such a "fruity" blend of last week's roast, last month's gammon, that salt and pepper would have been an insult to their fine flavor.

Prescription

To be eaten on top of a hill at sunset, between trios of "A Wandering Minstrel I" and "Onward Christian Soldiers," preferably before adolescence and its priggish queasiness set in.

17

Making the Perfect Fried Egg Sandwich

HOWARD DININ

dedicated to (n-1)

One egg.
The mammoth chicken gamete.
Primary color: yellow. Unary.
Pre-packaged,
Ingenious.
And
biodegradable.

A sustainer.
Life itself
and contained in that
a death.
Not a paradox:
a meal, even for the dying.
Indeed, a preferred repast.

It may be the simplicity.
The sustenance
in so many dimensions.
A perfect food.
Life.

Here's the recipe,
the one the dying prefer.
There's that one egg,

and butter.
That's it:
one egg,
one lump of butter,
walnut-sized,
sweet, mind.
Let the one dying add the salt.

The trick,
the cooking secret?
Frame of mind.

Think French.
The French for egg
requires three vowels,
the eggs of the alphabet.

The vowels open sounds,
throat and gullet unconstricted.
You can't say "egg"
and swallow one at once.

You can in French.

One consonant,
and those French:
they don't pronounce it,
but barely, a puff of air
between open lips, there
just to hold the word
together. The packaging.
An eggshell.

Think, consonant
with life.

Think French
for speed,
or rather pace.
The perfect fried egg

takes time.
We all,
not just the dying,
have so little.

You must take your time.
Haste is dissonant.

Consider this.
Perfect means
no flaws.
Ovum? Perfect, no?

Continuity
Open vowel sounds
Open throat
No constrictions.
No velar stops.
No looking at the clock.

Ovoid. Use a pan
with curving sides.
Curves, mind.
Not slopes,
no crevices.
Here's a memory tip.
Curves are feminine;
it's all one:
the egg the female cell.

You need a cup,
small,
ovoid. An espresso cup.
French, remember?

Crack the shell,
and separate it
intimate as you please
just above the cup.
Glides right in.

Just fits.
Let it sit.
And while you're at it
let the butter sit.

The unary thing,
all one temperature
to start, once you start.
No hurry.

And for cooking,
keep it low to keep it slow,
the heat
a low flame, enough
to melt the butter.
Sufficiency.
No more, no less.
French.

Let the butter liquefy
till it's albumen clear,
no color.
The only color is the yolk.

Swirl the pan
gently,
let the butter lap
the sides.
Then once it pools,
hold the cup
above the surface,
intimate as you please,
and tip the cup,
slowly please,
and slide the egg out.

So far, all lubricity.

Slow.
Open.
Lubricious.

Just as the albumen sets,
gently, please,
swirl the pan
so the egg slides free.
The flame stays low,
no browning,
the white stays white
to the end.

Now gently as you please,
and intimate,
you should have the hang of it
by now,
spoon
the fat to top the yolk.

Repeat.
Repeat.
Repeat.

Slowly.

Watch the pan, and drop
one slice,
two?
of bread
into the toaster.
What does the dying diner
want?
Open-face?
Or classic, something to take
in the hands?

I'll remind you again.
No browning.
While the bread toasts,
spoon more fat
to top the yolk.

Repeat.
Repeat.

No browning.
Don't hurry now,
so close to being done.
No short-orders
for the dying.

And when the toast pops,
plate one slice for sure.

Kill the flame
and swirl the pan.
Make sure the egg is free
to glide around.

Now here's the tricky part.
Simple, but you'll need
dexterity,
and a very thin
bladed spatula,
which you slide beneath the egg;
plate with toast
as near the pan as you
can get.
Slide the egg onto the toast,
and leave the fat behind.

Top it with the other slice,
if that's what's called for.

Ok
Now!
Quick!

French, think French.
The order's done.

Get it to the bedroom
where the dying diner
waits.

18

All It Took Was a Road / Surprises of Urban Renewal

From *If I Can Cook / You Know God Can*

NTOZAKE SHANGE

> From the very start, black music authorized a private autonomous, free, and even rebellious rhythm on the part of the listener or dancer, instead of subjecting him or her to a dominant, foreseeable, or prewritten pattern.
>
> —Carlos Fuentes, *The Buried Mirror*

Between Managua and Bluefields there are many, many mountains. Until the short-lived victory of the Sandinistas in 1981, there was no road. So Nicaragua was a fairly schizophrenic little country with the black people on one side of the mountain and the mestizos and blancos on the other, while Amerindians made a way for themselves in the jungles as best they could. It was very important that there be no connection between the East and West Coast populations. That way myths and distance could weaken any resistance to the reign of the dictator Somoza, if the threat of being "disappeared" was insufficient. When the freeways came through our communities, the African-American ones, my home was disappeared along with thousands of others. We were left with no business districts, no access to each other; what was one neighborhood was now ten, who lived next door was now a threatening six or eight highway lanes away, if there at all. Particularly hurt were the restaurants and theaters where a community shares food and celebrates itself. This we already know is a deathblow to our culture, extroverted, raucous, and spontaneous.

Anyway, I was in Nicaragua traveling to the house in which Nicaragua's revered poet Rubén Dario was born and raised before his sojourn to Europe. Here, a black North American coming from Managua going vaguely in the direction of the Atlantic coast, where people like me lived, would eventually see me, too. I was anxious, divining this reunion of another lost portion of the Diaspora. This anxiety didn't last long, however, for no sooner had I begun to be acutely aware of my "racial" difference from everyone around me (poets though they were, like me, in a nation of poets), than someone's radio blasted Willie Colón and Celia Cruz singing "Usted Abuso." The bus rang out with every imaginable accented Spanish singing, all swaying to my *salsero preferido* (favorite salsa singer). The South Bronx had survived and pulled a trick on the Major Deegan. The blockade against Cuba lacked a sense of rhythm. But it didn't stop there. Next came Stevie Wonder and Michael Jackson rockin' our little bus through a war-torn, earthquake-ravaged land. The tales of our people's incompetency and addiction to failure must be very bad jokes indeed.

Even more important was running into Nicaraguan poet Carlos Johnson. He reminded me of a painter friend of mine from Nashville, except for the West Indian tinge to his English. At the front porch of his house, Rubén Dario met us with a poem. Then came many poems from me, that to this very day stem from that moment of underestimating who and what I come from.

"My Song for Hector Lavoe"
Mira / tu puedes ir conmigo /
hasta managua and / the earthquake was no more a surprise /
than you / con su voz / que viene de los dioses / and the
swivel of hips de su flaca / as you dance or / when she
sucks the hearts / out of the eggs of / tortugas / anglos die to
see float about / while all the time we dance around
them / split up / change
partners and fall madly in love . . . porque
nosotros somos an army of marathon dancers / lovers / seekers
and / we have never met an enemy we can't outlive.

It turned out that Carlos used the racismo of the ruling class to his own advantage by wandering "aimlessly" around Managua as if he were an itinerant musician, like all black people, saxophone case in hand. Only this poet's musical instrument was an AK-47, which was used strategically to undermine the Somoza regime and lead to what we nostalgically now call La Victoria. I heard this story and others like it once we'd made it back to Managua, full of deep, sweet black rum, black music, and relentless appetites.

In what we could call a tropical ice house, a dance hall under a thatched roof, open to the night air and the call of romance, we dance to something called Nicason, a *mezcla* (mixture) of reggae, beguine, and cumbé with a ranchero overlay. You see, road or no road, we connect to the culture of the people we live with, whether they like us or not, or even if they've never seen one of us: they know James Brown. In the sweat and swivel of dancing, being hungry for more of life, and each other, we are *huevos de tortugas*, everybody.

TURTLE EGGS AND SPICES

This is very simple to prepare because there is nothing to cook. Gather some young turtle eggs (substitute quail eggs where necessary). Lay them on a bed of fresh, clean, dry lettuce, spinach, arugula, it's up to you. Place 4–6 eggs on the greens. Pierce the top of the eggs gently so that the whole egg doesn't crack—we don't want that. Make your presentation as extravagant or simple as you choose, placing edible flowers, orange or lemon peels, fruits or dried fish, in an attractive manner about the eggs. In another area prepare small dishes of crushed nuts, pico de gallo (a mixture of tomatoes, peppers, onion, garlic, and cilantro), peppers, pimiento, chopped olives, fish roe, and so forth, to be placed in the small holes we've made in the eggs by our guests who will leisurely "suck the hearts and spices" out of the eggs at their whim. This is a very sexy little dish. Sits well on the tummy, lightly, so to speak, so that dancing and romancing can continue without mitigation. (Please be aware that raw eggs may contain salmonella bacteria.)

That night in Managua we were able to cover the scars of war with poetry, music, and abandon ourselves to the impulses of our bodies in the night heat and each other's arms. The volcano where Somoza dropped the bodies of anyone for any reason was covered with mist and clouds. I only thought once about the house I grew up in that had disappeared and been resurrected as a police station. The thought broke my heart, but the fact of all of us let me hold my head high.

19

Poison Egg

TENAYA DARLINGTON

I can say this now: the best mornings of my childhood began with bird-calls, my father's boyfriend practicing his hoots at the stove. He was a fish and wildlife man, a game warden, and when he moved into our house, he brought a suitcase of duck calls and a Hefty bag full of flannel shirts. It was not an easy transition for a girl of twelve, whose mother had vanished. Well, not vanished exactly, but she had traded in domestic life earlier that year for surfing and sunning, on the premise of finishing a doctorate in Hawaii. Her letters, full of pressed flowers as big as my hand, contained wonderful descriptions of marine life but never the plane tickets she kept promising to send my older brother Jacob and me. *Wait until you see the Toucans,* she wrote. *They feed right off my porch.*

When our father came out to us, it was not even six months after she had left. I was still hoping they would get back together, that we would all move to Hawaii and leave behind our drafty rental house in Madison, Wisconsin, where our father had a visiting position in the university art department. After our mother left, we only saw him at breakfast. Otherwise, he was either teaching classes or painting in his studio all day, and rarely had time to help with homework or cook for us, except soft-boiled eggs and buttered toast. All other meals were foraged affairs or brother-sister team efforts that ended in messes: baked beans with red hots, canned chowder with croutons.

"Janine," my father began, drawing fingers down his beard. I still remember the way his lips twitched as he reached for my hand across the kitchen table, then took Jacob's. Behind our father's narrow form, a pan of water boiled, the toaster gave off its smell of burnt crumbs, and sunlight spilled through the high windows, across a row of wine glasses by the sink.

"I've met someone," he said, closing his eyes. "His name is Bjorn. It's a man, yes. I wanted you to hear this from me."

Jacob didn't flinch—at fifteen, he was reserved, sensitive, always reading Proust—but I screamed. An ear-splitting note, I held it for as long as I could, in the hopes of shattering the glasses winking happily on the counter. I suppose what I really wanted to do was knuckle and bruise my father's heart. Under my bed, I had a secret chart for all the times I'd cried since our mother had left: a grid of boxes and dates, tear-smeared, each splash like a small notary stamp.

"Janine," my father said again, pulling his hand back and running it over his shaved head. "Janine, please."

I screamed louder, and my father—the kind of father who rolled his own cigarettes and wore sandalwood beads and read books on meditation—put his fingers to his ears and turned away to finish making breakfast.

When I ran out of steam, my father served up his usual morning fare: soft-boiled eggs and toasted rye. No bacon—he was vegetarian. It was my mother the cook who always made us bacon, frying it in maple syrup.

Without looking me in the face, my father told me he hoped I'd come around. In a few days, Bjorn was coming to dinner.

I decided to poison myself. As I sat at the kitchen table, watching my toast harden and my egg grow cold, I considered options: certain mushrooms, the pits of peaches, bleach. Jacob proceeded to interview our father, Barbara Walters–style.

"So tell me about Bjorn," he said. "How did you meet him? What does he do?"

This time, I was the one who stuffed fingers in my ears. I focused on the egg before me, its shell seamless and perfect, and I thought about what might happen if I kept the egg with me until the night of Bjorn's dinner. If I ate a spoiled egg, would I die?

I was a dramatic child. I loved *Hamlet* and *Macbeth*. My bedroom was decorated with programs from children's theater productions, and thanks to my mother, I had a closet full of costumes. To fall asleep at night, I listened to bootleg cassette recordings of *Masterpiece Theater* so that I could memorize the inflections of a proper British accent, and when I awoke, I often performed various vocal exercises I'd learned at summer theater camp, singing "Aluminum Linoleum" as loud as I could. It gave Jacob a reason to save up for a cork-lined room.

When my father stood up to take his dishes to the sink, I slipped the soft-boiled egg into my pocket.

After the coming-out breakfast, I carried that egg with me for four days and spent hours in the window seat of my bedroom, planning my demise. At school, I ran the egg through the flame of a Bunsen burner during science class.

"Janine, are you torturing an egg?" asked Mr. McCoy, my science teacher.

"Not exactly," I said. "But it's part of an experiment."

Mr. McCoy drew together his thick, blond eyebrows. He wore saggy corduroys, balding at the knees, and patrolled the room with a feline presence. As long as we didn't blow up the building, he didn't care what we did. "Interesting," he said, his voice flat as Kansas. Then he strolled over to the next table, where a group of boys were hard at work on a prototype electric chair.

In gym class, I set the egg on a tree stump to make sure it got direct sunlight; while I played soccer, I imagined the molten core beginning to curdle. In home ec, I slipped the egg into the oven on low heat. While I made no-bake cookies with a partner, I imagined the white part of the egg shriveling up. In English, I asked Barry Congee to hide the egg under his armpit. "Keep it warm," I said. "As warm as possible."

"Is this, like, one of those projects where you take a raw egg and pretend it's a baby so you can practice mothering?"

"No," I said. "It's the opposite. It's soft-boiled."

"Gross." Barry flexed his nostrils. He was captain of the football team.

"I want to make it totally disgusting."

"Cool." His eyes lit up.

"Yeah, I'm planning to poison someone," I said, leaning my elbows on his desk. "Think it'll work?"

"I dunno," Barry said, adjusting his football jersey so that he could tuck the egg further up into the folds of his skin. I smiled at him, all teeth like a shark.

After school on our walk home, Jacob said, "Barry told me what you're up to. Don't you think this is going a little far?"

"Barry doesn't have a clue," I said, cradling the egg in the front pocket of my hoodie. "He thinks he does, but he doesn't."

"You're planning to poison Bjorn. That's so obvious," Jacob said. He adjusted his wide, tinted glasses, hiding what I was sure was one of his big-brother eye rolls. "Look, Janine. Dad is experimenting sexually. It's probably just a phase."

"Good-bye," I said, sauntering ahead of him in my best imitation of Holly Golightly.

"This isn't a big deal," Jacob called, running a few steps to catch up. "We live in Madison. Half of our class has experienced same-sex parenting. You're just stuck in a heteronormative schema."

"Am not." I stuck my tongue out. "And don't go all AP on me. This is our family, not a sociological study."

Jacob exhaled hard through his nose. "Actually, it is. Bjorn works for the Fish and Wildlife Commission. He hunts, which really puts Dad off. It probably won't last."

The rest of the way home, we walked in silence—past prayer flags flapping across unkempt lawns, past clouds of marijuana smoke hovering outside huge gabled housing co-ops, past Lake Monona where two cabbies sat kissing on a park bench and a girl covered in tattoos fed ducks a bag of stale croissants.

~

On the day of Bjorn's dinner, my father took the afternoon off. He soaked garbanzo beans and brought out some wild yeast he'd harvested to make bread. While a pot of curry simmered on the stove, he took a very long bath in essential oils. When he came out of the bathroom, he stood in my doorway, steam rising off his shoulders and petals in his beard. He said, "I would really appreciate it if you would put your latent prejudices aside this evening and join us for a peaceful supper," sounding as if he'd rehearsed the line.

I looked at the runes tattooed on my father's arms rather than in his eyes, and I said, "This has nothing to do with prejudice. I just don't think it's fair for you to be dating."

"What do you want?" my father's voice was measured. "A pledge of celibacy? I can tell you this: your mother—" but then he put a hand up, closed his eyes. "Listen," he said. "Please, listen. Will you at least pretend to be accepting?"

I thought, *In twenty-four hours, I'll be dead. Then we'll see who's accepting.* "No," I said, giving him a director's-chair scowl. "This is a family, not a play—I won't pretend that I'm not suffering."

"And what is it that you want?" he asked, cocking his head and holding up the towel knotted around his waist.

"A normal life," I said, as softly as I could, using the whisper technique from camp. "For once, just for once."

My father blinked, his lips a tight line. Then he left as if I had just said something unspeakable.

~

Palming my egg, I paced my room and listened for the doorbell. Would I die quickly, like Queen Gertrude in *Hamlet* drinking from a poisoned cup? Or would I experience crazy visions as Lady Macbeth had in the dark halls of her castle? I shivered. What if the egg didn't work? What if I just got sick and had to go to the hospital to have my stomach pumped? But I had run the egg through a Bunsen burner and left it out in the sun and cooked it in an oven and entrusted it to Barry Congee's armpit. Toxic.

I stood before my bedroom mirror and pictured my face green. I had my mother's pointy chin and her kinky red hair. I thought of her in Hawaii, wearing a lei and writing her dissertation on ancient goddesses, and I wondered if I should bother mailing her a suicide note. It would take days to reach her, and she probably wouldn't even get it before she flew back for my funeral. I withdrew the tear chart from under my bed and set it out on my desk; I made sure to underscore the day's date in a wobbly hand.

When the doorbell rang, I cracked my bedroom door. Sitar music drifted up the staircase, followed by the sound of low voices in the foyer. I listened as Jacob introduced himself and my father said, "Can I take your coat?" I was outnumbered by men. Cast out.

There had been a time when my mother had "ruled the roost," as she liked to say, but then she joined a group of Wiccans and realized she had no cultural power—only spiritual power—and so she went off to study ancient religions. I thought about the many times she had taken me thrifting, just the two of us girls, and how she never let me buy anything feminine (no fairy pink dresses, no floral bathrobes) unless I promised to wear them as costumes. She said she didn't want me turning into a stereotype. I was too smart for that.

For my last hours on earth, I decided on a wine-colored Gunne Sax dress with a lace bodice that my mother had hated. Using my fountain pen, I wrote on my blotter, "The queen, my lord, is dead."

"Oh, she's upstairs," I heard my father say. "She's not hungry. She won't be joining us for dinner." That's when I closed my door, crawled into bed, and prepared to peel the egg that would kill me. First, though, I arranged a goblet and a jewel-handled letter opener on the nightstand. The scene was set.

As I chipped away at the shell, I smelled sulfur, a deathly stink. The white of the egg was a dull, sinister gray. Surely, this egg had the power to kill me, but now the problem was getting it down the hatch. I was an adventurous eater, except for tofu—blocks of which my father stored in murky containers along the inside door of the fridge—and the gray-white of this particular egg looked a little bit like tofu. Mushy. Ashen. I couldn't fathom eating it.

I turned to the letter opener on the nightstand and wondered if I could trick myself into falling onto its sharp tip, but then I pictured the process of being disemboweled. Surely that would be a very painful death.

And so I wrapped the egg in Kleenex and wept. I applied several new tears to my chart and stared at the smudgy checkerboard that chronicled my sorrows of the last four years. *No one should have to suffer as much as I have,* I thought. Pushing aside my comforter, I marched into the hall with new resolve: I would throw myself down the stairs.

For at least ten minutes, I stood at the top of our wooden steps, looking at the dust balls that had gathered in the corners. Those dust balls would rise like ash. I could picture them floating up and then settling, my body a heap of crimson fabric at the base of the staircase.

As I was just about to let go of the banister, I heard footsteps below, and then a face appeared at the bottom of the stairs. It was a very handsome face—square jaw, close-cut dark hair set off against a tight white T-shirt. His eyes widened, and I felt mine widen in return—he looked a lot like the young Lawrence Olivier.

"What specter is this? Are you Janine?" His voice was raspy, slippery around the *s*'s. I liked the way he grinned rakishly up at me, his teeth glimmering like polished stones.

"Bjorn?" I coughed.

He approached me, one step at a time, like a gorgeous monster rising from water. The staircase was dim, and all I could see was his shining skin, his eyes fixed on mine—they seemed to glow. When he reached the step beneath me, he held out his hand and fingered the velvet piping on my Gunne Sax sleeve. "Nice," he said. "I had no idea you would be so beautiful."

"Oh," I said, pretending to be taken aback by his forwardness. "Am I?"

He nodded, pursed his lips, and pinched me on the nose. His hair was graying at the temples, and his aftershave had a clovey smell. My palms grew moist.

"I brought you something," he said, leaning down by my ear. "Something I picked out just for you," he whispered. "For breakfast."

"What is it?" I could barely breathe.

"You'll see," he said, winking big like a Hollywood hero.

"Really?"

He nodded and then skirted around me to the bathroom. I held onto the banister, waiting, breathing, fixated on the dust balls, wondering if my hands stunk of rotten egg, listening to the sound of dishes clanking in the sink below. Then Bjorn emerged from the bathroom, shaking his head at me. "I don't blame you for skipping dinner," he said. "Your father's cooking is atrocious."

"He made beans, didn't he?" I could feel my nose wrinkling at the word "beans." It felt like a secret between us.

"They were disgusting." Bjorn rolled his eyes, as dramatic as my brother. Then he said, "Get your beauty rest, princess. Morning will be here before the lark."

Without meaning to, I laughed and even lunged out to swat his arm, but he was already halfway down the stairs, whistling a birdcall.

~

That night, I listened to every recording of *Hair* that I owned. Dancing before my oval mirror, I practiced imitating Bjorn's sibilant *s* as I sang along with "Age of Aquarius." I didn't want to be Lady Macbeth anymore, dark in spirit; I would be Sheila, spreader of love. When the front-porch light flickered off and the voices downstairs dissipated, I tiptoed down the staircase with my poison egg, and behind my mother's potting shed I buried it in one of her paisley scarves.

Later, I would bury her letters there, too.

In the morning, I woke up to the sound of my record player crackling with static, and the smell of something warm and smoky rising from the kitchen. Bacon. It was a scent I had almost forgotten.

"You're right on time," Bjorn called from the stove when I appeared. He was alone, and from the other side of my father's bedroom door, I could hear heavy snoring. Not even Jacob was awake, although it was almost eight, the hour when he usually began his routine of calisthenics in the front room. Bjorn flashed a lopsided smile—perhaps he had slipped something into their drinks last night, a sleeping potion? On his feet, Bjorn wore my father's Chinese slippers. Around his neck, loosely tied, was my mother's old apron—still streaked with flour from the last time she made Beltane cookies.

"And how does m'lady like her eggs?" he crooned, pulling out a chair for me at the table.

"An omelet?" I shrugged.

"Coming right up," he sang, and then he reached into the breast pocket of his white T-shirt and withdrew two of the smallest eggs I had ever seen. "These are for you," he said, extending his palm, the eggs nestled against his pink skin. They were mottled in color, brown and cream, shaped like a pair of tears.

"Quail eggs," he said. "I found them in a nest yesterday." He raised a finger to his lips. "I only brought them to impress you, so don't tell."

"You did?" I said and frowned as deeply as I could, although I was delighted.

Bjorn rested a hip against the counter and eyed me. His hair was spiky, mussed from sleep, and in the daylight his face looked craggy. "I know thirty-seven different birdcalls," he said, turning to crack the eggs into the hot grease. "Want to hear them?"

"Yes," I said and lifted a cup of tea to my lips, closing my eyes to sip it delicately as I had seen women do in British musicals. Bjorn began with a riff of low calls, then a series of high-pitched ta-weet-ta-weets. His melodious voice was perfectly in tune, and he stopped only to say "here," as he walked over and slid the tiny omelet onto my plate, along with two strips of bacon and four squares of toast. The omelet was the size of a fortune cookie and very tender, more yellow and more velvety than any other omelet I had ever eaten.

"Delicious," I said, looking out the window toward the potting shed and thinking of the egg, wrapped in silk, buried beneath a brush pile. Would anyone ever find it? Would the squirrels dig it up? Would the hawk that lived in the pine tree gut it greedily some winter night when the rodents were deep in their burrows? Should I tell Bjorn that I was glad to be alive? When he stopped, I said, "Sing it again." And he did. I counted: he really did know thirty-seven. "Tah-wheet-wheet-wheet," he called, and slowly I sang the notes back to him, trying to match his low trill with my high one.

QUAIL EGG OMELET FOR ONE

Quail eggs are known for their bright yellow yolks and fluffy texture when cooked. It takes about five quail eggs to equal one chicken egg, so this omelet will be quite small, but very light and flavorful. Try serving this alongside a lightly dressed salad (tossed with olive oil and a little fresh lemon juice) and some toasted baguette.

6 quail eggs
3 tablespoons milk
½ teaspoon butter
1 teaspoon oil
½ teaspoon chives or other herbs, chopped
Parmesan, finely grated
lemon slice
sea salt

Whisk quail eggs and milk in a small mixing bowl until well combined. Heat a small nonstick skillet over a medium flame until sizzling hot (test it by tossing a few drops of water on it). Add oil, then butter—this prevents the butter from burning. Pour egg batter into the pan, then lift the pan an inch off the flame and shake it vigorously in a circular pattern, so that the batter keeps moving.

When the omelet is almost set, flip it over. Slide onto a plate; top with herbs, Parmesan, salt, and a few drops of lemon juice. Serve it open-faced, like a small pancake.

PART IV

Main Dishes

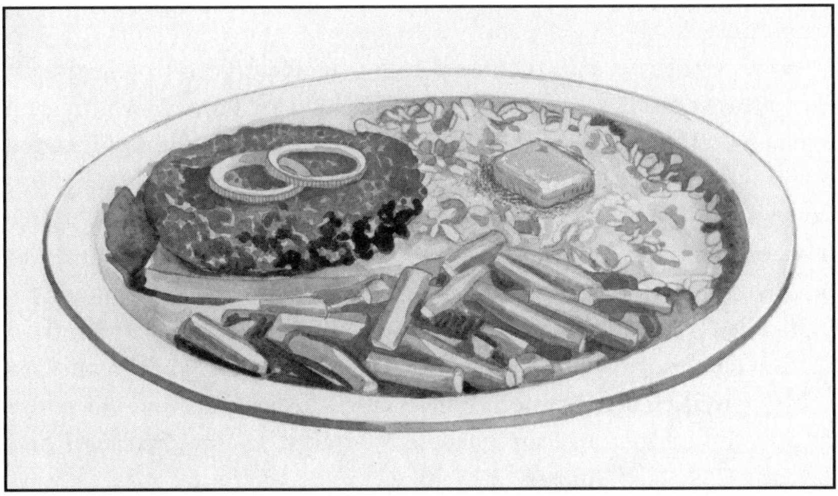

Prior to the European colonization of the Americas, natives of North America ate locally and seasonally, without imagining their meals in courses or parts, such as main dishes, side dishes, and salads. In the Northeast, Native Americans routinely dined on the "three sisters" of maize, beans, and squash, which were planted together—beans twining up the corn stalks, squash unfurling around the bases. In the Northwest, tribes caught salmon; Plains Indians ate buffalo; and natives of the Southwest relied on rabbits and raccoons as well as potatoes and corn. Despite these dietary differences, however, across all regions, Native Americans ate only a single large meal each day. The modern American custom of dining throughout the day—planned around a dinner with a main course—is an Old World import.

In the 1620s, the Pilgrims attempted to follow the fare of their homeland: breakfasts of bread sopped in ale; large midday dinners of a little meat, pudding, or savory pies; and smaller, just-before-sundown suppers of cold leftovers, all washed down with buckets of beer.[1] A combination of harsh winters and the inability to grow English grains meant that the Pilgrims had to trade for seeds, meat, and recipes with native peoples—and, as such, their diets changed dramatically. North American main dishes came to consist of bear, venison, goose, rabbit, or fish, all cooked with maize, beans, or squash.

Yet with the rise of nationhood in the eighteenth century, American wealth rose as well. Now some citizens could enjoy more variety in their mains—particularly in the quality and quantity of their meats. Since the medieval period, meat had been a marker of social status throughout Europe. The more money, the more meat. Medieval and Renaissance monarchs and the *haut monde* were known for the copious amounts of meat at their banquets. In the fifteenth century in England, one menu for a "franklen" dinner—meaning that of a landholder of the lesser gentry—consisted of brawn (pork or boar) served with mustard, a bacon-and-pea soup, stewed beef or mutton, boiled chicken or capon, roasted goose or pork, and either a capon bakemete (cooked in a pastry crust) or a Custade Costable (an open tart with egg filling).[2] These six dishes were merely the first course. From here, the franklen's guests could look forward to a second course of meat or fish pudding and many roasts—of veal, lamb, kid or rabbit, chicken, and pigeon—before tucking into a third course of even more tarts and pastries, with fruit, bread, cheese, and cakes to finish.

Accordingly, class-conscious Colonial Americans cooked up ever more meat for their mains. As is clear from the beginning of Amelia Simmons's *American Cookery*—published just two decades after the British colonies became the United States—beef, mutton, lamb, veal, pork, poultry, turkey, goose, duck, cock, partridge, pigeon, rabbit, salmon, shad, cod, flounder, oyster, lobster, eel, and trout all came to the new nation's table, whereas vegetables were considered merely a garnish. Some founding fathers welcomed this fleshy abundance as well: in 1801, Thomas Jefferson (perhaps America's first foodie) spent $3,000 on wine and $6,500 on groceries, much of it meat—even though Jefferson himself was a borderline vegetarian. Although he was known to nosh on Guinea fowls, beef, mutton, and lamb, in a letter to his doctor in 1819, Jefferson wrote, "I have lived temperately, eating little animal food, and that not as an aliment, so much as a condiment for the vegetables which constitute my principal diet."[3]

Jefferson's preference for main-meal salads proved to be the exception, however, and not the rule. In nineteenth-century America, a formal dinner would have consisted of a multitude of beefy, porky, fowly, and fishy mains. Rather than enjoying an appetizer or two, a soup or salad, an entrée, a bit of bread, a few select side dishes, and a distinctive dessert—as most modern Americans expect when attending a dinner party—a Victorian guest would have begun with oysters and terrapin soup before spending the rest of the evening, until confectionary time, masticating on meat. A lot of meat. Cookbooks of the period, such as Fannie Farmer's *Boston Cooking-School Cook Book*, list recipes for beef, veal, pork, poultry (pheasant, quail, squab, turkey, etc.), game, lamb, mutton, and fish—all of which might be offered sequentially as main courses of a single dinner.

Such dishes of critters and beasts were not merely a symbol of class status for Anglo-Americans; they also simply loved meat—its fatty sizzle and its juicy cut. In Mark Twain's 1880 account of a "Grand Tour" of Europe, *A Tramp Abroad*, he sings the praises of American beef over the tasteless Continental approximation, exclaiming:

> Imagine a poor exile contemplating that inert thing; and imagine an angel suddenly sweeping down out of a better land and setting before him a mighty porterhouse steak an inch and a half thick, hot and sputtering from the griddle; dusted with a fragrant pepper; enriched with little melting bits of butter of the most unimpeachable freshness and genuineness; the precious juices of the meat trickling out and joining the gravy, archipelagoed with mushrooms; a township or two of tender, yellowish fat gracing an outlying district of this ample county of beefsteak; the long white bone which divides the sirloin from the tenderloin still in its place . . .—could words describe the gratitude of this exile?[4]

Thus, even in the nineteenth century, a mighty mountain of muscular beef is what was (often) for dinner.

It was with the rise of industrial and globally influenced foodways in the twentieth century that American cuisine (and its main dishes) finally became more diverse. With a large urban and suburban middle-class market and many housewives or double-shift mothers in charge of their kitchens, ironically the American food economy shifted from the homemade to the industrial as canned foods became the new status symbol: "pure," "clean," and supposedly more healthful. Hence the rise of the Campbell-soup casseroles of the 1930s, '40s, and '50s as well as the blockbuster success of Irma Rombauer's *Joy of Cooking*, which, by the time she died in 1962, had sold six million copies.[5] Rombauer empowered the World War I and II generations of amateur cooks, drawing on their access to a cornucopia of foods both out of season and far beyond their locale to allow them greater experimentation than ever before. In the selection represented here from the 1931 first edition, Rombauer writes that, with her cookbook, she has "attempted to make palatable dishes with simple means and to lift everyday cooking out of the commonplace." So while meat was still the thing, Rombauer offers flavorful recipes for Southern-Style Fried Chicken, Rabbit à la Mode, and Yorkshire Pudding.

What Rombauer suggests here might be called the very beginnings of a fusion menu—Frenchified rabbit, soul-food southern fried chicken, and a pudding recipe from Merrie Ol' England. Rombauer's recipes point toward what will eventually evolve into American main dishes as diverse as our contemporary population, from Italian-Indian and Asian Fusion to Tex-Mex and even Germano-Vegan.

The diversity of our modern cuisine was initiated and inspired by waves of immigrants from all over the world, first Europeans and African slaves and then, after 1965, Asians and Latin Americans. Now, the centerpiece dish for any American's meal might be an Italian pasta, lasagna, or garlic-and-basil-based meat dish, such as in David Citino's "Poem of Chicken Breast with Fettuccine"—an honorific to his Italian family's culinary heritage. Or a cook might rustle up a little Cajun food, such as the new-ritual-making "Turkey Bone Gumbo" of Sara Roahen's essay on familial displacement and the human desire to belong. Or, perhaps, an eater might be faced with the "Boiled Chicken Feet and Hundred-Year-Old Eggs" in Shirley Geok-Lin Lim's piece: traditional foods first rejected and then powerfully remembered by the writer. Or, too, a main dish might be a completely made-up thing, akin to the Thai egg-and-pork mash-up recipe from Paul Hanstedt's short story "Half-Life." Or, in a kind of modern-day return to original Native American practices of hunting and foraging one's own dinner from local flora and fauna, a postindustrial, yet organically minded, eater might follow Gary Snyder's poetic directions on "How to Make Stew in the Pinacate Desert" or choose to cook Ellen Meloy's Riparian Roast—a recipe she provides as the culmination of her sardonic essay on eating as locally as possible, "Eat Your Pets." Regardless, however, of the ethnic, familial, global, local, industrial, or homegrown sources of these writers' main meals, interestingly and importantly, the (still) mostly meat mains bubbling up from these creative pieces come, as Teresa Lust suggests in "A Good Roast Chicken," not "from a recipe," per se, "but from a way of life."

On the one hand, the "way of life" integrated into these writers' recipes for fish, chicken, lamb, and pork is one that seeks connection: connection to memories, to family, to community, to animals, and to the land. Through the heartiest of dishes—that is, the main ones, the ones that take the most time, that symbolize the meal as a whole—these writers revive dead relatives, create new homes, speak difficult things, and even remake their own bodies in the shape of their mothers and fathers. In every piece, there is an attempt to get at the "meat" or center of things: to communicate and to connect with the human through hunger, hunting, harvesting, cooking, and eating. As Roahen writes, "I experienced one of those full, soul-moving, Virginia Woolfian moments of being. Here we were, establishing a new tradition for our family: Thanksgiving weekend turkey bone gumbo. How important and gratifying."

On the other hand, however, there is also in these selections a "main" point that focuses on what is lost or broken—on what is missing from the collective table. In Sherman Alexie's poem "13/16," all mains are the cookie-cutter foods of white-bread culture: those "U.S. Commodities, white cans / black letters translated into Spanish" that prompt the poet's recurring character, Lester FallsApart, to ask, "Does this mean I have to learn / the language to eat?" Alexie's recipe is a dark criticism of the illusion many Americans have that they possess a thriving indigenous cuisine: "[the] directions for preparation are simple: / a. WASH CAN; b. OPEN CAN; c. EXAMINE CONTENTS / OF CAN FOR SPOILAGE; d. EMPTY CONTENTS / OF CAN INTO SAUCE PAN; e. COOK CONTENTS / OVER HIGH HEAT; f. SERVE AND EAT." Ravi Shankar further questions any idealized national identity contained within American mains by rejecting the idea of a traditional recipe altogether. In "American Liver Mush," his ingredients include such elements as "3 cowboys," "2 narcotics officers," "1 Jimmy the Greek," and "4 channels NASCAR coverage." His resulting "meal" is a mordant comment on the politics of that greatest of imaginary main dishes: the American melting pot.

Yet what recurs most across all these selections is hope: hope that what mainly matters in a main meal is, in fact, that matter within the dish—what is sacrificed and what is shared. In "Spirit-Fried No-Name River Brown Trout," David James Duncan writes, "You are preparing to eat an animal that gave up its beautiful river and only life for your pleasure. Pleasure ought, therefore, to be maximized. Open your palate to the trout's flavor and your heart to its riverine essence, and that essence will charge through you like spring runoff, flushing every artery you've got." He counsels, "It is never 'heart smart' to refuse to open your heart."

In approaching these poems, essays, and stories, then, one is well advised to open the heart. One must be open to the beautiful and the terrible, to the living and the dead, and make the "main event" of these main-dish writings a readerly feeling of fullness and of satisfaction—of satiety.

NOTES

1. Sherrie McMillan, "What Time Is Dinner?," *History Magazine*, October–November 2001. <http://www.history-magazine.com/dinner2.html>.
2. John Russell, *Boke of Nurture*, ed. Frederick J. Furnivall (c. 1460; Bungay, UK: John Childs and Son, 1867), 54–55.
3. Thomas Jefferson to Dr. Vine Utley, 21 Mar. 1819, in *The Writings of Thomas Jefferson*, ed. Andrew A. Lipscomb and Albert E. Bergh, 20 vols. (Washington, DC: Thomas Jefferson Memorial Association of the United States, 1903–1904), 15:187.
4. Mark Twain, *A Tramp Abroad*, 3rd ed. (London: Chatto & Windus, 1880), 221–222.
5. Andrew F. Smith, *Eating History: 30 Turning Points in the Making of American Cuisine* (New York: Columbia University Press, 2009), 138.

20

From *The Joy of Cooking: A Compilation of Reliable Recipes with a Casual Culinary Chat*

IRMA S. ROMBAUER

Preface

Whenever I leave home and begin to move about, I am appalled to find how many people with a desire to write feel impelled to share their emotions with the general public.

Time and again I have been told with modesty and pride, or with both, that I was entertaining a literary angel unawares, until one day, recognizing the glint of authorship in a man's eye and anticipating his imminent confidence, I forestalled him by saying rapturously, "Oh, do you know, I am a reader!"

And now, after all, I am a writer—of a kind.

For thirty odd years I have enjoyed cooking as an avocation, and as I moved about from place to place I found myself encumbered with an ever increasing supply of cook books—domestic, foreign, published and unpublished.

The result of this encumbrance was an anthology of favorite recipes, which disposed for all time of my ambulant library. These recipes have been developed, altered and created outright, so that the collection as it now stands may make a claim for originality—enough, it is hoped, to justify its publication, and to hold the interest of those who encouraged me to put it into book form.

In this practical outgrowth of a pleasant experience, I have attempted to make palatable dishes with simple means and to lift everyday cooking out of the commonplace.

In spite of the fact that the book is compiled with one eye on the family purse and the other on the bathroom scale, there are, of course, occasional lapses into indulgence.

Good cooks at home and abroad have contributed to this collection, and many a recipe is coupled in my mind with a grateful thought of the friend who gave it.

Fowl and Game

If you are a new cook and are called upon to dress a chicken, remember, please, that among other things it has a crop that must be removed—(I am speaking from experience). The following is the best way to prepare a large chicken of doubtful age.

Stewed Chicken

Clean a chicken and cut it into pieces. Drop the pieces into boiling water, to which an onion, a carrot, a rib or two of celery with leaves and seasoning have been added. As the liquid will increase in volume, the chicken need only be covered to the depth of ½ inch. Cover the pot closely and simmer the chicken until it is tender (2 hours or more), but do not boil it at any time. Remove the chicken from the pot and make the gravy . . . adding milk or cream to it. When it is boiling add the chicken and serve it at once, preferably with dumplings, or rice.

Roast Chicken

Stuff a large chicken—about 3½ pounds—with Boiled Rice, Bread or Potato dressing. . . . Rub it well with salt and with 3 tablespoons butter, creamed with 2 tablespoons flour. Truss the chicken and place it uncovered in a roasting pan in a hot oven 475°. When it is well browned (about 25 minutes) baste the chicken with ½ cup of seasoned stock, cover it and reduce the heat to 325°. Baste it with the drippings in the pan every ten minutes, adding a little additional stock, if the pan threatens to become dry. Turn the chicken so that it may brown evenly. A thicker crust may be had by dredging the chicken with flour while it is cooking. If a glazed skin is preferred, omit the flour. Time for cooking about 1½ hours.

Chicken Stock

Boil 3 cups of water, 3 ribs of celery with leaves, ½ onion, a carrot and 3 sprigs of parsley. Add the chicken giblets, neck and wing tips. Simmer this until the giblets are tender. Remove the giblets and the neck and strain the stock.

Chicken Gravy:

Strain the drippings, pour off the fat.

To 6 tablespoons of fat add 4 tablespoons of flour and 2 cups of stock.

The giblets may be chopped and added to the gravy. . . .

Young Chickens Baked

Cut the chickens into quarters. Season them with salt and pepper and brown them well in butter in a hot skillet. Place them in a covered pan in a slow oven 325° for 1 hour or more. Add ½ cup of hot stock, or water, and baste them frequently. Make gravy with the drippings, adding cream to the stock, if desired.

Broiled Spring Chicken

Select chickens weighing about 1 pound. Rub them with butter on both sides and sprinkle them with a very little salt (if the butter is unsalted). Place them in a pan, skin side down. The skin side will brown quicker than the under side. Broil them until they are brown, under a good flame, turning them frequently, after 15 minutes add butter, if needed, and put ½ cup of stock in the bottom of the pan. Cover the pan and bake the chickens in a slow oven 275° basting them every 10 minutes. This will require about 30 minutes. Very small chickens may be broiled for 20 minutes and require no baking. . . .

Sautéd Chicken

In ordinary parlance—Fried Chicken

Do not attempt to sauté chicken in this way unless it is young and tender.

Season chicken that has been cut into small pieces and dredge it with flour. Place butter, or bacon drippings in a skillet and when it is hot, add the chicken, turning it in the hot fat until it is brown. Reduce the heat, cover the skillet and continue cooking the chicken until it is done, (from 20 to 30 minutes, according to size). Remove the chicken from the pan and make the gravy. . . . Serve the chicken garnished with parsley.

Sautéed Chicken (Fried) Southern Style

Cut a young chicken into small pieces. Sprinkle it lightly with flour, pepper and salt. Beat an egg with ¼ cup of milk. Dip the chicken in this and then in fine bread or cracker crumbs. Brown the chicken in hot butter or lard. Place ¼ cup of boiling stock or water in the bottom of the pan, cover the skillet and bake the chicken in a slow oven—325°. A two and a half pound chicken calls for about one hour's cooking in all—30 minutes on top of the stove and 30 minutes in the oven.

Smothered Chicken

A good way of preparing middle-aged chicken.

Cut a chicken into quarters or small pieces, roll them in flour and season them well. Brown them in fat which has been heated in a pot and to which several slices of onion have been added. Combine stock, cream and a sprig of parsley. Heat this to the boiling point and pour it over the browned chicken until the bottom of the pot is well covered. (Boiling water may be used in place of stock and cream.) Cover the pot and simmer the chicken until it is tender. Make gravy with the drippings . . . , adding stock or cream and a few drops of Kitchen Bouquet. Pour it over the chicken before serving it.

Frog Legs

Season frog legs—roll them in flour and sauté them in hot butter—onion may be added to the butter, or the skillet may be rubbed with garlic. When they are brown, reduce the heat, pour ½ cup of boiling stock over them and cook them closely covered for about 10 minutes. They may then be rolled in sautéd bread crumbs to which a little lemon juice and chopped parsley have been added, or they may be covered with rich boiling cream sauce flavored with Sherry and served garnished with parsley.

Broiled Squab

Split the birds down the back and flatten the breasts. . . . Allow 25 to 40 minutes for cooking squab.

Baked Squab

Rub squab with salt, both inside and out. Stuff them with wild rice, or with bread dressing. Brush them with melted butter and sprinkle them with flour and place them in a closely covered pan. Bake them in a hot oven 450° for 45 minutes, reduce the heat to 400° and bake them for about 45 minutes longer. Baste them frequently with melted butter.

To Clean Ducks:

Clip the wing tips and remove the coarse guard feathers, leaving the ducks covered with down. Melt a cake of parafine and paint the ducks, using a brush and covering the entire surface of the birds with the hot wax. Allow the parafine to harden and pull it off. It will carry the feathers with it.

Wild Ducks

Stuff ducks with apples and raisins, or with sweet potatoes and apples. . . . Place the ducks on a rack in a roasting pan. Sprinkle them with salt and pepper and cover the breasts with thin slices of salt pork or bacon. Place them in a hot oven for ½ hour—460°. Reduce the heat to a moderate oven 325° and pour ½ cup of boiling stock over the birds. Cook them uncovered and baste them frequently (1¼ hours are usually required for roasting). Make the gravy . . . , adding sour milk or cream. Serve the ducks with currant jelly or cranberries.

Roast Goose

Stuff a goose with raw, quartered and cored apples, with bread or chestnut dressing. Truss it and sprinkle it with salt and pepper. Put 6 thin slices of salt pork over the breast and place the goose in a rack in a dripping pan in a hot oven 500° for ½ hour. Reduce the heat to 300°, cover the pan and roast the goose, basting it frequently until it is done. Uncover the pan and remove the pork for the last ½ hour of roasting. If the fowl is young and fat it will require no stock or water for basting. If it is not, add the stock before covering the pan. A goose will require from 1 to 4 hours' roasting.

Roast Turkey

Clean a turkey and fill it with bread or chestnut dressing. Spread the entire surface of the fowl with salt and follow this with a coat of ⅓ cup of butter creamed with ¼ cup of flour. If the fowl is lean, a piece of salt pork may be put across the breast. Place the turkey on a dripping rack in a roasting pan in a hot oven 500°. If the turkey browns too fast, cover it with a piece of buttered paper. When it is well browned (15 minutes) reduce the heat to a slow oven 275°, pour 1 cup of stock . . . over it, cover it and roast it until it is done, basting it every 15 minutes. Remove the pork and cook it uncovered for the last half hour (optional). Turn the turkey so that it may brown evenly. Add additional stock, if necessary. The time for cooking a 12 lb. turkey by this method is approximately 3 hours.

Rabbit Stew

Cut a rabbit into pieces. Season and dredge them with flour. Sear them in hot drippings, or butter, on top of the stove until they are well browned. Cover them to the depth of ¼ inch with boiling stock, or vegetable stock . . . and place a lid over them. Simmer them until they are done, but do not boil them at any time. Remove the rabbit from the pot and make gravy with the drippings . . . adding sour milk or cream and a few drops of Kitchen Bouquet.

Rabbit Sautéd

If rabbit is young, follow the rule for Sautéd chicken, adding sour cream to the gravy.

Smothered Rabbit and Onions

1 rabbit cut in pieces
Salt
Pepper
Flour
Butter or bacon drippings
Sliced onions
1 cut thick sour cream

Sprinkle the rabbit with salt, pepper and flour; brown it in butter or bacon drippings. Cover it with a thick layer of onions, sprinkle the onions with salt and pour the cream over them. Cover the pot closely and simmer the rabbit for one hour, or place the pot in a slow oven—325°—and bake the rabbit until it is tender (about 1 hour).

Rabbit à la Mode
Haasenpfeffer

Cut a rabbit into pieces and place them in a crock or jar. Cover them with equal parts of vinegar and water, add a sliced onion, salt, pepper corns and a bay leaf. Soak the rabbit for 2 days, then remove the meat, keeping the liquor. Follow the rule for Rabbit Stew, using the vinegar water in the place of stock and adding sour or sweet cream to the gravy.

21

American Liver Mush

RAVI SHANKAR

Ingredients:

3 cowboys from PRCA rodeos
2 narcotics officers in a LAPD squad car
¾ hour's worth of "Yellow Rose of Texas"
1 pierced skinhead, chopping
1 Jimmy the Greek
8 Lynyrd Skynyrd fans, packed into 1 minivan
1½ tins of Skoal's Bandit Wintergreen
1 demographic pie chart from a meeting of Board of Trustees
½ gallon corn mash moonshine, homemade
4 channels NASCAR coverage (or 2 stuffed deer heads & 2 Yosemite Sam mudflaps)
3 hours of church per week, minimum

Add in:

An election year, hurricane season
1 Subaru Forester
1 clothesline in front lawn containing:
  6 tube tops
  1 John Deere hat
  1 Gondola textured Jacquard polo shirt
  ½ a bandana
  2 monogrammed cardigans, his and hers
  1 set of patched overalls
  2 pairs argyle wool socks

Set aside:

Last season's Uggs & Birkenstocks
2 luxury box seats, fifty-yard line
1 jar whole pimentos, drained
1 bug zapper, gift-wrapped
5 hours of testimony by Alberto Gonzalez before the Senate Judiciary Committee
1 large bay window

Preparation:
Start with the cowboys in a pickup truck with mudflaps, roaring to the Deke Latham Memorial, Kaycee's biggest annual event, sponsored by Dodge. Juxtapose with the police cruising Slauson Avenue, stopping each male walking alone or together to put a flashlight in his face. Years before, throwing dice in a dim room in Steubenville, Ohio, and perfecting his theories on breeding, Jimmy Snyder is being dreamt of by Brent Musberger, who won't remember the dream. Add the bug zapper, now unwrapped and hanging on a porch, high-voltage electric current turning its wire-mesh into airborne insect particles that when breathed in are allergenic. After two hours, add the Skynyrd fans, including Kid Rock who, hammered on moonshine, hair tied in a rag of bandana, breaks the bay window playing street hockey with the chew tin. If the closet stays lined with shoes, it may well be time for a tag sale. Only the New Balance are timeless for those who will never run a marathon. All this should be made in sweltering summer heat.

Once they've browned, reserve in a ditch. Add the skinhead scouring himself with a sponge to rid himself of dirt splotches. Keep the "Sweet Home, Alabama" and the "Yellow Rose of Texas" blaring; the tube tops and the daisy dukes hula-hooping. When the Board of Trustees vote without abstention to hold their next meeting in Palm Springs and applaud the lady who brought the scones, grind the minutes in a mortar mash. Sprinkle between "I can't recall's," the attorney general's smug reply to Arlen Spector that "there is no express grant of *habeas* in the Constitution." Allow this to sink in like a golf ball in a water hazard or overalls in manure.

When the dialogue has been reduced by half, think WWJD. What would Jeff Gordon do. Or what would Jimmy Johnson do, depending on your view. Pull on the cardigan and argyle socks, pile into the Forester, and sit in a church pew next to children who smell like cake frosting. Listen to the organ and choir singing *Nova Vita*, "Breathe on me, breath of God." The marquee outside reads, "Choice, not chance, determines Destiny" or "Wal-Mart isn't the only saving place!" or "If evolution were true, mothers would have three arms." The song could fill the Louisiana Superdome.

Keep it cooking until the end of kali yuga. Garnish with sliced pimentos for adornment.

Serves well under three hundred million.

22

Eat Your Pets

ELLEN MELOY

Standing in a million acres of remote, rock-throttled, lizard-gnawed Utah desert, I think back to a recent time in southern California, when I was stuck on a freeway with three lanes of halted cars spewing several millennia of fossilized plant beds from their exhausts, the fumes popping my few remaining brain cells like bubble wrap, nearly knocking me unconscious so that if the traffic ever did move again, I, slumped over the steering wheel, dripping stalactites of drool onto the rental car's tasteful silver shag carpet, would incite gridlock anew, and the other drivers, their bloodstreams raging with espresso, would hate me and start shooting. I now stand in the intense heat on alkaline soil sprouting shrubs so sparse, thorny, scruffy, and stumpy, they seem more like green bones than plants, and remember the car ahead of me in that California traffic jam, a sleekly ovoid, Teutonic marvel with in-dash fax and Jacuzzi. Its bumper sticker said, "I'd rather be hunting and gathering."

Californians dine by a sacred creed: eat fresh ingredients, procured locally, grown seasonally. "We don't shop at supermarkets anymore," they sniff. "We forage," and it's off to pluck zinfandel grapes and *fraises des bois* with gloves made from the underbellies of bilingual alpacas, to buy fetal aubergines from Buddhists, oysters shucked by the Holy Ghost, and olives cured in the spittle of Himalayan puppies. Even if the nation's food distribution system were suddenly paralyzed, forcing everyone to eat locally, Californians would still be pate-plump and hot-tub poached while the rest of us stumbled about in weasel pelts. Californians may have overcrowded their own nest, but they will always eat better.

Every region in the world that has produced a flavorful, healthy cuisine, the foodies claim, has based that cuisine on local materials. Notice, however, that people are not rioting for an indigenous Northern Rockies cuisine, for example, for bloody bison blubber, jerked beaver, or tennis-ball tomatoes sponsored by hormones in a thirty-two-day frost-free season. Nor do they crave what might be procured in this parched sandstone canyon in Utah, where I am trying to live by the Creed and prepare a meal with native resources. Compromises have been made.

We float through this canyon on a white-water raft, packing in all food and supplies, as we do in a series of trips during my husband's seasonal job as a backcountry river ranger. The wilderness must be left intact. It would be rather unseemly, not to mention illegal, for a federal agent to be tilling crops or killing possibly endangered mammals for dinner. Another reason for packing in our food is that shopping in a rural supermarket, where I supply each river trip, poses many challenges.

In a land of high birth rates, baby products consume considerable shelf space. There is a marked absence of crustaceans and a notable preponderance of "white food," such as processed sandwich spreads, pre-whipped topping substances, and Frisbees of pallid cheese and dough in the frozen pizza bin. There are hard balls of colorless lettuce with the charisma of a barnacle and many items in nugget form. Say "tofu" around here and everyone will think you have sinus problems. Fresh summer produce can be luscious but limited in repertoire. Good wines? One's brain hemorrhages with any attempt to explain Utah's liquor regulations, which in complexity lie one rung on the purgatorial ladder below tax laws. Nearly every election year, a citizens group launches an effort to "legalize adulthood in Utah" and ease the moral vise of an abstemious theocracy. Every year they fail.

News of a fallen Berlin Wall has not arrived here yet. We shop in a town where, in the seventh year of the worst drought in a century, with the local reservoir shrunk to the size of a hand mirror, the city council proposed to ban xeriscaping. To these devotees of suburban botanical orthodoxy, native plants constituted ecoterrorism and weeds grew only in communist plots. When we lose green lawns, they warned, democracy will crumble. In the supermarket checkout line, where one's patriotism is routinely tested, the few interesting items I scrounge have bought me exile to Bulgaria.

"Did you, like, find these *here*?" the clerk asks, holding up in "icky" position a pack of dried corn husks (for *tamales negros*) as if they were the carapaces of hundreds of sun-fried African grasshoppers. As she empties my cart we begin a food identification rite.

"Astroturf?" she asks.

"No, cilantro," I answer.

"Caulk?"

"Feta cheese."

Reversed, the rite becomes even more idiotic.

"Styrofoam?" I ask a clerk who is stocking an aisle.

"No, Wonder bread." He presses a code into his waistband beeper, the code that summons the agent who works for the Bulgarian airline.

"Sheetrock?" I ask. "Small internal combustion engine?"

"No, Velveeta. Family pack."

Despite a reputation for being meatloafed on the steppes of culinary mediocrity, the intermountain West has slowly begun to buck the cholesterol tide. My own demands are not unreasonable. I merely want reasonably fresh, flavorful, minimally carcinogenic food. I want to eat like a Fremont.

The Fremont Indians lived in the Great Basin and Colorado Plateau from around the seventh to the thirteenth century, roughly contemporary with the Southwest's fabled Anasazi. Archaeologists working on Utah's Fremont River first recognized the Fremont as a distinct variation of the Anasazi culture and gave it the name. These seminomads hunted mule deer along the river corridor where I now travel and stalked bighorn sheep in its highlands and tributary canyons. When conditions were favorable they grew squash, beans, and corn, which they stored in masonry cists under protected ledges in the canyon walls. They pecked magnificent and enigmatic rock art on the faces of sandstone boulders and cliffs, made baskets and ceramic pots, and gathered wild plants for culinary, medicinal, and ceremonial purposes. Beyond these generalizations it is reckless to define the Fremont for, like the Anasazi, they were opportunistic, diverse, and adaptable in a harsh, arid environment of great variety: mountains, alkali basins, deep canyons, juniper-pinyon forests, and this broad, silty river wedged between thousand-foot-high cliffs.

What if, like the Fremont and Anasazi, you were entirely responsible for procuring your food from your immediate environs? What if you failed and went hungry? I cannot speak from experience because I grew up and remain well fed. We were not a "think of starving children in China" kind of family, each meal dredged in béchamel and guilt. The Great Depression was my parents' tribal history. They understood necessity and never used hunger as punishment. They never sent us to our rooms without dinner, only without dessert. If they served up a lesson with the green beans, it was to appreciate my mother's labors. While her peers tripped over their aprons in the post–World War II rush to industrial foods, my mother drew on an eclectic cuisine known in our household as "from scratch." My young lips never touched Jell-O or orange squares of petronuclear cheese smelted between two slabs of snow-white, inflatable bread.

Only as a young adult did I first see true hunger. At a city diner I once sat across the room from a shabby vagrant who was nursing a cup of coffee, the only food he could afford. When he thought no one was looking, he uncapped a bottle of ketchup set among the table condiments and drank it down like a cold beer. A vegetarian, obviously.

In the river canyon, California reverie ended, I look around at the hunter-gatherer's larder. Cattle grazed these river bottoms for a century, selecting for certain forage, so there is a mix of native and exotic flora, a postgrazing plant succession also influenced by erosion and drought. Things are not exactly as they were a thousand years ago. Nevertheless, the Fremont Indians would have eaten ricegrass, squawbush berries, the greens of four-wing saltbush or its ashes in a cornmeal-based bread. They may have chewed the roots of globemallow to strengthen broken bones, washed their hair with yucca root, and painted with beeplant, cliffrose, or greasewood dyes. They used yucca fibers for twine, cattails for mats, rabbit hair for coats. The Fremont wore the desert; they ate it.

What would it be like to eat everything you could lay your hands on? What if, standing on this sunny alluvial fan spilling into the sinuous river, I were very, very hungry? For a start I could stuff a few darkling beetles into my mouth, nail the black tailed jackrabbit under the greasewood bush, gnaw sugary mariposa bulbs, clobber a great blue heron, strangle a chukar, pillage the cooler of a random river runner, or bag a Rocky Mountain bighorn sheep, replacement to native desert bighorns wiped out decades ago by overhunting and domestic livestock diseases. Supplement this diet with wild onion, yucca pods, and the fruit of the prickly pear cactus. I could go fishing. While the Fremont fished native squawfish, I would catch introduced species—carp, catfish, and other exotics that have since overtaken native river habitat. This eclectic ecology affects the purity of tonight's menu. My husband and I will eat like the Fremont, with adjustments. Pockets full of plump, pungent juniper berries, I return to camp.

The menu is roast lamb, the closest legal meat to a bighorn sheep, baked with juniper sauce in a very un-Fremontlike cast-iron Dutch oven, fresh corn roasted in the husk then eaten with dashes of cumin and squeezes of lime, and *posole* with black beans and *chipotle* peppers. I stuff the leg of lamb according to a recipe rehearsed on a different ranger patrol. On that river trip we discovered that we had no string to bind the roast. Since the nearest town was a sixty-mile death march from our camp, we searched our gear for a string substitute. Duct tape? Nylon webbing boat straps? The cable on the come-along the ranger uses to peel flipped rafts off boulders? We tied the roast with dental floss.

Tonight's *posole* simmers while the grill awaits the corn. The roast bakes under a crown of bright cottonwood embers, double-stacked with a second Dutch oven of peach pie. We pop the wine cork, turn the gnats and mosquitoes over to the bats, and watch this gorgeous river flow by. Is this living by the Creed?

The gourmet fetishism of the 1980s turned us into food snobs. There is nothing new about this condition—diet has had a centuries-long relation to class and status—except its irony. Organ meats, edible flowers, blood sausage, and the like, once the fare of peasants, now sizzle the palates of the affluent, who scorn cheap mainstream bologna; PAM; SPAM; anything pink, puffy, or partially hydrogenated; and other foods containing the oil-based flavors we fought Iraq for. The food elite have adopted the cuisine of the poor. But they have left the poor with the ketchup bottle.

To irony add the illusion that we *can* live off the land or eat food close to the source. Not too many people remember what the source is. Not much of either the source or the land is left. Imagine everyone in Newark foraging. Imagine yourself wringing the necks of chickens or grappling with bleeding, bleating goats.

Behind the excesses the foodies launched an awareness of food politics and the relation between diet—what we eat, how it is grown, the resources consumed to produce it—and individual and planetary health. A diet less dependent on the mass-food apparatus also may require an apocalyptic eradication of food taboos. To pull us back from the ecocidal brink, writes Calvin Schwabe in *Unmentionable Cuisine*, we must put more songbird, reptile, roadkill, rodent, dog, cat, tongue, brain, and gonad—that is, fresh ingredients, locally procured—on our tables.

It may not be possible to eat like a Fremont, but their adaptability, resourcefulness, and intimate knowledge of this harsh desert environment are instructive. Surrounding me, in fact, lies the ultimate "from scratch" cuisine. Carp ceviche and raven confit. Jerked kit fox. Tanagers *en croûte*. Bunny fajitas. Lopped-off haunch of feral cow or the nearest Labrador retriever. Eat your pets!

RIPARIAN ROAST

Remove the excess fat from a leg of lamb and throw the fat to the catfish. Rub the outside of the meat with olive oil, the inside with salt and pepper, then stuff it with garlic cloves and a thatch of cilantro. Tie the meat with dental floss—unflavored, unwaxed. Crush a few tablespoons of juniper berries in your fingers. If you are not employed by the federal government, take off your clothes, rub your juniper-scented fingertips all over your body, and flit about on the beach. Pour an inch or so of red wine into a Dutch oven; add the juniper berries and meat. Cook with embers below and on the lid, replenishing embers as needed. When the meat is done, dispose of the fat in an environmentally appropriate manner. The sauce: Add more wine, some water or stock, and stir, scraping bits off the bottom of the pot. Simmer until reduced.

23

How to Make Stew in the Pinacate Desert: Recipe for Locke and Drum

GARY SNYDER

A. J. Bayless market bent wire roller basket buy up parsnips, onion,
carrot, rutabaga
and potato, bell green pepper, & nine cuts of dark beef shank.
They run there on their legs, that makes meat tasty.

Seven at night in Tucson, get some bisquick for the dumplings.
Have some bacon.
Go to Hadley's in the kitchen right beside the frying steak—Diana on
the phone—get
a little plastic bag from Drum—
Fill it up with tarragon and chili; four bay leaves; black pepper corns
and basil;
powdered oregano, something free, maybe about two teaspoon worth
of salt.

Now down in Sonora, Pinacate country, build a fire of Ocotillo,
broken twigs and
bits of ironwood, in an open ring of lava: rake some coals aside (and if
you're smart)
to windward, keep the other half ablaze for heat and light.
Set Drum's fourteen-inch dutch oven with three legs across the embers.

Now put in the strips of bacon.
In another pan have all the vegetables cleaned up and peeled and
sliced.
Cut the beef shank meat up small and set the bone aside.

Throw in the beef shank meat,
And stir it while it fries hot,
lots of ash and sizzle—singe your brow—

Like Locke says almost burn it—then add water from the jeep can—
add the little bag of herbs—cook it all five minutes more—and then
throw in the pan
of all the rest.
Cover it up with big hot lid all heavy, sit and wait, or drink budweiser
beer.

And also mix the dumpling mix aside, some water in some bisquick,
finally drop that off the spoon into the stew.
And let it cook ten minutes more
and lift the black pot off the fire
to set aside another good ten minutes,
Dish it up and eat it with a spoon, sitting on a poncho in the dark.

24

Spirit-Fried No-Name River Brown Trout: A Recipe

From *My Story as Told by Water*

DAVID JAMES DUNCAN

Like Christ (aka ><>), and unlike most of the rest of us, a pan-fried trout is utterly forgiving. If you use too high a flame, the skin takes the abuse and the flesh is still delectable. Too low a flame and it still makes decent sushi. Even overcooked for hours in British *Babette's Nightmare* simmer-it-to-mush style, the structural integrity of muscle that spent its entire life fighting river current is nearly impossible to reduce to goo.

Secret ingredients? There are none. Indispensable ingredients? There are two. The first? Honest butter. Forget margarine, forget olive oil (the cultural dissonance!), forget *I Can't Believe It's Not Coagulated Petroleum With Yellow Dye!*®, forget cholesterolic and caloric paranoia, period. Wild trout frying is not a meal, it's a rite. You are preparing to eat an animal that gave up its beautiful river and only life for your pleasure. Pleasure ought, therefore, to be maximized. Open your palate to the trout's flavor and your heart to its riverine essence, and that essence will charge through you like spring runoff, flushing every artery you've got. It is never "heart smart" to refuse to open your heart. Butter aside, there are no Trout Frying Commandments. Almonds, garlic, and cornmeal offer interesting counterpoint if you like fried almonds, garlic, and cornmeal; needless distraction if you don't. The flesh under discussion requires no trick additives. If you open your heart and use enough butter, a trout fried in a dredged-up chrome fender over an acetylene torch is worth eating.

Due to the chef-friendly equation between ease of prep and splendor of result, the trout is considered by many to be an easy fish to fry. It is not. The reason it's not is that butter is only one of the two essential ingredients, and the other is frequently overlooked. What is the mystery ingredient? *The trout itself.*

The cause of this shocking omission is the corporate-spawned delusion that those blotchy, cellophane- and styrofoam-swaddled, dented-Grumman-canoe-colored fish-corpses at the local chain supermarket are, as the label claims, "trout." Don't believe it! The supermarket product is mass-manufactured, half-embalmed pond-spawn. Raised on obscene industrial pellets, "toned" by flaccid, poop-flecked waters, these hapless victims of genetic Mcdiddling bear as much resemblance to wild river trout as does a drug-bloated, shit-smeared, feedlot moo-cow to a wild bull elk. *True trout frying cannot take place until a food-worthy species has been identified and a choice specimen taken.* Trout frying can begin, in other words, only with the catching of a *wild* trout, which can be obtained only after a journey to clean wild water. We have of necessity moved, in a single paragraph, from a tube-lit, corporate-owned refrigeration unit to the most unspoiled lake, river, or stream within range of your home. This is what I call "Progress"! We're still not quite ready to catch a fryable fish. But we are at least now safe to begin considering their true variety.

Trout species vary from drainage to drainage, as Highland Scots and Indian tribes once did and by choice still do, and as any conceivable long-term, slow-time, sustainable inhabitant of the "Americas" will one day do.

Even the same one trout species takes on surprisingly different characteristics and flavors from river to river. The reasons for this are myriad, sometimes holy, and far beyond the scope of a single human mind, let alone a single human recipe. Suffice it to say that in my little home niche here in western Montana, I catch seven kinds of wild trout (the brook, the Mackinaw, the cutthroat, the rainbow, the bull, the cutthroat-rainbow hybrid, and the brown); that two of these are native to these waters, four introduced from elsewhere, and one (the hybrid) a little of each; that all seven are well able to sustain themselves without human assistance if human ignorance and avarice give them half a chance; and that it is self-sufficiency that has earned the best of them the beautiful designation "wild."

But, ah, Industrial America! Of the seven local species, the indigenous bull trout is endangered, the indigenous West Slope cutthroat threatened, and the introduced Mackinaw lousy eating, so the first two I release and the third I culinarily ignore. I'm so stunned by the blazing colors of the occasional brookie I catch that I'm as likely to kill it as I am likely to kill a mountain bluebird or western tanager. And almost every time I set the hook to a bread-and-butter rainbow or hybrid cuttbow, it pirouettes skyward and so does my heart, so that by the time I land it I'm as likely to kill and eat it as I am to kill and eat a member of the Joffrey Ballet.

Six of seven species landed, six of seven released, and my frying pan still empty. The reader begins, perhaps, to see the difficulty in obtaining that second Trout Fry Essential. Who wants to kill and eat beauty? Who wants to kill and eat one's dance partner? I am one of those people who finds the American rodeo clown a wildly more romantic figure than the Spanish bullfighter, since rodeo clowns not only refuse to mince and posture, but practice—with far bigger, far more dangerous bulls—the art of catch-and-release. I am also, however, one of those people who, like the trout themselves, eats flesh. In honor of this unanimity, I now turn, with all the appetite that's in me, to the seventh and last local wild-trout possibility: the brown.

~

Our Montana brown trout—like most nineteenth-century arrivals—began the long journey westward by crossing the Atlantic in ships. There were two distinct immigrant families. I call them the McBrowns and the Brauns. The more silvery, red-spotted Loch Leven McBrowns originated, like a lot of Montanans (the clans Craighead, McClay, McGuane, Maclean, Doig, Duncan, etc.), in Scotland. The more buttery-colored orange-spotted Brauns hail from Germany. And to this day, if you gently squeeze the living bellies of either, they let out a croaking sound that brings Scottish broguery and *Deutsch* umlauts to mind.

What I love best about McBrowns and Brauns, though, is not the Old World heritage or remnant dialect: it's the fact that these fish, unlike most European introductees to this land, did not follow the Pioneer/Plunderer, Industrial Robber Baron, Missionary Zealot, or Racist Cracker models. *Mirabile dictu*, brown trout chose the Native American model. From the moment of their release upon this continent, the McBrowns and Brauns opted, belly-croak brogues and umlauts notwithstanding, for sly, adaptable indigenous ways. And indigenousness, by *Gott*, is what they got.

Moving from oak barrels into America's sweet rivers, lying deep and still when in doubt, brown trout set out not to invade their new continent but to *belong* to it. They carved out a niche among the competing species. They achieved balance with the food supply. They learned to sidestep the pantheon of predators. They learned to migrate elk- or Indian-style to beat the harsh seasons. They survived river-stopping ice-ups, riverbed-scouring ice-outs, multiyear droughts, hundred-year-floods, irrigation overallotment, placer and open-pit mines, 75,000 American dams, generations of polluters, generations of political representation by river-molesting nudniks, generations of bombardment by cow-asses uncountable, generations of bombardment by Sportfishing Huns.

Despite all such assault, they thrive. There are rivers, streams, and spring creeks all over America that have, in a single century, become as impossible to imagine without their wild browns as the waters of the Pacific Northwest were once impossible to imagine without their salmon. There is no veteran fly fisher conversant with the various salmonid species who does not consider browns the Coyote of North American Trout. The McBrown's and Braun's swift transition from Highlander and Deutschlander to ineradicable American Native bypassed the usual Outlander Phase. It took a *fish* to do it, but brown trout are living proof that a gracious and native harmony—to the European immigrant who daily seeks nothing else—is attainable not just in theory, but in body, tooth, and soul.

Another thing to love about browns: there are private "game ranches" in many states, Montana included, where you can hand over a MasterCard, borrow a rifle, use the roof of your luxury sedan to steady your sights, shoot a terrified, fencebound deer, elk, or buffalo, climb back in the sedan, order the beast professionally gutted and cleaned if your shot killed it—professionally executed, gutted, and cleaned if it didn't—then order a haunch of it cooked to specs, on site. For the right kind of money you may even be able to order your haunch professionally pre-chewed. So what a pleasure to report that *there is no analogous way to purchase or pretend to dominate or sink your pointy teeth into a wild brown trout.* Brown trout are not for sale. For 99 percent of their lives they're not even visible. Hiring an ace angler to kill one for you is socially difficult and legally illegal. And hiring a professional fishing guide to lead you to one suitable for eating is an excellent way of enticing the guide, who is almost certainly a poker-faced, closet brown-trout worshiper, into making sure you get skunked.

The wild brown is, then, as egalitarian a quarry as happiness itself. To catch in order to fry in order to eat one of these indigenous beauties, even the most prodigiously portfolioed oligarch in America has to slip into a Gore-tex fartsack and stagger out into a cold, wild river, where, with his brain the size of a cantaloupe and fiscal grasp of continents, he'll find the Coyote of Trout, with its brain the size of a peppercorn, anything but willing to rise up and die.

Even for those of us who live here, plying the rivers for browns over the course of a Montana summer is no way to keep steady meat on our tables or healthy egos on our ids. Brown trout are delicious—to my palate, the tastiest species of my legal local four. But of the local trout species, they wear the most perfect camouflage, have the teeth most likely to cut through a leader, prefer the snaggiest lairs, and almost invariably, when hooked, head for the nearest sunken tree. They have the keenest eyesight and the greatest paranoia about what's going on up onshore. They're often nocturnally voracious but uncatchably ascetic by day. Upon achieving trophy size they turn cannibalistic, nearly immunizing them to the efforts of us insect-imitating fly-slingers. And when they *are* rising, they have the subtlest of rise-forms, making them the most difficult trout to locate and stalk. As a result, those who would consistently catch browns must own more than a pedestrian itch to wet a line. Of fly fishers especially, these fish demand not just interest but obsession. Not a pretty obsession, either. In order to become one of the rare maestros who can deceive these beasts at will, one must immerse oneself for years and to the eyeballs in the sort of obsessive fish-speak I've been scribbling this whole past paragraph—

Unless one happens to know a wicked secret: *even the oldest and most sagacious of browns grow temporarily crazed—by sex.* No fooling. Every mature brown trout that swims makes a spawning run in fall. This seasonal change of metabolic and existential purpose transforms the Coyote of Trout into the most imbecilic of impulse shoppers. It's a tragic but all-American malady: you can sell a spawn-minded brown damned near anything.

I'd heard stories, before moving to Montana, about how aggressive browns grow in October. Being from the Northwest coast, I imagined a belligerence akin to that of salmon, who purposefully stand guard, after arriving at the spawning grounds, around their redds. There is no similarity. Like all but the kinkiest humans, a brown wants no other species of creature in its bed of love except other browns. Unlike most humans, the brown considers its *entire visible world* to be this private bed, remains open-eyed and armed (to the teeth) round the clock, and at the sight of trespassers aims to kill. It's a strange behavior to transpose into human terms. If my wife and I were to become the sexual equivalents of brown trout tonight, our foreplay would consist of attacking and swallowing seven pet chickens, five goldfish, a guinea pig, a Dalmatian, a pony, and a horse. *Vive la difference!*

I know a gin-clear creek, near a highway I often travel, that meanders through a quarter-mile-long meadow too pretty to pass by. I called it Three Fish Meadow, because the eight or ten times I'd plied it, I caught an average of three pan-sized trout, none of them browns. One crisp day in early October, I stepped into the same meadow, obeyed an impulse to tie on a fat orange jack-o'-lantern of a fly called an October Caddis, cast it into a pool-table-sized pocket behind a wheel-barrow-sized rock, and immediately hooked a nice brown. After landing and releasing the fish, I cast into the same little pocket—and instantly hooked another good brown. This happened five more times. Each of the seven browns raised hell in the pocket, crashing into and dragging line across its cohorts. Each subsequent fish nevertheless savaged my pumpkin fly. Continuing up through Three Fish Meadow, I caught and released twenty-six trout averaging thirteen inches. All but two were sex-crazed browns. The meadow, in spawning season, needs a new name.

I remember, midway through the meadow, a female brown who had claimed as her boudoir a side-channel so shallow I never thought to fish it, and so nearly stepped on her as I came hiking along full speed. *Yet she didn't spook!* At the sight of a seventy-two-inch human splashing down upon her with a hundred-and-eight-inch fly rod in hand, this fourteen-inch creature shot to the foot of her bedroom-sized glide, did a one-eighty then zipped straight back at me, *as if to scare me off by charging*. If she'd been a few inches longer, it might even have worked!

Since I didn't bolt, the horny she-trout halted in eight inches of water not four feet to my left, and proceeded to glower up at me. I tried to glower back, but her eyes began to unnerve me. *If I lay some eggs in a nest in the gravel here*, she seemed to be thinking, *will you swim over 'em and do your part?*

Deciding we both needed a reality check, I choked up on my fly rod like a baseball hitter who's been given the bunt sign and dropped my big orange fly, *plonk!* Right on top of her head. This was not fly fishing. This was terrorism. I was doing to the little trout about what Brom Bones did to Ichabod Crane in *The Legend of Sleepy Hollow*. A sane trout would, like Ichabod, have fled for miles. My flirtatious friend grabbed the pumpkin fly as if it were a tossed bridal bouquet. I began laughing so hard I lost her—a relief to us both. But talk about sexual aggression! The Chinese ought to be grinding up October browns instead of elkhorn to restore wilted Eros.

Much as I enjoyed catching those browns, and much as I would have further enjoyed eating a few, I encounter a moral quandary with regard to the brown trout's seasonal nincompoopery: what fly-fisherly honor is there in catching and eating a creature whose peppercorn outsmarts our cantaloupes forty-eight weeks out of the year, by simply waiting for the sex-drunk four weeks when it couldn't outsmart a fly-fishing Orvis shop mannequin? What honor is there in matching wits with and deceiving a normally inspiredly elusive creature while it languishes in a lovesickness so severe that a fourteen-inch specimen considered *me* a potential mate? Many of us could whomp Shaquille O'Neal at one-one-one basketball while *he* was having sex, too. Is this cause for pride? When a brown in the throes of its own mania to create life slashes my fly in late autumn, it is not a fly-fishing conquest by me: it's a biological conquest of the brown trout by the brown trout itself.

That said, I must make a confession. When it comes to fly fishing, I'm an addict, hence a pretty low-rent guy. My impulse to fish is so strong that I'll admit it: it's *fun* for me to attach my fly to a brown trout's biological conquest of itself. What I must ask myself and all honest fly fishers, though, is whether there is a more and a less honorable way to proceed with this low-rent malady of ours. Is there a sustainable way for us, and for this sex-stoned brown, each to pursue our very different addictions and live to tell the story?

I believe so. I believe the sustainable solution is a recipe: I discovered, one day in late fall, that it is not only possible but enormously pleasurable to spirit-fry and eat a brown trout, then release it unharmed. It happened like this:

~

One October day I slipped into my waders, drove to a certain never-to-be-named brown-trout river, hiked down to a certain logjam, dropped a fly in the eddy behind this jam, lost sight of my fly when it drifted behind some willows, heard a slurping sound behind the willows, raised my rod at the sound, watched the rod slam downward, and felt the angry headshakes of a solidly hooked fish.

Those headshakes excited me for three reasons. First, I recognized them to be the headshakes of a brown—my fry-pan favorite. Second, judging by the slow authority of the shakes, this brown was sizable: I pictured salmon-sized trout steaks sizzling in Le Creuset. Third, the logjam it was hiding in happened to be a logjam I'd built myself earlier in the summer, by chain-sawing and dismantling a dry-docked upstream jam and walking its logs a quarter-mile downstream to this deeper site and getting hung up en route in half-drowned, abandoned barbed-wire fences and driving into Missoula and cruising the hock shops and finding an ancient pair of bolt cutters and dickering the guy down to twelve bucks and driving back to the river and cutting and coiling and removing drowned barbed-wire fencing till I got my hands punctured and shins dinged up and logs right down where I wanted them. This jam was, in other words, an act of indigenous fly-fishermanly madness. And the wild animal on my line was evidence that Mother Nature had noticed my madness, and approved of it.

A big brown in summertime, hooked in the very same place, would have bolted into the logs and snapped my line in short order. The October brown, however, shot directly away from the logs into the snagless center of the run, where nothing good could possibly happen to it, and proceeded to veer from side to side, not as if looking for escape, but as if looking for something to attack and kill. Typical spawning-run brown behavior. I worked my way through willow brush to the hole's tail-out, forded the little river, waded back up to the pool, and waited for the big brown to come up with a new idea.

It never did. It came up with desire, anger, beauty, size, and that was it. After five or six minutes of furious veering, it tired. I led it down to the tail-out, eased it into the shallows in front of me.

I looked at the brown. The brown looked at me. I saw by the oversized, totemic jaws that the fish was a male. I took him in my hands, turned him gently on his side, measured him against the marks on my fly rod: twenty-two inches. Filleted out, quartered, and fried with almonds, he'd sate my entire family. Released, he would create his own.

The little stones in the stream were bronze in the October sunlight. The brown, against those stones, was brilliant yellow, white, and gold. His pelvic fins, translucent amber, were the size of silver dollars. The orange spots scattered down his side shone, as Richard Hugo once said, "like apples in a fog." He was so old he'd developed a gaze like a cougar, a redtail, an eagle. One does not capture an animal like this every day. I was able to pluck out the fly, right him in the water, keep my grip loose so as not to harm him. I was not able to let him go.

I dropped to my knees in the water beside him, my waders fending off the cold. The current swirled around half of me and all of the brown, coming in small, uneven surges that gently rocked my body; it felt like riding a quiet horse. Though I held him captive, the brown stayed perfectly in rhythm with this horse. Since he faced upstream, I turned that way too, and looked in the direction the brown trout was looking. Ours was an eastward-flowing stream. It was evening. The sun was turning orange before us in the west. Mountains veed to the water on both sides of the river, the northward-sloping ridges yellow with last summer's grass. As the flow swirled down toward us, reflected sun turned its surface into a blinding sheet of orange-flecked silver. As the silver came closer, reflected sky turned it into broken shards of blue. Closer yet, the blue vanished, the water went as clear as air, and the sunlit stones beneath us became a bed of shining gold. All this beauty, all these riches—and I was *still* not sure what I would do with my brown.

Then I noticed, right in front of us, a fresh-dug, trout-length excavation in the bed of gold. It was his redd. Or hers. His paramour's. And as I stared at this redd, beaten into the stones by a seemingly departed female trout's body, I realized for the first time in my life just who the animal in my hands would truly be making love to. Not to his mate. Hardly to a mate at all. She'd dug the redd, laid her eggs. But he would never touch her. All he would ever touch was this water and these stones. He was making love, as was his mate, to the blinding silver, the broken blue, the shining gold.

I touched his side with my finger. A drop of milt spilled from his vent and vanished downstream. He was in the throes, even as I held him. I saw why I'd considered spawning browns stupid. I saw it was I who was stupid. I saw that, at a certain time of year, the rhythm of the river becomes impossible for these creatures to resist; that the mere act of swimming, mere caress of cold water, becomes a long slow copulation; that their entire upstream journey is an arduous act of sex. The dip in the gravel, nest of eggs, spraying of milt, was just the culmination of that weeks-long act. I looked again at the mountains veeing down toward the water. The gravel beneath us was made of fragments of those mountains, the current flowing past made of their melted snows. The brown trout I held was making love to the mountains and snow.

I realized that, in consuming this fish, I'd be consuming part of everything that made him. I realized that everything that made him was precisely what, or who, he was making love to. I realized that this same everything is who we, too, are made of; who we, too, are submerged in; who we, too, daily eat; who we, too, seek to love and honor. The trout in my hands let me feel this. He was, through no intention of his own, a spiritual touchstone. And one takes such stones not to stomach, but to heart.

One doesn't want to kill beauty; one doesn't want to kill a dance partner. But one doesn't want to let them go, either. I held that brown way longer than I should have. Held him till my hands began to burn. I've said it before: I must say it once more: *there is a fire in water. There is a flame, hidden in water, that gives not heat, but life.* I held a trout, and my own two hands, in that fire. The cold flames ran through and past us. And I was fed, I was sated, I'd had all the nourishment and flesh I needed when at last I opened my heart, opened my hands, and let my beautiful brown trout go.

25

Half-Life

PAUL HANSTEDT

All he wanted was to be the good son. To make up for all those years of stupid mistakes.

"Dad," Gordon called from the kitchen, "are you out of canola oil?"

"What?" his father hollered.

Gordon could hear the TV blaring. *Wheel of Fortune*, maybe, or *Price Is Right*. "Oil," he said. His skull felt dry.

"What?" his dad hollered again.

Jesus. Gordon grabbed the counter, struggling up from where he'd been peering into the lazy susan. Exercise, he thought, that was another thing he needed to do. Not even fifty and he moved like an old man. Hobbling down the hall, he dug in his pocket hoping to find a loose Tylenol. It'd seemed like a good idea at the time: Debbie gone and his mom dead, he'd cook for the old man, make the guy a decent meal every couple of weeks. Not like Gordon had anything better to do.

He turned into his mom's old office, the shelves lined with shrunken heads and shell amulets, pottery shards and ceremonial spears—the usual anthropological clutter. His dad was on the couch, feet up, the buttons of his oxford stretched over his belly. His right hand fingered a glass of scotch on the end table. Somehow, unlike Gordon, his dad only ever had one.

"Oil," Gordon said.

"What?" His dad was still hollering.

"Jesus, Dad," he said. "Oil. Oil. Don't you have any oil?"

Still his father looked confused. Gordon wondered, not for the first time, if all the knobs and wires that'd made his dad one of the most respected judges in the state were finally starting to short.

"In the cupboard."

Gordon took a breath. "There's only an inch."

"So?"

"I need more."

His father's eyes flickered over Gordon's face. Those eyes. Still good-looking, too, even with all that fat. On the TV, Vanna or someone said something about sunny Florida. Gordon flashed to an afternoon maybe thirty years ago, his father on the beach reading a legal brief, his mother beside him on the porch talking about half-life and decay, how people used to think radiation was healthy. "If it hurts," his mother had said, "people figure it must be good for you."

Now his father set his glass down with a clink. "You want me to go?"

"Depends. How soon you want to eat?"

His dad sighed and pushed himself forward on the sofa. It took him a second to heft himself up, long enough that Gordon considered going over to help. He didn't. His skull still hurt, that dull, familiar ache, like a sponge that'd been out of water too long. He turned and went back to the kitchen.

~

It was harder when his father was gone. He stayed away from the cupboard over the sink, didn't push a chair over, didn't even go to that side of the room. But he knew they were there, those bottles, Dad's occasional summer taste for gin, the accumulated gifts from friends left unopened, some foreign stuff a buddy had brought from Iceland tinged with caraway, good scotch. Really good scotch. There was probably beer in the fridge, too, maybe an open bottle of chardonnay in the door. Gordon made a point of keeping his eyes straight ahead when he went in for the pork and the eggs, concentrating hard when he was chopping the onions. It was an easy recipe, Kai Jeow Moo Sab: Thai pork cakes—four eggs, four tablespoons of fish sauce, a half cup of green onions, and a pound of ground pork dolloped into cakes in hot oil and fried. He was pretty sure that his father even had the Maggi seasoning that Gordon had brought over himself a few weeks earlier when this whole experiment had started. But the recipe only called for a teaspoon, and he wasn't about to start digging around in the cupboards, not with the old man gone, not with his head aching, not with that coppery taste in his mouth, the saliva gathering beneath his tongue.

In the end, he didn't even wait for the extra oil, frying the last two cakes in a fugue of grease that turned them black; it was dumb, he knew, but he couldn't handle the thought of standing there waiting, the cauliflower steaming, the salad dressed, nothing to do.

When his dad came in, smelling of Ohio winter, Gordon was arranging the cakes on the blue-and-white plate his mother had brought back from Italy.

"Sorry," he said. "I guess I could have gotten by without."

His dad shrugged, pulled off his jacket. "I took too long. Bumped into Derek Broughie. Hadn't seen him in years."

Gordon nodded, finished with the pork and surrounded it with the cauliflower. Opening the fridge, he dug through the crisper until he found some parsley. He broke off a stem, shut the doors, and turned, dropping it on the plate. When he looked up, his father was watching, lips pressed together. Gordon raised his eyebrows. His father shrugged, not quite grinning.

"It matters," Gordon said.

"I'll bet."

"It does."

"I believe you." His father slipped a hand under the blue plate, carried it to the table where Gordon had already placed the silverware. Gordon followed with the salad and a glass of water. After they'd said grace, Gordon's dad nodded at the food. "I never understood why you didn't do this."

"Do what?"

"This. Cook. Fancy stuff. You always liked it."

Gordon looked at the food in front of him. The cauliflower was the right color of old parchment, the salad smelled of apples and vinegar. Even the pork didn't look bad, dark as it was.

"I do it."

"For a living, I mean."

Gordon drew a breath, pasted under by a litany of old excuses—cooking was too easy; there wasn't enough money, not enough prestige, not really a job compared to, say, banking or law. What came out surprised him: "I couldn't be your son and be a cook."

His dad's chin jerked up. Gordon drew a breath. His old man, the guy who'd seen it all—from meth moms who'd placed the pipe to a toddler's lips to country boys who'd driven an old lady off the road because she was in their way—his old man stared at him, startled. Gordon tried to think of something to say, some way to backtrack. Nothing appeared.

“What the hell does that mean?”

“Nothing.”

“Your mother and I, we never pushed you.”

“That’s—”

“We loved you.”

“Dad—”

“You could have been a plumber for all we cared. A mechanic. A cook. You were our son.”

“That’s not—”

“Don’t go blaming us for this mess. This isn’t our fault.”

Then his dad cursed, a word Gordon had never heard him use in his entire life. It was like seeing the dead rise. Gordon wondered again about Alzheimer’s, if this wasn’t some essential slip of his father’s personality, but then he recognized the slightly rehearsed sound of his father’s voice. This was something his dad had thought about—something he’d been thinking about for a long time.

“It’s not your fault,” Gordon said.

“Damn right, it’s not,” his dad said.

Gordon didn’t think he’d ever seen the man so angry—not the time he’d caught his son breaking all the windows in a neighbor’s garage, not the first time Gordon had come home drunk and thrown up in the foyer, not when Debbie had left him or when he’d been fired from the bank. His dad sat stiff in his chair, dug his fork into the omelet, took a bite, chewed furiously. He followed with some cauliflower, a sip of water, slices of loin stabbed with his fork two at a time. His dad kept his eyes on the wall beside the table, examining the wallpaper maybe, or the photograph Gordon’s mom had taken of their hike up Kilimanjaro, a small African porter—a boy, really—curled up with a pack at his back, his feet bare, his red shirt faded to a soft pink. Gordon wondered, not for the first time, what that boy was doing now. He must have been about five years younger than Gordon then, which would put him in his early forties today. Was the boy married? Did he have kids? Was he even still alive?

That same summer, just before Gordon’s sophomore year, there’d been a party down by the coal yard, a bonfire, the air gray in the headlights of a dozen cars, music thumping from someone’s box. When he’d taken that first sip of Southern Comfort, it was like a boulder lifted from his shoulders: he was the judge’s son, the professor’s son, the perfect boy with the perfect grades, this despite a learning disability the doctors had said would make it hard for him to read beyond a sixth-grade level—ever. But he'd shown them, his mother had made sure of that, his father standing back, keeping an eye on the whole thing. Gordon had studied and been tutored and memorized and studied and restudied and vomited before almost every test he'd ever taken in middle school. Then someone—Scott Torgeson, maybe?—had handed him that bottle, and he'd wiped the rim and slipped it in his mouth and swallowed and—

Freedom.

Gordon knew, right then, that food still in front of him, his father still staring at the wall, that he'd stop at the Quik Trip on the way home. Knew he'd go inside and propel himself toward the cooler, knew he'd pull it open, grab whatever was closest, have it on the counter before he could think. Knew he'd finger the bottle caps as he drove the rest of the way home, exhilarating in their rough edges, knew the way his cuticles would catch on the cardboard as he lifted the six-pack from the car, still propelling himself forward, still consciously unconscious, moving, moving, until that moment when he was in the kitchen with a bottle uncapped, the rim at his lips before the opener even hit the counter.

"The thing is," his father said. He was looking at him again, his eyes clear, the lines on his forehead gone. "The thing is, you were always so hard on yourself."

Gordon almost laughed. "And who do you think taught me that?" he wanted to ask, but didn't. "I know," he said.

"I mean," his father continued, leaning forward, "you never let yourself fail. So much pressure. Always putting pressure on yourself."

"I know," he said again. And again, he wanted to say, "And?"

His father had been about to continue, actually had his hand up, his mouth open, his next argument lined up and ready to go. Instead they stared at each other. The old man with the handsome white hair, the square jaw, the blue eyes that would be startlingly beautiful even in a woman—the old man who'd cruised through law school and risen to the bench as though it'd been made from him, who, if he'd failed, ever, had done it quietly and where no one could see. And his boy, soft shouldered, soft bellied even when young, much less now when he was middle-aged. Unemployed, divorced from a woman who'd been too good for him even when he was sober, even before he'd been caught pilfering from his employer's coffers, the boss who'd hired him as a favor to his judge father, to his anthropologist mother with all those shrunken heads on the den wall.

"I know," Gordon said again because it was what he'd said his whole life when his parents had caught him out of line, had tried to lecture him on how to make his life better. "I know," he said because usually it shut them up, usually it ended the conversation sooner rather than later.

As it did now. Because when he said it this time, Gordon could tell, his father got it.

Which was something, of course. Two men sitting across from each other in this kitchen painted blue by a woman who'd been dead for nearly a decade, the table layered with pork and salad and vegetables soaked in butter and that single stalk of parsley set just right. These two men, the one old but not really, never having seen the short end of the stick, never having been told, "This gold is not for you." And the other, younger, born failing, born falling like a runner with a gimp leg. Dead before he'd even begun.

26

The Poet in the Kitchen and The Poem of Chicken Breast with Fettuccine

DAVID CITINO

The Poet in the Kitchen

Especially during the holidays, I'm reminded that writing a poem is much like preparing a meal. The poet may not always wear the funny hat, but he or she is still very much the chef. I assemble, arrange on counter and table, then prepare the various ingredients. I measure, weigh, decant, top off, fold in, pour over. I beat, peel, pare, knead, squeeze, wring, pound, slice, chop. I sauté, brown, braise, bake, roast—performing that old dance whereby something raw and cold is brought, over a period time, to a state of heat or at least doneness and completion, so that just in time I can meet others at the table where we've all come together to celebrate.

Let's say I want to write a poem about my family. I'll conjure up and assemble the ingredients: Nonna and Pop, their duplex on West 105th in Cleveland, their tales of life on the South Side before that, and in Italy before that. The warmth of Nonna's kitchen. The fragrance of her apron as she bakes bread, puts up in Ball jars tomatoes festooned with shreds of deep green basil, makes blood soup, cranks sausage into long casings of intestines she purchased at the slaughterhouse.

At sixteen, when I got my permanent driver's license, I would take Nonna to the import store, Giovanni & Mario's near downtown. She'd been shopping there for a half a century. I recall the potent force of garlic, olive oil in kegs and gallon cans, great baskets of live snails, tripe, dates, and figs—sights and scents I'll never get out of my head.

To get to my high school, Saint Ignatius, I took a bus and the Rapid Transit train from my home near West 140th. I got off at the West 25th Street station, then walked through the West Side Market on 25th, past stalls of swinging cheeses and sausages, salamis and hams gleaming like stalactites in a great cave, and joints of meat, hog jowls and snouts, squid, and gleaming fish whose baleful eyes seemed to turn to regard me as I passed by. The train ride that transected the west half of the city took me from newer times to olden, and the market aisles and stalls represented, even to the young man I was becoming, a place whence my parents and grandparents came. Traveling and food were visible, auditory, olfactory, and gustatory manifestations of history.

Pop had a garden in back of his house, with grapes on trellises above, little fig trees, and a crowd of vegetables in progress. He'd throw pebbles from the paths we'd walk, showing off individual plants of which he was particularly proud. "*Agilo*" (garlic), "*fico*" (fig), "*pomidoro*" (tomato), he'd announce. Each treasure had two names, one from Calabria and the other from Cleveland. He was trying to teach me culture, a respect for labor and soil, and he was trying to give me the words.

He worked for the B&O Railroad for fifty-two years. I remember the twelve pairs of tracks my little legs had to climb over to visit his signal shack, my fingers firmly trapped in the fat hand of my father. I know the rich stink and glow of the potbellied stove where he burned old railroad ties to keep warm, and the gnarled Italian cigars that took my breath away. The blare and glare of diesels, the U.S. Steel and Jones & Laughlin blast furnaces, Sohio's refinery flares, bellowing ore boats and tugs twisting up and down improbable curves of the Cuyahoga—these are my ingredients. So pure and elemental are they, each time I arrange them together I can make something with a different texture and taste.

I fuss and fume with these memories, recall and recall some more, fiddle, cut and paste, chop, grate and dice, head over to the oven of my feelings for these two dear immigrants with the thick accents and the world they created, which made me and mine.

If I'm lucky, if I watch the clock carefully, if I trust my training and taste through each step of the process, then I may end up with the poem pleasing to me and to others who will come to partake of it.

If I wish to cook the Christmas dishes Grandmother taught me, I proceed in similar fashion. For poets as well as comedians, timing is everything. I can't wait too far into December to visit the Italian specialty store—in Columbus it's Carfagna's on Route 161—for the essential parts of the meals. The store is packed—wall-to-wall paisans, often three generations pushing the cart down the terribly narrow aisles, looking over the offerings of holiday fare. We eye each other and recognize the familiar features of the tribe, most of us less than tall, curly haired, dark eyes expressive and secretive at once. I take a number and enter the throngs at the long fish and meat counter.

Back in the day, Christmas Eve was meatless, by church decree, and dinner consisted of various kinds of fish. I purchase a hard, flat slab of salt cod, *baccala,* of which always there is a goodly supply at this time of year. This was—is—the fare of the peasant and poor immigrant. It keeps forever. I'll soak the fish for three days, changing the water often to wash away the salt, so that the finished product will wrinkle the noses of the children only a little. I select shrimp and silvery smelt and perhaps a piece of white fish, and of course clams or anchovies for the pasta.

I select hot Italian sausage and a tough old stewing hen for the tomato sauce for the Christmas Day lasagna. This dish is made with tiny meatballs that take forever to make. Grandmother Carolina would criticize those of us who helped her roll the meatballs. They must be small as the nail of her little finger, she would show us. (I'm ashamed to say that today I crumbled browned Italian sausage rather than use her more demanding and time-consuming method—sometimes I'm a lazy but expedient chef.) I prepare and add the hard-boiled eggs and various cheeses for this lasagna, which is the signature dish of my family. It tastes of us, and we of it. It dates back to the grandparents in Calabria, to the grandparents of their grandparents in that land in the toe of the Italian boot.

Before I leave, after filling my cart with leaves of oregano, basil, Italian parsley—and some *fino vino* (Chianti Classico for the lovers of red, pinot grigio for the others), I purchase boxes of *torrone,* rectangular Christmas candies made of nougat.

When it's time to put together this year's version of the old Christmas poem, a meal, I go through the steps of preparation and execution, timing, boiling, and stewing that I undertook for the poem I wrote about my grandparents, Michele and Carolina. A poem must have distinctive flavor. A meal is a poem. Not every meal is great. Not every poem. From both we ask something of the authentic, something that changes us at least a bit.

The Poem of Chicken Breast with Fettuccine

After work has hollowed you,
sit a moment, thinking hard
of the simplest things. When
enough time passes, rise,

go into the kitchen.
Take two chicken breasts.
Pound, dust with pepper, salt,
dredge lightly in flour,

brown in a heavy skillet
with olive oil
extra vergine—
fragrant as Tuscan autumn—
with chopped garlic

and Crimini mushrooms
redolent of dank woods.
Add a half-cup of pinot grigio,
bright as late sun,

and lemon, squeezed
by hand so the liquid
blesses your fist. Cover,
simmering no more than

twenty minutes. Thoughts
of cream, butter, cheese,
intricate timbales?
Put them out of your mind.

This will be so simple
it will take you back to what
you were. Serve over
pasta. Kiss with basil

and parsley that swayed
in a garden moments before,

grated pecorino Romano.
Sit now with someone

you care for, or could,
given the right words,
heat, savor, light—blessings
meant to be shared.

27

A Good Roast Chicken

From *Pass the Polenta: And Other Writings from the Kitchen*

TERESA LUST

The day my grandfather brought home the Rhode Island Reds is the day my mother learned to be a Singer. You might read this and think I mean *singer*, one who belts out show tunes, but I'm talking poultry plucking here, and I do mean one who singes over an open flame. Her job, she said, when I asked her please to tell me again about her day as a poulterer's apprentice, was to singe the pinfeathers off the chickens once they'd been plucked. She'd rather have been a Waxer, which Mrs. Sebastian down the road, who kept White Leghorns, said was better than being a Singer. Mrs. Sebastian said the pinfeathers slipped right out when you painted the naked birds with melted paraffin and then peeled back the hardened wax. But my grandmother Teresa was saving her paraffin for making grape jelly. Besides, she said, putting up chickens made mess enough without a pot of hot wax underfoot.

A generation and a half later, I pulled a roast chicken from the oven and found myself thinking not of my mother singeing off pinfeathers but of all the ways I could have prepared my chicken that night. Could have made Chicken Kiev or Chicken Cordon Bleu, Chicken Chasseur or Chaud-Froid. I could have ballottined the breasts and fried the thighs and Buffaloed the wings, or served it up coq au vin'ed, or jambalaya'd or vindaloo'd, but nothing would have captured the simple essence of a chicken quite like my roast.

It was going to be a good one, I could tell. Skin crisp and the color of dark toast, drippings sputtering in the bottom of the pan and the scent of it like my grandmother's house minus the tomato sauce. You could call it a preparation deceptive in its simplicity. I didn't even use a recipe, just rinsed and patted dry a four-pound roasting hen, brushed it with melted butter and sprinkled it inside and out with coarse salt and cracked pepper. Then I set it breast-side up on a bed of rosemary sprigs in a roasting pan and drizzled it with the juice of a lemon. I tucked the spent lemon inside the bird's cavity along with a few fresh sprigs of thyme and some garlic cloves, and set the pan in a 400-degree oven for an hour or so until the juices ran clear when I poked it in the thigh. A meat thermometer, if I'd remembered to use it, would have read about 170 degrees. Then I let the roast rest for ten minutes and put it on a platter with some parslied new potatoes and buttered carrots. That's it.

But I'd gone to the farmers' market and sprung for a free-range chicken, one who'd had the run of the barn and eaten a few slugs in its day—a chicken with some real meat on its bones and not some junkie chicken shot up with hormones and antibiotics. The garlic and the potatoes and the carrots came straight from my garden that morning, and the herbs grew in pots on my front porch. It occurred to me that a good roast chicken dinner is not got from a recipe, but from a way of life—a life full of vegetable gardens and barnyards and meals rushed from the farm to the table. By extension—and this is when I envisioned my mother holding a freshly plucked chicken over a candle flame—it is a life where there's no denying that what lies succulent and crisp on a bed of rosemary sprigs once scratched in the dirt.

If you had asked my grandfather Joe as he crated up chickens on an August day now fifty years deep in my mother's memory, he might have added that not only can barnyard birds scratch in the dirt, they can peck like the devil. In fact, some of them, the old biddies, are just too ornery and tough for the roasting pan, and they need a good long simmer in a pot to cook the meanness out of them.

Joe was not a chicken farmer by trade, although he raised a few Banty hens for eggs. An Italian immigrant to Washington State, he worked first as a butcher over in Cle Elum, and then as a ferry-crosser down on the mighty Columbia before he ended up a self-taught electrical engineer in the Yakima Valley—which, he liked to say, just goes to show how far you can get on a little spit and elbow grease. He tended irrigation systems for many of the fruit growers in the area, orchardists who harnessed Cascade

Mountain snowmelt to overcome the fact that their rain-shadow valley received only eight inches of precipitation a year.

Joe set out for the orchards that morning to have a look at some farmer's pump. After a brief period of inspection and consultation, he agreed to make the necessary repairs for a fee of seventy chickens. Now, in the cash-strapped wake of World War II the barter system was alive and well in the valley. Joe had been known to take occasional payments in apples or firewood or even cherries. As for live chickens, well, these birds were a first. But why not? he thought, in this life you take what you can get.

When it came time later that day to collect his wage, I like to think my grandfather summed up his efforts and decided the pump just wasn't quite a seventy-chicken job. Or else I imagine him sizing up those birds and finding one of them just wasn't quite up to snuff. But most likely he simply miscounted, because one of my aunts swears he returned to town at the end of the day with only sixty-nine Rhode Island Reds in the back of his '37 Dodge pickup. And by the way those Rhodies squawked and flapped and carried on, you'd have thought they knew they were off to meet their Maker. Which they were.

It was my grandmother who did them in. She took one hard look at my grandfather and that truck and those birds and muttered, "Joe Picatti, if I 'adda gun that'd shoot around corners you'd-a been dead long ago." But then she reached for an apron to cover her housedress and set to work right there in the driveway. One after another, she held each plump, wriggling body between her knees and grasped with determined fingers the sweet spot partway up its scrawny throat. Then she administered a sharp, clean yank, up and out just so, which broke the bird's neck and killed it instantly. She never winced. Did not even issue a barely audible gasp; neither as each chicken breathed its last, nor afterward, during those long slow seconds when the dead creature convulsed wildly in her clutch before falling limp.

Don't get me wrong, my grandmother Teresa would much rather have spent her time stirring risotto or counting her rosary or growing scarlet runner beans than snuffing out life. Her comment about the corner-shooting pistol notwithstanding, she wasn't a violent sort, wasn't one to commit what some would call cold-blooded murder with her bare hands. She had to wear gardening gloves—though not so much out of squeamishness, or out of a desire to distance herself from such a disagreeable task, but to keep from getting hangnails. And on that sun-baked afternoon with sixty-nine dead Rhode Island Reds growing warm under her aquiline nose, she would have had no time for explaining the difference between murder and putting dinner on the table.

She and Joe strung the chickens by their feet from the clothesline and let the blood drain out onto the grass. Instead of lamenting the moral implications of the food chain, Teresa promised to fix Joe a mess of cockscombs for dinner that night. Too bad she hadn't any artichokes, for cockscombs and kidneys sautéed with artichokes was the favorite royal feast of none other than Catherine de Medici. But Teresa would dredge the combs in flour, fry them in the olive oil she saved for special occasions, and that would be feast enough.

Dinner would just have to wait, though, for she had a flock of chickens still to be dressed and drawn. It seems to me a curious fact that while poultry dressing is the sage and cornbread stuffing you eat at Thanksgiving, dressing poultry is what you do when you clean a bird of all its feathers; but so it goes. Teresa put a kettle of water on to boil. She soon had the whole kitchen smelling of chicken soup as she plunged each bird headfirst into the bubbling pot of water and swirled it around for a few seconds until the feathers slipped away without tugging. Two of my aunts, who had been enlisted as the Pluckers, took the dripping birds back to the driveway and plucked out wet feathers by the handful. The feathers dried in the August heat and wafted upward, scattering across the lawn. Feathers hung from the zinnias in the flower bed and caught in between the slats in the picket fence. They clung to my aunts' pedal pushers and my grandmother said, careful now, don't be bringing them in the kitchen.

Next, my mother came in as the Singer. She was a twiggy child of eleven, all knees and elbows and wide brown eyes. She still had a dark, thick head of Shirley Temple curls that summer, and not the flat, limp strands that grew in after her bout a year later with typhoid fever—Grandma warned her what happened to naughty children who went off swimming in the irrigation ditch. Joe lit one end of a tightly twisted newspaper like a torch. He held a naked bird upside down, then showed my mother how to sear off the nubbly pinfeathers and the soft down without charring the skin. When the flame burned down close to his fingers, he dropped the newspaper to the cement driveway and finished the job by turning the chicken over the flame like a roast on a rotisserie spit.

All afternoon my mother singed away. And as she singed, her nose wrinkled up and her lips drew tight and my grandfather said, "Come now, honey, they don't smell that bad. Your face is bound to freeze that way, you keep scrunching up your nose like that." She blushed, handed him another bird to be drawn, and tried to concentrate on the sounds he made while he worked—the smooth scrape of metal on metal every time he honed the blade of his boning knife against his carbon butcher's steel, the knuckle-pop-pop as he snapped off the feet at the knee joint, and the soft slap every time he plopped a chicken on his cutting board. Grandma leaned toward my mother and said, just watching him you'd have thought only a day and not twenty years had passed since he worked as a butcher up in that coal town of Cle Elum. Which was the job, and don't you forget it, that kept him out of the mines.

Sixty-nine times he laid a chicken across the table and ran his knife down the length of its neck. He pulled out the windpipe and the gullet and then the crop, which he split open, revealing to my mother the grains of corn that had been the bird's last meal. He made an incision at the chicken's tail end and extracted the entrails, setting aside the giblets—the liver, heart, and gizzard, that is. He'd always been a shoo-in for giblets in tomato sauce. Occasionally he found a string of yolks inside a laying hen. These he placed in a bowl so that Teresa could whisk them with marsala and a touch of sugar into the custard she called *zabaglione*. But the intestines, which he had never learned to like, not even in a frittata with cheese, so help him, he threw out with the rest of the viscera. Finally, he scooped out and discarded the oil sac at the heart-shaped base of the tail, the part he called the pope's nose, then handed the birds to one of my uncles, who wrapped it in heavy paper and packed it for the meat locker they rented from the butcher.

I like to linger on this image of my grandfather, of him working with nimble fingers, wielding a knife with a competent hand. His hand, my mother recalls, could take a pocketknife and whittle off the entire skin of an apple in one long strip. As children, she and my aunts would lie sprawled on the floor, mouths agape like nestling sparrows, while he dropped the fleshy peel onto their tongues. He had a stroke just about the time I was old enough to shape my own memories, and in those memories his hand rests on the arm of a green La-Z-boy rocker and squeezes an orange ball, never quite recovering its strength.

I regret not having known my grandfather back when he possessed a hand steady enough to draw a chicken. But I am not so sentimental as to pine for a time when women in starched aprons wrung the necks of chickens out of necessity, no matter how farm-fresh the resulting meal. I find my terra-cotta herb pots, my vegetable patch and my farmers' market chicken a healthy compromise. So does my mother, who never pursued her career as a Singer, and now prefers to leave the unpleasantries of dressing and drawing to the abattoir. Yet she doesn't use her back-then-we-really-had-it-rough voice, the one she uses when she mentions gasoline rationing cards and hand-me-down boys' saddle shoes, when she recounts her day as the Singer. Rather, her voice takes on a warm lilt—if not of nostalgia, then at least of bemusement.

My mother's chicken-singeing tale came back to me just the other day while I waited at the meat counter in the grocery store. Actually, I thought of my grandfather, because I stepped in line behind a woman who made me think the art of sizing up a chicken is still alive and well.

She was a wisp of an old woman, clad in weathered pea coat and galoshes, and wearing a scarf over her head tied tight underneath her chin. All she wanted, I heard her ask, was five pounds of chicken. Drumsticks with the thigh attached. You see, she was partial to dark meat.

A clean-cut fellow behind the counter, looking fresh out of the laundry in his starched white shirt and his bleached apron, was trying his best not to lose his patience with her. She hunched forward and peered with squinty eyes through the glass display case while he reached his plastic-gloved hand into a pile of chicken parts and held up drumstick-thighs for her inspection. Time and again I watched her scrunch her wizened mouth into a pout and shake her head. "No, son, not that one," she said, or, as he showed her another, "No, that one won't do either." But occasionally she gave a nod, smacked her lips and said, "Yep, now there's a keeper," after which, the attendant gave a not-so-subtle roll of his eyes and set her selection on the scale.

After several minutes of this, the clerk had finally had enough. "Lady, excuse me, but what's wrong with the rest of these hindquarters? All nice and fresh. Why, they're free-range; what more could you want?"

The woman pulled herself back upright and looked him in the eye. "Sure," she said. A little strutting around and exercise would give a chicken some honest taste, indeed. But what she was after, as she'd already mentioned, was some choice dark meat. She could tell at a glance the leg upon which a chicken roosted each night, and that was the one she wanted. "That's the leg where all the flavor goes," she said. "You learn to pay attention, son, and you can tell the difference."

"Well, I'll be," he said, raising his eyebrows. He stood quiet for a moment, then apparently decided it best to humor her, for he shrugged his shoulders and set back to sorting out the rest of her five pounds. He reached for a leg, then glanced at the pile on the scale and his face broadened with a toothy grin. "Ohhh, I get it. All we've got up here is right-sided hindquarters. That must mean chickens always roost on their right foot. Why didn't you just tell me?" He inspected the piece in his hand, saw it was a left leg, and tossed it back into the bin before the woman could stop him.

"Ah, ah, ah. Not so fast, you," she said. "I'll be wanting that one. That chicken was a lefty."

ROAST CHICKEN

1 four-pound chicken, preferably free-range
1–2 tablespoons melted butter or olive oil
Salt and freshly cracked pepper
1 lemon
3–4 rosemary sprigs
3–4 thyme sprigs
3–4 cloves of garlic, no need to peel

Rinse the chicken and pat it dry. Brush it lightly with melted butter (or use olive oil). Sprinkle it liberally with salt and pepper, inside and out. Place chicken breast-side up on a bed of rosemary sprigs in a roasting pan. Drizzle the chicken with the juice of the lemon. Tuck the lemon halves inside the bird's cavity, along with the thyme sprigs and garlic cloves. Roast in a 400-degree oven for one hour, until the juices run clear when you insert a knife at the thigh. Let the bird rest for ten minutes before serving.

28

Turkey Bone Gumbo

From *Gumbo Tales*

SARA ROAHEN

You *Can* Take It with You

January 2007

On the morning that I surrendered my New Orleans citizenship by leaving my house keys with a property manager and then driving toward my husband, I stopped for coffee. And a lagniappe. Almost as soon as Katrina hit, I began stockpiling New Orleans mementos, starting with any old cookbook I could find in Manhattan's used-book stores. Once I returned to New Orleans, I expanded my range: rarer cookbooks, bumper stickers, photographs, oyster shells, a bottle of Mississippi River water. The frantic collecting was as much an endeavor to hold on to my own identity as it was to preserve what I loved about the city. As I waited for my coffee on that ultimate morning, I scanned the café for a last-minute souvenir, something symbolic that would help make sense of the day, and I found it rolled up in a basket on the floor: an earthy clay-colored T-shirt with "Be a New Orleanian Wherever You Are" printed across the chest in orange lettering.

The phrase had become a mantra for many New Orleanians who had reluctantly started their lives anew elsewhere after Katrina, first because their homes hadn't survived and then later because of lost jobs, poor schools, uninhabited neighborhoods, unhappy spouses, mental and physical health concerns, better career opportunities, common sense. I had already collected a pile of stickers with the same slogan, and I intended to vandalize Philadelphia with them.

When I tried to imagine what it would mean to be a New Orleanian wherever I was, creating my own Monday red beans and rice ritual by inviting our new neighbors to dinner came to mind. Shrimp boils in the courtyard of our rented townhouse came to mind. Also baking fig cakes and building my own altar to Saint Joseph on March 19; gumbo z'herbes on Holy Thursday; another resolution to make coffee and chicory my morning wake-up beverage. In other words, I would eat and drink like a New Orleanian wherever I was, which seemed thematically appropriate, considering how I had bonded with the city.

So on the day before my departure, I went grocery shopping, heading first to Angelo Brocato's in Mid-City for cookies, then out to Jacob's in Laplace for andouille, tasso, smoked turkey legs, and beef jerky for the drive. On the way back into New Orleans, I stopped at Dorignac's supermarket in Metairie, where the shelves always heave with local staples: Cajun Crawtator potato ships from Zapp's, hot pickled okra, smoked and fresh hot sausage, Louisiana pecans, Bulgarian-style yogurt from Bittersweet Plantation Dairy, honey from a beehive in Uptown, Union coffee and chicory, pickle meat, crab boil, Creole mustard, Tony Chachere's seasoning, and Camellia brand red beans. At the checkout, the cashier glanced at my loot and said, "Oh baby, you must be leaving town."

A final dozen raw and a final dozen fried at Casamento's, that coffee stop, a farewell wave to the Superdome, and that was it. If I hadn't been bolstered by wearing my "Be a New Orleanian" T-shirt while crossing the Potomac—that damn Yankee river—I'm certain I would have turned around.

I continued to wear the T-shirt in Philadelphia, but the message began to lose its hold on my resolve immediately. Such as once I learned that you can't buy beer on Sundays here or legally drink anything alcoholic while walking down the street. And once I learned that navigating the city according to the position of the Schuylkill River doesn't get you where you want to go—Philadelphia streets fall into a tidy grid pattern, with right angles and signs at every corner, an efficient system so unfamiliar after seven years in the Crescent (shaped) City that my inner compass refused to adjust. When a rusted seal broke on a water pipe in our basement in the middle of the night, causing a flood to soak all the belongings that had remained dry during Katrina, it felt somehow poetic. When I had to relinquish my Louisiana ID in order to get a Pennsylvania driver's license, in order to get a Pennsylvania license plate, in order to get a parking permit, in order not to get towed—that was the final nail. My identity had officially been jacked.

The worst of it was that somewhere during the move I had misplaced my will to cook like a New Orleanian. I had shoved those groceries from Jacob's and Dorignac's into the freezer upon my arrival, and there they had stayed. I wasn't in New Orleans anymore, no matter how often I wore that T-shirt, so what would a pot of red beans prove? Why bother the stomach with cayenne? What was the point of pickle meat? What *was* pickle meat? Instead I tried my hand at curry cauliflower pasta, lamb stew, pork tenderloin, broccoli soup, and roast chicken. And it was awful, all of it. Food without a narrative just tasted like food. Matt lost weight; I was lost.

I did experience some moments of emotional clarity during this period, moments when I understood that I was not making New Orleans proud. What kind of born-again loses her faith the first time her prayers aren't answered? Where was all that wisdom I reportedly had gained while learning to like mayonnaise, kill crawfish, manage silver-dollar-sized oysters in one mouthful, eat soup with a fork? I despised my stupid T-shirt because it reminded me of where I wasn't; at the same time, I knew that there must be some way to repossess my inner New Orleanian—to remember why partaking in tradition, delighting in community, and finding meaning in family had seemed so obviously the best way to live.

During one of those clear moments, in mid-November, a solution startled me out of the dark side: turkey bone gumbo. An e-mail exchange with my dad's brother Danny, still the turkey chief in our family, gave me hope. Danny agreed to save me two turkey carcasses from the Thanksgiving dinner we would eat together in three weeks, and I resolved to save myself by making turkey bone gumbo out of them. Settled.

~

In preparation for another cross-country drive, this time from Pennsylvania to Wisconsin, Matt and I repacked the car with the andouille from Jacob's, a baggie of Louisiana bay leaves (which are milder than the California variety), and a canister of seasoning mix called Slap Ya Mama, which, despite the fact that I hadn't never used it before, I hadn't been able to leave Dorignac's without buying.

A few days later, in the afterglow of our traditional Thanksgiving mish-mash-mush, Danny placed the two turkey carcasses in a white garbage bag, and I hauled them across town to my parents' house.

Turkey bone gumbo is not a specialty of Louisiana as much as it is a given there. Like turkey and cranberry sauce sandwiches, cold pumpkin pie, and Stove Top re-mish-mash-mushed with creamed onions and sweet potatoes, turkey bone gumbo is what you make from Thanksgiving leftovers because they are there and because Thanksgiving dinner is always better the second time around no matter where you live.

The next day I woke early to fire up a stock using the turkey bones plus some onions, celery, and bay leaves. It simmered while the rest of the family and I joined my dad's other brother, Jay, in his favorite event of Thanksgiving weekend: a typical Wisconsin tavern lunch of beer and brats. My uncle Jay is the only one of the three Roahen brothers who moved away from Wisconsin as a young adult, and it's never seemed accidental that he's the one who drives the most Wisconsin-centric ritual of our family's annual reunion. Place-specific traditions allow you to hold on to home—to taste it, even—long after you don't have a bed there anymore.

As usual, I didn't allow enough cushion time to make the gumbo myself without risking the loss of another thumb tip. You can't do anything else without risking the loss of another thumb tip. You can't do anything else while you're preparing your roux—no phone calls, no bathroom breaks, no pleasantries—and so it was a happy coincidence that the family's newest babies went down for naps just as I was beginning the process. This freed up Stephanie and our cousin Jenny to cull the good turkey meat from the two boiled carcasses, separating out the bones, a fussy job. Matt worked at the counter alongside them, peeling potatoes and hard-boiled eggs for the potato salad that he insists accompany any gumbo we make at home. I manned the stove, a slave to my roux, while the three of them chattered behind me.

"Is this an onion or a tendon?" I heard Jenny ask as she picked through the strained stock remains.

We're in that important middle generation now—Stephanie, Jenny, Matt, me. The generation that gets fewer presents and less sleep: the generation charged with carrying on those little traditions that have been passed down from our parents and grandparents, so that our own children, and their children, can begin to understand where we all came from. So that *we* can understand where we all came from. Listening to them prattle on like kids in art class as they pitched in to help me make this dinner, I experienced one of those full, soul-moving, Virginia Woolfian moments of being. Here we were, establishing a new tradition for our family: Thanksgiving weekend turkey bone gumbo. How important and gratifying. As long as I didn't burn the roux.

Shoot, the roux!

Some Louisianans believe that making a proper roux requires hours of continuous stirring over a low flame. I learned to make roux using a more aggressive, borderline violent method by following the instructions in a Paul Prudhomme cookbook to cook the fat and flour together quickly over high heat. I always wear long sleeves for safety, and I acquire the gastronomic equivalent of a runner's high in the process. This time was no exception. My mom's steel whisk clanged against her heaviest-bottomed aluminum pan at a frantic tempo as I conjured up the photographs of differently colored rouxs printed in Chef Paul's cookbook, so as to recall the difference between brown and burned.

You must rely on your nose as well as your eyes, though judging a roux by its aroma is trickier, as the smell of *burning* nuts is a good sign when making a roux while the smell of *burned* nuts is the kiss of death, and only a millisecond separates the two. I called Matt over to take a whiff as the nutty aroma peaked. "You better stop now! You better stop now!" he yelled. "Not yet, not yet!" I yelled back, as is our roux-making routine. Then, just a moment before absolute terror, I dumped my chopped seasoning vegetables into the pot, stopping the roux from cooking any further and inducing a puff of moist, earthy, caramel-scented steam. My roux never approaches black like I want it to, but this one was nevertheless a pride. A respectable brown.

Next I added the stock; an hour later, in went the turkey and the andouille. An hour after that, the company began to arrive, twenty-nine people in all. Every one of them tried the gumbo. Even children who had been too finicky for plain roast turkey on Thanksgiving tried the gumbo. Some people slapped some Slap Ya Mama on theirs. Others garnished with Tabasco. I set out a bowl of "the green stuff"—chopped green onion tops and parsley. Matt persuaded nearly everyone to marry their gumbo and their potato salad in the same bowl, and no one seemed to find it offensive. I watched the room from a stool at the kitchen counter, content for the first time in a long time. Here were all my people, eating like all my other people. My dad served brandy old-fashioneds.

When I lived in New Orleans, I believed that a meal like this—Louisiana turkey bone gumbo made and eaten in Wisconsin—was less relevant because it was out of context. Though I haven't changed my mind entirely, I know that I experienced an emotional breakthrough the night that twenty-nine members of my extended family partook of my Louisiana turkey bone gumbo in Wisconsin, and I know it was possible only because of what living in New Orleans had taught me about connecting with people by cooking and eating together.

I've never loved books with happy endings, and this isn't one of them. But new beginnings are important. And what is a roux if not a new beginning? What is a New Orleanian, wherever she is, without a reason for gumbo?

29

Boiled Chicken Feet and Hundred-Year-Old Eggs

SHIRLEY GEOK-LIN LIM

"You mustn't eat chicken feet until you are a married woman!" my aunts warned me. "Otherwise you will grow up to run away from your husband."

They sat around the dining table, an unstable jointure of old planks stained by years of soya-sauce drips and scorched by the ashy embers that always fell out of the small coal oven under the metal hot-pot which was fetched out once a year for Chinese New Year family feasts. They chewed on gold-brown chicken feet that had been boiled with ginger, garlic, sugar, and black soy. The feet looked like skinny elegant batons with starred horny toes at one end, their speckled skins glossy with caramelized color, but chicken feet all the same. My aunts and stepmother gnawed at the small bones, grinding the jellied cartilage of the ligaments audibly, and the bone splinters piled up beside their plates.

I would not stay to watch them. I had seen hens and roosters pick their feet through fungal monsoon mud, stepping on duck and dog and their own shit.

My stepmother raised poultry on our leftovers and on chopped swamp vegetation which sprouted lavishly in the greenish slimy wasteland behind our house, and on festival days she slaughtered at least two fat chickens for us—her five stepchildren, two sons, and cherished husband. Chicken was a luxury we tasted only on these days, on Chinese New Year, Ch'ing Ming, and Mid-Autumn Festival, and the Feast of the Hungry Ghost. And then, as my aunts told us was the practice even when they were children, the chickens were divided according to gender, the father receiving the white breast meat, the sons the dark drumsticks, and the daughters the skinny backs, while the women ate the feet and wings.

As the only daughter in a family (then) of seven boys, I was excused from such discrimination and took my turn equally with the drumsticks, the favorite meat for all of us. Chicken was always sold whole and freshly slaughtered, and no one imagined then that one could make a dish solely of drumsticks or of chicken breasts. Such mass marketing was possible only with the advent of refrigeration, and although coffee shops in town held large industrial-sized refrigerators for serving shaved iced concoctions and cold sodas, popular refreshments among Malaysians to fend off the humid equatorial temperatures, Chinese Malaysians, like most Asians in the 1950s, would eat only fresh food. We thought of frozen meat as rotten, all firm warm scented goodness of the freshly killed and gathered gone, and in its place the monochromatic bland mush of thawed stuff fit only for the garbage pail.

Still, while no one sold chicken parts separately, fresh chicken feet were always available in the wet market; you could buy them by the kilos, a delicacy to be enjoyed, according to my elders, only by married women. Well, let my aunts and stepmother suck on those splintery bones. I was never comfortable at the table when those feet appeared, when the women waved me away from them. My mother had run away from her husband. A bad woman, a runaway wife, a lost mother. A young girl, I was not to be trusted with those chicken feet, not when I had my mother's history in my blood, my mother's face on my face, still recognizable to my aunts, my father's brothers' wives, good wives and mothers, even though it had been five, six, seven years since she ran away.

I could not face the leathery skin, tightly bound to the long femurs after hours of simmering. And the soft padded soles that my aunts delighted in chewing—it was here that the chicken came closest to the human anatomy: pads like the fat feet of my stepmother's babies. Even now, now that I have grown to become a wife and mother like my aunts and stepmother, like my runaway mother, I will not eat chicken feet, no matter how much wine, cardamom, cumin, honey, or ginger has steeped them. I remember the tiny bones, the crunch of skin and cartilage. I remember my mother.

Almost forty years later, living in the United States, I am constantly reminded of how "Chinese" has become a fetish for Americans looking for a transcending experience of difference and otherness. Ranging from white models with stark black eyeliner and chopsticks in their chignons to "happy" dressing gowns that copy karate-type uniforms, things associated with Chinese culture pervade mainstream American imagination, suggesting, through the fixed acquirement of a traditional middle-class taste—for blue willow-pattern china, for instance, or take-out shrimp in lobster sauce—that Americans are omnivorous consumers rather than Eurocentric ideologues.

Purveyors of such U.S. "multiculturalism," however, usually disguise the material sources of their goods. Difference has to be softened, transformed, before it can be assimilated into Middle America. So also with Chinese food, which, before Nixon's visit to China in 1972 was sold in thousands of small restaurants outside of Chinatowns as egg rolls, egg foo yung, chow mein, and fortune cookies, none of which was recognizable to me who had grown up eating home-cooked Chinese food in Malaysia. Influenced by the increase in Asian immigration to the United States after the 1965 Hart-Celler Act, and thirty years after Mao Tse-tung intoxicated the Nixon presidential party with *maotai* and exotic ten-course banquets, many Americans have learned to dine on "authentic" Chinese food across a number of regional cuisines, from the mild, flavorful fresh steamed dishes of Canton, to the salty fiery peppers of Szechwan and Hunan and the rich elaborate food of the Shanghainese. But mid-Manhattan restaurants and Chinese cookbooks never note the particular dishes peculiar to Old One-Hundred-Name, what the Chinese call the man in the street. These dishes have been the ordinary fare for billions of poor Chinese through the centuries, and for myself as a hungry child in a family of too many children and never enough money.

While the chicken feet my aunts feasted on was forbidden to me, I was repeatedly coaxed to taste *pei ta-an*, the only other dish in my famished childhood that I could not eat. These duck eggs, imported from China, had been selected for their large size, covered with a mix of mud and straw, then stored in a darkened space for at least a month, covered with cloth that had been impregnated with sodium carbonate. You had to knock the dried grey mantle of mud gently off, wash the eggs in cold water, then crack and peel the bluish-white shells. What emerged was a clear glistening gelatinous black oval enclosing a purple-green-black yolk, and a sharp reek of sulfuric vapor, a dense collection of chemicals from decaying things, like the air-borne chemical traces that trigger the salivary glands of scavenging wolves or turkey buzzards.

Father was especially fond of *pei ta-an,* what the expensive restaurants called hundred-year-old eggs, which my stepmother always served sliced thin in sections of eighths accompanied by shredded pinky young ginger pickled in sugar vinegar. He believed it was *poh,* full of medicinal properties that stimulated blood circulation, cleansed the liver and kidneys, sharpened the eyesight and hearing, and elevated the male libido, and my stepmother, a generation younger than he, diligently served it as a cold relish to accompany steaming rice porridge, or alone, as a late-night snack.

Occasionally Father shared this delicacy with us. My brothers hung greedily over him, waiting for their one-eighth sliver of slippery shining jet-black egg, which was served draped with a vinegary-moist ginger shred. Approaching *pei ta-an* for the first time, I thought its glistening black carapace and iridescent green-black yolk beautiful, a magical gem cut open for inspection. But then its acrid stench shot up my olfactory glands, opening passageways more powerfully than a tongueful of green mustard, and I gagged, as close to vomiting over food as I would ever get. Unlike boiled chicken feet which I could ignore by resolutely leaving the table, *pei ta-an* pursued me out of the kitchen, out of the living area, and out of the house, a smell of pollution I feared each time Father called out for us to come and eat some hundred-year-old egg.

At some point in my childhood, however, drawn by my brothers' lust for *pei ta-an,* I pinched my nostrils closed and opened my mouth for the sliver. Its flavor and texture was like nothing I had ever tasted, the combination of the jellied white-turned-to-black and the tightly packed purple-black heart igniting on my taste buds as an intricate instantaneous sensation of bitter and sweet, rawly and densely meaty, yet as delicate as air-spun cotton-candy, primitively chemical and ineffably original. I was hooked. But *pei ta-an,* although not expensive, was what my stepmother bought for Father alone: for his health, his pleasure, his libido. A morsel would always be our share of this pleasure.

Late on the evening that I first tasted *pei ta-an,* I walked out to the Chinese grocery store at the corner of the main road and spent some of my cache of coins hoarded from the dollars that my mother far away in another country mailed me once or twice a year. I bought two eggs jacketed in mud and straw. While my brothers were playing Monopoly in the front room, I sneaked into the kitchen, broke open the armor, carefully crazy-cracked the shells, peeled the pair, all the time marveling at the scent that had set my saliva flowing, and ate them slowly, reveling in the gentle chewy texture of the albumin and the heavy metallic yolky overload. My stepmother was right. Eating *pei ta-an* was a libidinous experience.

I have grown accustomed to the absence of strong flavor and scent in food, living in the United States. Many Americans appear to prefer their meals as antiseptic as their bathrooms. The movement toward "health foods" seems to me to be yet another progression toward banning the reek, bloodiness, and decay of our scavenging past and installing a technologically controlled and scientifically scrutinized diet. In some future time, humans may live to a hundred and fifty years, dining on a mass-produced nutritious cuisine of "natural foods" based on grains, vegetables, and roots. Boiled chicken feet and chemically preserved eggs will become gross memories from a horrible history of animal abuse and carcinogenic poisoning. But in the meantime, millions of Asians are still eating these dishes in search of, if not, as my poor father who died young of throat cancer believed, health and longevity, at least a diverse diet that can keep them body and soul.

Thus my eldest bother, by now middle-aged and middle-class prospering, promised me a memorable breakfast when I visited him in Malacca in 1989. It was Sunday, as in the West a day for leisurely gatherings and perhaps some family feasting. We drove to the center of town, up through a narrow side-lane, and parked by an open ditch. Under a galvanized tin roof, crowding with other families, we sat on low stools around a small round wooden table, as scarred and stained as the table around which we ate in our childhood. The hawker, a Chinese Malaysian, was busy stirring an enormous blackened iron pot from which clouds of steam puffed up. Smaller pots containing various dark and green mashes sat on smaller grills, all fueled by a propane tank. Pouring the boiling liquid from the teapot, Eldest Brother rinsed the bowls, cups, spoons, and chopsticks set before us. Then a woman—the hawker's wife? daughter?—filled our bowls with plain white rice porridge, watery, the grains soft but still separate rather than broken down into a glutinous mass. From the many pots she brought different bowls—salted cabbage cooked to a dark-green slush with slabs of pork fat edged with a little lean; salted pickled cucumber crunchy and sweet; hard-cooked and browned bean curd less chewy than the meat it was processed to imitate; salted dried anchovies smaller than my little finger, fried crisp with their heads on. Nothing was fresh; everything was freshly cooked.

A light in my head flashed and lit something I had always known but never understood. How poor the masses of ordinary Chinese have been for millennia and how inventive hunger has made them. How from the scraps, offal, detritus and leftovers saved from the imperial maw, from dynastic overlords who taxed away almost everything, peasant Chinese have created a fragrant and mouth-watering survival: dried lily buds and lotus roots, tree cloud fungus and fermented bean mash, dried lichen and salted black beans, pickled leeks and seaweed dessert; fish maw and chicken feet; intestines and preserved eggs. No wonder as a child I was taught to greet my elders politely, "Have you eaten yet, Eldest Auntie? Have you eaten rice, Third Uncle?" Speaking in our dialect, my stepmother still greets me, newly arrived from rich America, thus, "Have you eaten?"

The cook himself approached our table bearing two dishes especially ordered by my brother for me: soy-boiled chicken feet chopped into bite-sized pieces, and *pei ta-an* cut in eighths with a mound of pickled ginger on the side. My eldest brother had figured me out: that, even after decades of American fast foods and the rich diet of the middle class, my deprived childhood had indelibly fixed as gastronomic fantasies those dishes impoverished Chinese had produced out of the paltry ingredients they could afford. This is perhaps the instruction to an increasingly consuming and consumed planet that the cuisine from China offers: to eat is to live. And we multiplicious billions will all have to learn to eat well in poverty, turning scarcity and parsimony to triumphant feasting. Facing my morning's breakfast of preserved vegetables and hundred-year-old eggs, boiled chicken feet, and rice gruel, I knew my brother was offering me the best of our childhood together.

SOY-BOILED CHICKEN FEET*

10 pairs of chicken feet
1 teaspoon salt

* The same recipe can be used for chicken drumsticks, substituting eight drumsticks for the feet, and skipping the initial boiling.

1½ teaspoon pepper
one knob ginger as big as a large walnut
4 cloves garlic
¼ cup sherry
1 tablespoon sesame oil
2 teaspoons sugar
1 cup soy sauce
5 star-anise or 1 teaspoon five-spice powder (optional)

1. Wash chicken feet well, making sure that claws are clipped off and any small feathers plucked with tweezers. Strip the yellow outer epidermis off legs.
2. Fill a large pot with water and set it on high heat. When water boils, place chicken feet in the pot and cook for about 15 minutes, then drain.
3. Peel brown skin off ginger and slice thin in rounds. Peel garlic and crush lightly.
4. Put soy sauce, sherry, ginger, garlic, salt, pepper, sugar, star-anise or five-spice powder, sesame oil, and chicken feet in a large flat saucepan. Bring to a light simmer and leave simmering for about 30 minutes, by which time meat should be falling off the bones.
5. Cool. Then chop into bite-sized pieces.

Serves 4 to 6.

30

13/16

SHERMAN ALEXIE

1.

I cut myself into sixteen equal pieces
keep thirteen and feed the other three
to the dogs, who have also grown

tired of U.S. Commodities, white cans
black letters translated into Spanish.
"Does this mean I have to learn

the language to eat?" Lester FallsApart asks
but directions for preparation are simple:
a. WASH CAN; b. OPEN CAN; c. EXAMINE CONTENTS

OF CAN FOR SPOILAGE; d. EMPTY CONTENTS
OF CAN INTO SAUCE PAN; e. COOK CONTENTS
OVER HIGH HEAT; f. SERVE AND EAT.

2.

It is done by blood, reservation mathematics, fractions:
father (full-blood) + mother (5/8) = (13/16).

It is done by enrollment number, last name first, first name last:
Spokane Tribal Enrollment Number 1569; Victor, Chief.

It is done by identification card, photograph, lamination:
IF FOUND, PLEASE RETURN TO SPOKANE TRIBE OF INDIANS,
WELLPINIT, WA.

3.
The compromise is always made
in increments. On this reservation
we play football on real grass
dream of deserts, three inches of rain

in a year. What we have lost:
uranium mine, Little Falls Dam
salmon. Our excuses are trapped
within museums, roadside attractions

totem poles in Riverfront Park.
I was there, watching the Spokane River
changing. A ten-year-old white boy asked
if I was a real Indian. He did not wait

for an answer, instead carving his initials
into the totem with a pocketknife: J.N.
We are what we take, carving my name
my enrollment number, thirteen hash marks

into the wood. A story is remembered
as evidence, the Indian man they found dead
shot in the alley behind the Mayfair.
Authorities reported a rumor he had relatives

in Minnesota. A member of some tribe or another
his photograph on the 11 o'clock news. Eyes, hair
all dark, his shovel-shaped incisor, each the same
ordinary identification of the anonymous.

4.
When my father disappeared, we found him
years later, in a strange kitchen searching
for footprints in the dust: still

untouched on the shelves all the commodity
cans without labels—my father opened them
one by one, finding a story in each.

PART V

Side Dishes

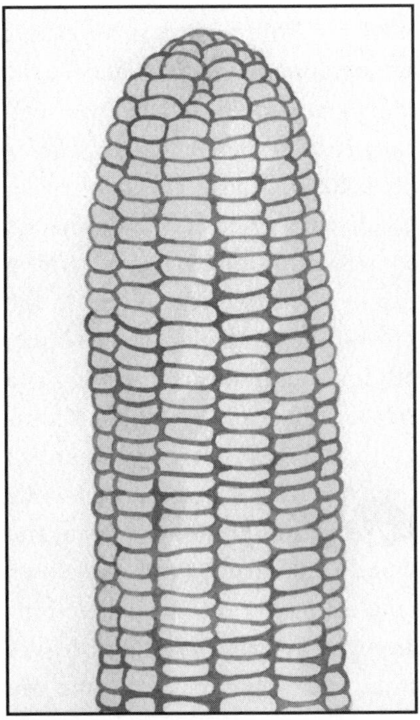

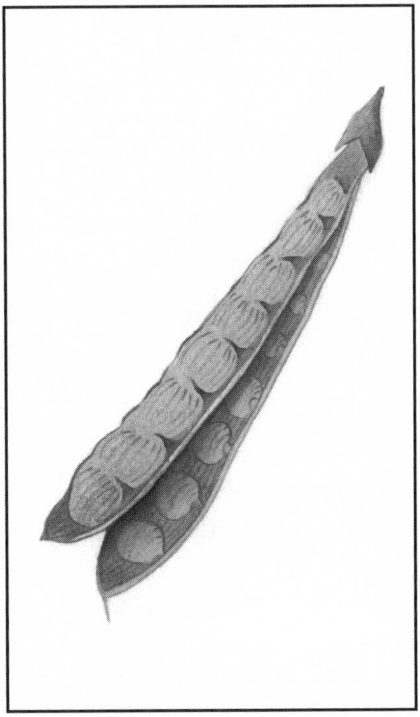

In *Borderlands: La Frontera,* Gloria Anzaldúa writes about living within the margins of modern America. Her specific margin is the "borderland" country between Mexico and the United States that is the American Southwest, as well as the linguistic and culinary fringes that define this community. Inhabiting what she terms a *mestiza* culture in which she speaks the "wild tongue" of Chicano Spanish and eats dishes defined by Tex-Mex foodways, Anzaldúa claims that it is centrally through language and food—what goes in and what comes out of *la boca,* the mouth—that each of us internalizes our identity. And just as her combined language of English and Spanish defines what she sees and says from the country's margin, Anzaldúa's food memories similarly show an amalgam of tastes and textures from distinct regions. She remembers her "sister Hilda's hot, spicy *menudo, chile colorado* making it deep red, pieces of *panza* and hominy floating on top."[1] Hilda's soup, with its Colorado red chiles, its bits of Mexican *panza* (pig belly), and its southern-inflected hominy, epitomizes what may be called a borderland dish.

For Anzaldúa, then, American identity is complex. It is an ethnic synthesis: an identity created "on the sides" of the national "mainland." To be someone *en el otro lado*, "on the other side," is simultaneously to be "sidelined" (trivialized, alienated) and also, potentially, to be someone who is "side-by-side" with someone else: close together, in collaboration, in solidarity.

Side dishes symbolize this borderland sense of both belonging and being apart—of being, as Ketu Katrak puts it, both at "home" and in "alien-kitchens." For Katrak, growing up in India before moving to the United States for graduate school, her cross-cultural identity comes out of a "pattern of belonging, of home-sounds and home-aromas." Living and working on the other side of the ocean from her extended family, Katrak returns to India "through the tastebuds, through the aromas" of the Indian dishes she cooks in her American kitchen, dishes she first learned while watching her mother adapt and make up recipes in Bombay. In turn, and in a kind of cultural turn-around, Deborah Thompson (a home-grown American) attempts to follow the broken-English, verbal instructions her mother-in-law gives for cooking Thompson's dead Bengali husband's favorite side dish, Moong Dal—a recipe all but forgotten. "This time you will remember?" asks her mother-in-law. At the margins of her husband's culinary customs and traditions, Thompson can only resurrect the memory of Raju fully when she makes the Dal as he would have liked it: "lot of chili, lot of turmeric." Yet her mother-in-law remains unconvinced that such resurrection magic can happen more than once unless Thompson actually records the recipe and does not just listen to it. "You must write it down," she insists.

And, in fact, within the selections presented here, other memories from the linguistic, ethnic, aesthetic, political, and culinary sidelines are both recalled and recorded through the writing down of side-dish recipes. Alice B. Toklas remembers within her 1954 memoir-cookbook the fourteen years that she and Gertrude Stein—as "sideline" expats—lived in Bilignin, France. Through her writing, Toklas restores and revives the French-inflected recipes she made out of their copious vegetable garden. Toklas recalls, "The first gathering of the garden in May of salads, radishes and herbs made me feel like a mother about her baby—how could anything so beautiful be mine. And this emotion of wonder filled me for each vegetable as it was gathered every year. There is nothing that is comparable to it, as satisfactory or as thrilling, as gathering the vegetables one has grown." A reader, too, feels a bit overcome by wonder—wonder, in part, that Toklas and Stein were able to sow, reap, and eat such abundance. As Stein says to Toklas upon surveying their harvest, "there were enough vegetables for an institution," reminding her that their household consists of only three people. "There was no question that, looking at that harvest as an economic question, it was disastrous," admits Toklas, "but from the point of view of the satisfaction which work and aesthetic confer, it was sublime."

Sublimity and pleasure are also the subjects of Julia Child's side-dish recipes for vegetables from her 1961 *Mastering the Art of French Cooking*. As Child extols, "Anyone who has been fortunate enough to eat fresh, home-cooked vegetables in France remembers them with pleasure." When Child brought her knowledge of French cookery and cuisine to America in the 1960s, the idea of a side dish as a pleasure unto itself was largely unknown and even disbelieved. Typical American sides of the period tended to consist of canned or frozen vegetables, invariably overcooked, or potatoes boiled to the point of mush. Within her cookbook, however, Child works hard to convince her middle-class, provincially minded cooks, "Returning voyagers speak of [French vegetables] with trembling nostalgia: 'Those delicious little green beans! They even serve them as a separate course.'" Perhaps some early readers may have given Child a sidelong glance, not quite convinced; but in the coming decades, particularly with the success of her TV show *The French Chef*, Child proved that middle-class Americans, and not just the well-to-do, could not only enjoy but also prepare French food. Through a union of French technique and American foodstuffs—as shown in the our selection of Child's various recipes for American-grown artichokes—amateur American cooks could slice, dice, steam, boil, and bake their own side-dish sublimity.

Cooking up sublimity is what Vertamae Smart-Grosvenor has in mind as well in her "Demystification of Food"—although her sublimity is a bit more sensual than Child's. "Food is sexy," she writes, "and you can tell a lot about people and where they're at by their food habits. People who eat food with pleasure and get pleasure from the different stirring of the senses that a well-prepared food experience can bring are my kind of people." Published just shy of a decade after *Mastering the Art of French Cooking*, Smart-Grosvenor's own *Vibration Cooking* actually takes on the likes of both Child and James Beard. "White folks act like they invented food and like there is some weird mystique surrounding it—something that only Julia and Jim can get to. There is no mystique. Food is food. Everybody eats!" she insists. Rather than fussing over whether food is high-brow or low-brow or whether it looks Martha Stewart–perfect on the plate, Smart-Grosvenor suggests that American cooks need to let their collective hair down. "When I cook," she explains, "I never measure or weigh anything. I cook by vibration. I can tell by the look and smell of it. . . . Different strokes for different folks. Do your thing your way." In other words, when it comes to the kitchen, everyone should walk the boundaries between what they know and what they feel; "marginal cooking," for Smart-Grosvenor, defines both creativity and happiness.

And, admittedly, sometimes it is true that one wants pleasure, solace, or sympathy over inspiration or awe in a dish. One wants comfort food. As Paula Dean and other American comfort-food peddlers know, certain side dishes have long served as a meal in themselves, especially when one is feeling sideswiped by love. As Nora Ephron describes in her disquisition "Potatoes and Love" from her novel *Heartburn*, at the end of a relationship, her main character, Rachel Samstat, always wants potatoes:

> Mashed potatoes. Nothing like mashed potatoes when you're feeling blue. Nothing like getting into bed with a bowl of hot mashed potatoes already loaded with butter, and methodically adding a thin cold slice of butter to every forkful. The problem with mashed potatoes, though, is that they require . . . hard work. . . . Of course, you can always get someone to make the mashed potatoes for you, but let's face it: the reason you're blue is that there isn't anyone to make them for you. As a result, most people do not have nearly enough mashed potatoes in their lives, and when they do, it's almost always at the wrong time.

Here, readers on the margins of love may well feel better, more centered, in eating to the bottom of a big bowl of mashed potatoes (that, hopefully, someone else has made for them), while being cheered with Ephron's comforting, confessional wit.

Humorous side dishes make their appearance as well in Laurie Colwin's "Repulsive Dinners," in which she asserts that "there is something triumphant about a really disgusting" feast and argues, sardonically, that her "life has been much enriched by ghastly meals." Watching her make her way through a semicooked rice-pineapple-breakfast-sausage dish as well as a squid-flounder-apple-onion-and-cinnamon pie, it is hard not to split one's side over the horrendous dishes she has felt obligated to eat. As with Ephron, Colwin's remedy upon returning from a hideous dinner out is potatoes—although this time they are shredded potatoes fried in half a stick of butter. (Julia Child would surely approve.)

In the end, however, perhaps the most profound way to reconcile what it is like to be on the boundaries of family, home, relationships, kitchen, or table is to employ a side dish to celebrate love. Kathy Fagan's poem is a hymn to the tomato—what she calls love's "apple," that "*swelling / Fruit*." Offered and shared during her wedding reception as part of a family recipe for insalata pomodoro, Fagan's focus on this rich-red fruit (on the boundary of a vegetable) symbolizes the heart: sweet and adaptable. In consuming this "love salad" along with the wedding guests, readers move from the margins of the poem to its center. Side-by-side with the writer, one recalls that lovely afternoon, everyone tilting "the bowls to their wet mouths," their collective *bocas*.

And even now, many years later and many miles away, Gloria Anzaldúa believes she can still envision her mother "spicing . . . ground beef, pork and venison with *chile*" when Anzaldúa cooks up her mother's *tamales*.[2] Her mouth, her *boca*, floods with memory, and just as when a reader follows Fagan's recipe for insalata pomodoro or Child's for artichokes or Ephron's for mashed potatoes, both body and mind remember and connect. In Ketu Katrak's words, "That is the boundaryless pleasure of cooking. . . . Yes, today, I cook this dish, but many hands and minds are part of its history and its success." In a sense, then, one could say that we humans are all side dishes—admixtures and component parts of the larger whole. And when we write these recipes down, when we say them in language and eat them as food, we feed the whole.

NOTES

1. Gloria Anzaldúa, *Borderlands: La Frontera* (San Francisco: Aunt Lute Books, 1987), 61.
2. Ibid., 83.

31

From *Mastering the Art of French Cooking*

JULIA CHILD, LOUISETTE BERTHOLLE, AND SIMONE BECK

Légumes

Anyone who has been fortunate enough to eat fresh, home-cooked vegetables in France remembers them with pleasure. Returning voyagers speak of them with trembling nostalgia: "Those delicious little green beans! They even serve them as a separate course. Why I'll never forget the meal I had . . . ," and so forth. Some people are even convinced that it is only in France that you can enjoy such experiences because French vegetables are somehow different. Fortunately this is not the case. Any fine, fresh vegetable in season will taste just as good in America or anywhere else if the French vegetable-cooking techniques are used.

The French are interested in vegetables as food rather than as purely nutrient objects valuable for their vitamins and minerals. And it is in the realm of the green vegetable that French methods differ most radically from American. The French objective is to produce a cooked green vegetable so green, fresh-tasting, and full of flavor that it really can be served as a separate course. They do not hesitate to peel, boil, squeeze, drain, or refresh a vegetable, which is often upsetting to those very Americans who weep in delighted remembrance of vegetables in France. For many Americans have been taught that by performing any of these acts, one is wickedly "throwing away the best part."

Blanching

You will note that before anything else in the way of cooking or flavoring takes place, all the green vegetables in this chapter are blanched—dropped into a very large kettle of rapidly boiling salted water. This is the great secret of French green-vegetable cookery, and also happens to be the same process used in America to prepare green vegetables for the freezer. Success is entirely dependent on having a great quantity of boiling water: 7 to 8 quarts for 2 to 3 pounds of vegetables. The more water you use in proportion to your vegetables, the quicker the water will return to the boil after the vegetables have gone in, and the greener, fresher, and more full of flavor they will be. Baking soda is never necessary when you cook green vegetables this way.

Refreshing

A second important French technique is that of refreshing. As soon as green vegetables have been blanched, and if they are not to be served immediately or are to be served cold, they are plunged for several minutes into a large quantity of cold water. This stops the cooking immediately, sets the color, and preserves the texture and flavor. If the vegetables are not refreshed in this manner and sit steaming in a saucepan or colander, their collective warmth softens and discolors them, and they lose their fresh taste. Following the refreshing technique, then, you can cook all your green vegetables well in advance of a party, and have only the final touches left to do at the last minute.

Overcooking

A cardinal point in the French technique is: *Do not overcook.* An equally important admonition is: *Do not attempt to keep a cooked green vegetable warm for more than a very few moments.* If you cannot serve it at once, it is better to set it aside and then to reheat it. Overcooking and keeping hot ruin the color, texture, and taste of green vegetables—as well as most of the nutritive qualities.

Scope of Vegetable Chapter

This chapter does not pretend to offer a complete treatise on vegetables. The French repertoire is so large that we have felt it best to go into more detail on a selection than to give tidbits on all. Most of our emphasis is on green vegetables. There is a modest but out-of-the-ordinary section on potatoes. Other vegetables rate only one or two recipes—but good ones—and some we have not mentioned at all.

Green Vegetables

Artichokes (Artichauts)

French or globe artichokes are in season from October to June. April and May are the peak months when their prices are most attractive. A fresh, desirable artichoke is heavy and compact, with fleshy, closely clinging leaves of a good, green color all the way to the tips. The stem is also fresh and green.

As baby artichokes are not generally available in this country, all the following recipes are based on the large, 10- to 12-ounce artichoke which is about 4½ inches high and 4 to 4½ inches at its largest diameter.

SERVING SUGGESTIONS

Hot or cold boiled artichokes are served as a separate course, either at the beginning of the meal or in place of a salad. Most wine authorities agree that water should be served with them rather than wine, for wine changes its character when drunk with this vegetable. But, if you insist, serve a strong, dry, chilled white wine such as a Mâcon, or a chilled and characterful *rosé* such as a Tavel.

PREPARATION FOR COOKING

One at a time, prepare the artichokes as follows:

Remove the stem by bending it at the base of the artichoke until it snaps off thus detaching with the stem any tough filaments which may have pushed up into the heart.

Break off the small leaves at the base of the artichoke. Trim the base with a knife so the artichoke will stand solidly upright.

Lay the artichoke on its side and slice three quarters of an inch off the top of the center cone of leaves. Trim off the points of the rest of the leaves with scissors. Wash under cold running water.

Rub the cut portions of the artichoke with lemon juice. Drop it into a basin of cold water containing 1 tablespoon of vinegar per quart of water. The acid prevents the artichoke from discoloring.

ARTICHAUTS AU NATUREL

[WHOLE BOILED ARTICHOKES—HOT OR COLD]

Artichokes should be boiled in a large kettle so that they have plenty of room. It is not necessary to tie the leaves in place. Because they must cook a comparatively long time, artichokes turn an olive green. Any Frenchman would look with disfavor on a bright green boiled artichoke, knowing that baking soda had been added to the water.

6 artichokes prepared for cooking as in the preceding directions A large kettle containing 7 to 8 quarts of rapidly boiling water 1½ tsp salt per quart of water Washed cheesecloth	Drop the prepared artichokes in the boiling salted water. To help prevent discoloration, lay over the artichokes a double thickness of cheesecloth; this will keep their exposed tops moist. Bring the water back to the boil as rapidly as possible and boil slowly, uncovered, for 35 to 45 minutes. The artichokes are done when the leaves pull out easily and the bottoms are tender when pierced with a knife.
A skimmer or slotted spoon A colander	Immediately remove them from the kettle with skimmer or spoon and drain them upside down in a colander. Boiled artichokes may be served hot, warm, or cold.

How to Eat an Artichoke

If you have never eaten an artichoke before, here is how you go about it. Pull off a leaf and hold its tip in your fingers. Dip the bottom of the leaf in melted butter or one of the sauces suggested farther on. Then scrape off its tender flesh between your teeth. When you have gone through all the leaves, you will come to the heart, which you eat with a knife and fork after you have scraped off and discarded the choke or hairy center growth.

To Remove the Choke before Serving

It is not necessary to remove the choke, but it makes a nicer presentation if you wish to take the time. To do so, gently spread the leaves apart enough so you can reach into the interior of the artichoke. Pull out the tender center cone of leaves in one piece. Down in the center of the artichoke, at the point where you removed the cone of leaves, is the choke or hairy growth which covers the top of the heart. Scrape off and remove the choke with a spoon to expose the tender flesh of the artichoke heart. Sprinkle salt and pepper over the heart. Turn the cone of leaves upside down and set it in the hollow formed by the top of the artichoke.

Sauces for Hot or Warm Artichokes

Beurre Fondu, melted butter

Beurre au Citron, lemon butter sauce . . .

Sauce Hollandaise . . .

If you have removed the choke, you may wish to spread the leaves apart enough to expose the heart, then heap 3 or 4 spoonfuls of the hollandaise into it and top with a sprig of parsley.

Sauces for Cold Artichokes

Vinaigrette, French dressing . . .

Sauce Ravigote, vinaigrette with herbs, capers, and onions . . .

Sauce Moutarde, mustard sauce with olive oil, lemon juice, and herbs . . .

Sauce Alsacienne, soft-boiled egg mayonnaise with herbs . . .

Mayonnaise . . .

ARTICHAUTS BRAISÉS À LA PROVENÇALE
[ARTICHOKES BRAISED WITH WINE, GARLIC, AND HERBS]

Most of the many recipes for braised artichokes follow the general lines of this one. You may, if you wish, add to the casserole a cup of diced tomato pulp, or ½ cup of diced ham, and, 10 minutes before the end of the cooking, ½ pound of sautéed mushrooms. Another suggestion with different vegetables follows this recipe. Braised artichokes go well with roast or braised meats, or they can constitute a first course. As they are rather messy to eat with the fingers, guests should be furnished with a spoon as well as a knife and fork, so the flesh may be scraped off the artichoke leaves.

For 6 to 8 people

6 large artichokes
A large kettle containing 7 to 8 quarts of rapidly boiling water
1½ tsp salt per quart of water

Prepare the artichokes for cooking as directed at the beginning of this section, but cut off the leaves so that the artichokes are only about 1½ inches long. Then slice the artichokes into lengthwise quarters and cut out the chokes. Drop the quarters in boiling water and boil for 10 minutes only. Drain.
Preheat oven to 325 degrees.

1 cup (4 ounces) diced onions
6 Tb olive oil
A 10- to 11-inch covered fireproof casserole large enough to hold the artichokes in one layer
2 large cloves minced garlic
Salt and pepper

Cook the onions slowly in olive oil in the casserole for 5 minutes without letting the onions color. Stir in the garlic. Arrange the artichoke quarters in the casserole. Baste with the olive oil and onions. Sprinkle on salt and pepper. Cover casserole and cook slowly over low heat for 10 minutes, not allowing artichokes to brown.

¼ cup wine vinegar
½ cup dry white wine or dry white vermouth
1½ cups stock, canned beef bouillon, or water
An herb bouquet: 4 parsley sprigs, ½ bay leaf, and ¼ tsp thyme tied in cheesecloth

Pour in the vinegar and wine. Raise heat and boil until liquid is reduced by half. Then pour in the stock, bouillon, or water. Add the herb bouquet. Bring to the simmer, then lay the waxed paper over the artichokes. Cover casserole and place it in the middle level of the preheated oven. Casserole should simmer slowly for 1¼ to 1½ hours, or until liquid has almost entirely evaporated.
* If not to be served immediately, set casserole aside, its cover askew. Reheat when needed.

2 to 3 TB minced parsley

Discard herb bouquet. Serve from casserole or on a warm serving dish. (The artichokes may be surrounded with baked tomatoes and sautéed potatoes.) Sprinkle with parsley before bringing to the table.

VARIATION: ARTICHAUTS PRINTANIERS
[ARTICHOKES BRAISED WITH CARROTS, ONIONS, TURNIPS, AND MUSHROOMS]

Except for the addition of other vegetables, this recipe is the same as the master recipe. You may wish to use butter instead of olive oil, cut down on the garlic, and omit all or part of the vinegar, increasing the wine accordingly.

- Ingredients for the preceding braised artichokes, including diced onions, oil (or butter), wine, stock, and seasonings
- 12 small white onions, about 1 inch in diameter, peeled
- 3 or 4 carrots, peeled, quartered and cut into 1½-inch lengths
- 3 or 4 white turnips, peeled and quartered

Following the preceding recipe, quarter and blanch the artichokes, and cook the diced onions in the olive oil (or butter). Then add the artichokes and place the whole onions and the other vegetables around the edge of the casserole. Baste with the diced onions and oil (or butter), and season with salt and pepper. Proceed with the recipe.

- 12 to 18 mushroom caps lightly sautéed in olive oil or butter

About 10 minutes before the end of the cooking, add the mushroom caps. Finish the sauce and serve the casserole as in the preceding recipe.

→ 32 ←

The Vegetable Gardens at Bilignin

From *The Alice B. Toklas Cook Book*

ALICE B. TOKLAS

For fourteen successive years the gardens at Bilignin were my joy, working in them during the summers and planning and dreaming of them during the winters. The summers frequently commenced early in April with the planting, and ended late in October with the last gathering of the winter vegetables. Bilignin surrounded by mountains and not far from the French Alps—from higher ground a few miles away Mont Blanc was frequently visible—made early planting uncertain. One year we lost the first planting of string beans, another year the green peas were caught by late frost. It took me several years to know the climate and quite as many more to know the weather. Experience is never at bargain price. Then too I obstinately refused to accept the lore of the farmers, judging it, with the prejudice of a townswoman, to be nothing but superstition. They told me never to transplant parsley, and not to plant it on Good Friday. We did it in California, was my weak reply. They said not to plant at the moment of the new or full moon. The seed would be as indifferent as I was, was my impatient answer to this. But it was not. Before the end of our tenancy of the lovely house and gardens at Bilignin, I had become not only weather-wise but a fairly successful gardener.

In the spring of 1929 we became tenants of what had been the manor of Bilignin. We were enchanted with everything. But after careful examination of the two large vegetable gardens—the lower on a level with the terrace garden in front of the house, and the other on a considerably higher level and a distance from the court and portals—it was to my horror that I discovered the state they were in. Nothing but potatoes had been planted the year before. Poking about with a heavy stick, there seemed to be some resistance in a corner followed by a rippling movement. The rubbish and weeds would have to be cleaned out at once. In six days the seven men we mobilised in the village had accomplished this. In the corner where I had poked, a snake's nest and several snakes had been found. But so were raspberries and strawberries.

A plan was made for plots and paths. The French are adroit in weeding and gathering from paths a few inches in width. It was difficult for me to accommodate myself to them. A list of what vegetables and when they were to be planted had to be made. We had brought with us sacks of seeds of all the vegetables Gertrude Stein and I cared for and some with which we would experiment. To do the heavy work a boy from the hamlet had been found. After fertilisers had been turned into the ground and the topsoil raked to a powder, with a prayer the planting commenced. The seeds for early gathering had scarcely been disposed of when it was time to plant the slips bought from farmers' wives in the square at Belley at the Saturday-morning market. There were two horticulturists in Belley, one an over-educated ambitious pretentious youngish man who never ceased believing he was to be the next Minister of Agriculture, and an old woman who had no more preparation for her work than experience which had taught her little. The slips we had from them were not all vigorous; we planted twice as many as we intended to grow.

The wind blew the seeds from the weeds in the uncultivated fields that surrounded the gardens. The topsoil was of made earth and heavy rains commenced to wash it away. These were the two disadvantages we should have to overcome. The weeds remained a tormenting, backbreaking experience all the summers we spent at Bilignin. After the autumn gathering was over, the topsoil would be renewed. Fortunately there was plenty of water. Only once was there a drought, when the ox cart brought water in barrels from the stream in the valley below. For watering we had bought three hundred feet of hose.

The work in the vegetables—Gertrude Stein was undertaking for the moment the care of the flowers and box hedges—was a full-time job and more. Later it became a joy, Gertrude Stein asking me what I saw when I closed my eyes, and I answered, Weeds. That, she said, was not the answer, and so weeds were changed to strawberries. The small strawberries, called by the French wood strawberries, are not wild but cultivated. It took me an hour to gather a small basket for Gertrude Stein's breakfast, and later when there was a plantation of them in the upper garden, our young guests were told that if they cared to eat them they should do the picking themselves.

The first gathering of the garden in May of salads, radishes and herbs made me feel like a mother about her baby—how could anything so beautiful be mine. And this emotion of wonder filled me for each vegetable as it was gathered every year. There is nothing that is comparable to it, as satisfactory or as thrilling, as gathering the vegetables one has grown.

Later when vegetables were ready to be picked, it never occurred to us to question what way to cook them. Naturally the simplest, just to steam or boil them and serve them with the excellent country butter or cream that we had from a farmer almost within calling distance. Later still, when we had guests and the vegetables had lost the aura of a new-born miracle, sauces added variety.

In the beginning it was the habit to pick all vegetables very young except beetroots, potatoes and large squash and pumpkins because of one's eagerness, and later because of their delicate flavour when cooked. That prevented serving sauces with some vegetables—green peas, string beans (indeed all peas and beans) and lettuces.

There were exceptions, and for French guests this was one of them.

GREEN PEAS À LA FRANÇAISE

Put in a saucepan over medium heat 4 cups shelled green peas, 12 spring onions, a bouquet of 1 sprig of parsley and several stalks of basil, ¼ cup butter, ¼ teaspoon salt, ½ teaspoon sugar, 1 white lettuce cut in ribbons and 4 tablespoons water. Bring to a boil, cover and reduce heat gradually to low. Before serving remove bouquet and add 4 tablespoons butter. Tip saucepan in all directions to melt butter. Serve at once.

Or this one:

GREEN PEAS À LA GOOD WIFE

Put 12 young onions in a saucepan over medium heat with 3 tablespoons butter and ½ cup fat back of pork previously boiled for 5 minutes, drained and cut in cubes of ½ inch. When the onions are lightly browned, remove with the cubes of back fat. In the saucepan stir 1 tablespoon flour. Mix well and gradually add 1¾ cups veal *bouillon*. Allow to boil for 15 minutes and salt.

Then add 4 cups shelled green peas, the diced pork fat and the onions. Cover and cook from 15 to 25 minutes according to the size and age of the peas.

Here is still another recipe for

GREEN PEAS AS COOKED IN PROVENCE BY THE FARMERS

Put in an earthenware casserole, which has a well-fitted cover and which is fireproof, 5 tablespoons olive oil and 1 medium-sized onion. Brown the onion over low heat. Then add 6 medium-sized potatoes cut in ⅓-inch slices. Stir the potatoes until they are covered with oil. Add 4 cups boiling water, 4 cups shelled green peas, 3 cloves of crushed garlic, a bouquet of half a laurel leaf, a twig of thyme and a slice of fennel or a bunch of fennel greens, ½ teaspoon salt, ¼ teaspoon pepper and ½ teaspoon saffron. Cover and boil gently. When the peas are tender slide on the surface of the juice 4 eggs. They must not touch each other. Gently pour 2 tablespoons of the juice over the yolks of the eggs to form a film. Cut 2 slices of French bread ⅓ inch thick and place on the plates on which the peas and the sauce are to be served.

In summer there were about thirty different vegetables which had to be examined and gathered every morning as well as the berries. There were more berries than we could eat either in desserts or fresh, so I made jam of the little wood strawberries and jelly of the raspberries. The French have a perfect way of making

STRAWBERRY JAM (2)

Put equal weight of sugar and berries into an earthenware bowl. Stir gently not to bruise the berries until they are coated with sugar. Put aside for 24 hours. Pour off sugar and juice that has exuded from berries. Place over medium heat in enameled saucepan or pot and bring to a boil. Boil gently for 3 or 4 minutes. Remove from heat. Skim and place berries in glasses. Replace syrup over heat and boil gently until spoon is thickly coated. Fill glasses.

Ordinary strawberries may be cooked in the same way. They must of course be hulled or stripped and preferably not washed. They will require from 12 to 15 minutes boiling, depending upon their size and their ripeness. The hulls of the little berries remain on the stalks when the berries are picked.

Most of our men guests had their breakfasts served on the terrace. The breakfast trays were my pride, though the linen and porcelain were simple. In the market place in Chambéry we unearthed some amusing coloured glassware, 1840–1850, from Savoy, not at an antique dealer's but in a store that sold glassware. We bought all there was. Berries, fruits, salads and vegetables served in them were subjects for still-life pictures. For French guests an abbreviated American breakfast was served, somewhat more ample however than their usual coffee and rolls or *croissants* with butter, jam, marmalade or jelly. *Croissants* are a delicious accompaniment to breakfast or to tea.

CROISSANTS OR CRESCENTS

Heat ½ cup milk. When it is warm mix into it 1 package of compressed yeast. Sift 1 cup flour and mix with the yeast to make a sponge. Allow to rise, for about ½ hour. Sift 3 cups flour into a large bowl. Put the yeast at the bottom in the centre of the bowl and gradually work in 3½ cups milk and the flour. Put aside until it has risen to twice its size. Then place it on a lightly floured board and knead thoroughly until the dough no longer sticks to the hands. Roll out and place ¼ cup butter, which has been worked with the hands into a square, in the centre, fold the dough from the sides to meet in the centre. Roll with the hands into a ball and keep in a cool place for several hours or even for the night. Then roll out again and divide into pieces the size of an egg. Roll each one into a cylinder and put aside for 10 minutes. Then very lightly roll them out to ⅓ inch thickness. Roll from one corner, bend into the shape of crescents and put aside for 35 minutes. Place on a lightly buttered baking sheet, paint with pastry brush dipped in slightly beaten egg mixed with 1 tablespoon water. Bake in preheated 425° oven.

String beans with a sauce is a desecration, especially string beans grown in France. Even in my well-loved California they were less tender, less flavoursome, and not as free from strings. Still they could be cooked—with our French friends in mind—disguised to my mind as

STRING BEANS IN THE PROVENÇAL MANNER

Heat 3 tablespoons olive oil in frying pan. Add ¼ cup capers, ¼ cup boned anchovies, 1 crushed clove of garlic and 4 cups string beans previously boiled until tender in boiling water with ¾ teaspoon salt and ¼ teaspoon pepper in an uncovered saucepan. Toss them in the frying pan until they are well mixed with the various ingredients in it. Serve hot with chopped parsley and fine chopped spring onion sprinkled on them.

And this way:

STRING BEANS BROWNED IN THE OVEN

Boil in salted water uncovered 4 cups string beans. Do not overcook, but when tender remove from heat and drain thoroughly. Butter a fireproof earthenware dish. Sprinkle generously with grated Swiss cheese. Mix 1½ cups *Béchamel* sauce with 2 yolks of eggs. Pour ¼ cup of this on the cheese in the earthenware dish, then the string beans and on them the rest of the sauce. Sprinkle ⅓ cup grated Swiss cheese on the string beans, dot with 3 tablespoons melted butter and put in preheated 450° oven for 15 minutes.

These are very nice ways to cook string beans but they interfere with the poor vegetable's leading a life of its own. As for the cooking of lettuces, with or without sauce, the easiest way to accept this is to consider lettuce as two vegetables, raw lettuce and cooked lettuce. To me cooking lettuces is the sacrifice of the innocents. If cooked they must be, this way is always received with appreciation:

LETTUCE IN RIBBONS WITH CREAM

For 4 cups shredded lettuce put 4 tablespoons butter in a saucepan over medium flame, put the shredded lettuce in the butter and turn with a wooden spoon until all the lettuce is covered with butter. Reduce the heat to low, add ¼ teaspoon salt. Cover and simmer until all the moisture in the lettuce has been absorbed. Add 1½ cups thick cream sauce and 1 teaspoon onion juice. Stir well together. Place on a serving dish in a mound, and surround by large triangular *croûtons*.

BRAISED LETTUCE WITH ITALIAN SAUCE

Wash and dry 4 large lettuces having removed the green outer leaves. Pour into 4 tablespoons butter melted in a saucepan. Stir, reduce heat and cover. Simmer until all the water has evaporated, then add this sauce.

Chop coarsely ⅓ cup mushrooms. Place mushrooms in saucepan over low heat with 2 tablespoons olive oil and 2 tablespoons butter, 1 tablespoon chopped onion and ½ tablespoon chopped shallot. Mix well and add ⅓ cup hot dry white wine. Cover and simmer for 10 minutes, add ¼ cup tomato *purée,* ¼ teaspoon salt. Add ¼ cup butter in small pieces. Melt and mix by tipping the saucepan in all directions. Do not allow to boil.

This is a change—indeed a violent one.

There were lettuces for early gathering and for summer. For autumn not only Batavia and Romaine, but an endless variety of vegetables to be served raw or cooked.

For the early raw vegetables, we waited for tomatoes to ripen. Neither Gertrude Stein nor I cared for raw root vegetables, nor did we care for spinach in salad. Spinach and sorrel—blessed perennials that they are—could be gathered early. The second or third year at Bilignin I dug up the row of sorrel, keeping only one plant. Sorrel is not a delectable dish, but from time to time a few leaves in a mixed salad add an agreeable tang, or chopped very fine and sprinkled on cold fish they have their place. At Bilignin a friend looking over the two vegetable gardens was surprised that there was no Henry IV spinach growing in either of them. It was the first time it had been spoken of to me. So obediently the next year Henry IV spinach was planted. There was no difference between it and ordinary spinach except that the Royal kind, as we got to calling it, grew on poles and one could gather it without stooping. On the other hand it bore less prolifically. For several years it was planted as a curiosity and amusement for our American friends. After three or four years it was no longer planted.

There was still another spinach which grew in the hot summer months without going to seed, called in French *Tetredragon,* which was known in the only American seed catalogues in which it was listed as New Zealand spinach.

The good Madame Roux, who in these early days of my apprenticeship would come into the garden when I was at work, interrupted the washing and ironing she was doing to give me tactful advice. From her I learned all that was taught me. It was not until the Occupation that she had the satisfaction of seeing the fruits of her effort. *Á propos* of the New Zealand spinach, she said it required a good deal of fertiliser, that what suited it best was *la crème de la crème,* and when she saw that I had no idea what that was, she explained that it meant pig's manure. She came into the garden with a large wheelbarrow of it next morning, and having secured a second one, we hastily found space for two lines. The leaf is small and thick, shaped like the leaf of the ivy, and the plant has a tendency to creep and to climb. In the Bugey it grows on short poles, but it is wayward. Deliciously tender when cooked, it is best when boiled as it is, without the addition of water after washing. Ten minutes in a covered saucepan and drained, put under the cold-water tap and drained again, the water thoroughly pressed out and returned to the saucepan—that is the right way to cook it. Then salt should be added and sour cream or butter in quantity. A half teaspoon of salt, and a pinch of ground nutmeg or a pinch of ground ginger or both, give the necessary flavour. There are so few people who care for spinach, but this way of preparing it has seduced a number of my friends.

From the United States every year a kind friend sent a little packet of sweet-corn seed grown and gathered by his mother. It was a great treat for us. At that time there was no table corn in France. The French grew corn for animals—in the Bugey, for the chickens. When it was known that we were growing it and eating it they considered us savages. No one was seduced by the young ears we gave them to taste. But what did astonish and please them were the giant globe tomatoes, not only red but yellow and white, and the very large Chinese globe egg plants, which held nearly a pint of stuffing each.

It was after seeing gumbo (or okra) growing in Méraude Guevara's garden in the south of France that gumbo seeds came to Bilignin. The plants flourished, almost alarmingly so. We couldn't eat half of what I gathered, and it was quite beyond our budget to keep the number of chickens with which to cook them. There were few lobsters and crabs in a small town so far from the sea as Belley. They were used, then, with river and lake fish, with veal, and in a mixed vegetable stew—not because the vegetable stew requires more than a dozen different ones, but because one has to commence to eat them in rotation the next day.

This delicious dish does not include gumbos, but ¾ cup of them thinly sliced and 1 cup hot *bouillon* could be added.

MACÉDOINE OF VEGETABLES

Cooked with freshly gathered spring vegetables this mixed-vegetable dish is exquisite.

In a fireproof pot which has a well-fitting cover put 3 tablespoons butter and 3 medium-sized onions cut in rings. When brown, add 6 hearts of lettuce,

2 cups shelled sweet peas, 2 cups string beans, 2 small round carrots, 6 round turnips, 1½ cups small new potatoes, 2 cups asparagus tips and 1 cup butter. Cover and cook over low flame. Shake the pot frequently and stir gently from the bottom occasionally with a wooden spatula or spoon. Be careful that the vegetables do not burn or scorch. After 1¾ hours add salt and pepper and cook for ¼ hour—2 hours in all.

This is one of the very best of vegetable dishes.

This is a richer version of it:

MACÉDOINE OF CREAMED VEGETABLES

Boil 1¼ cups shredded carrots, 1¾ cups shredded turnips and 1¾ cups shelled peas in 1 quart milk. Boil 1¾ cups string beans and 1¾ cups asparagus tips in salted water. Steam 3 large potatoes, peel and dice. Do not overcook any of these vegetables. In a saucepan over low heat melt 2 tablespoons butter, add 1 tablespoon flour, stir with wooden spoon. Slowly add the hot milk that remains after cooking the carrots, turnips and peas. Stir carefully so that the sauce is perfectly smooth. Allow to simmer for 10 minutes, stirring constantly, and then add 1 cup heavy cream. Bring to the boil and mix with vegetables, and salt and pepper. Bring to the boil again, stir to mix but do not allow to boil. Remove from flame and add 2 tablespoons butter. Do not stir but tip saucepan in all directions to mix. Serve at once.

Also an exquisite dish.

The summer vegetables were often cooked simply, but in late August and through the autumn more elaborately. Spiced and richer ways seemed appropriate. Often fresh herbs were boiled with them, or chopped, for those cooked in the oven. My taste for garlic is pronounced—friends say exaggerated—and there never seems to be too great a flavour of basil in vegetables, fish or meat. This is for country cooking; cooking in town does not admit of so much condimenting, or spicing for that matter.

Italian squash (zucchini) and egg plant (aubergine) can be prepared in the same way as

STUFFED BRAISED PEPPERS

Put through the meat chopper 1 cup raw lean veal and 1 cup ham. Mix well with the yolks of 2 eggs, 2 tablespoons fresh basil chopped fine, 2 tablespoons white wine, 1 tablespoon parsley chopped fine, salt and pepper, 1 cup chopped mushrooms previously cooked in 2 tablespoons butter, the juice of ½ lemon, salt and pepper, 3 tablespoons grated Parmesan cheese, ½ teaspoon cumin powder and ¼ teaspoon saffron. Cut in half, lengthwise, 3 red and 3 green sweet peppers, remove seeds and boil for exactly 2 minutes. Drain and wipe dry. Fill the peppers with the stuffing. Melt 5 tablespoons butter in a casserole with a tight-fitting cover. Place the stuffed peppers, not overlapping, in it. Moisten with a cup of hot chicken or veal stock. Add 2 cups chopped tomatoes. Cook covered over medium heat for 20 minutes. Remove peppers, place alternating yellow and red peppers on serving dish. Reduce sauce for a few minutes, then strain over peppers and serve.

This is a pleasant change from the too-frequently-served vegetable browned in the oven. The flavours marry well.

We were very proud of the artichokes the garden produced, too proud to do much to them until late autumn, when we ate this version of

ARTICHOKES À LA BARIGOULE

For 4 large artichokes put in a casserole with a tight-fitting cover over medium heat 5 tablespoons olive oil, 1 chopped onion and 2 diced carrots. Place the artichokes on these, leaves up, salt and pepper. Pour a little of the oil over the artichokes. Cover stirring occasionally. When the carrots and onions begin to brown add 1 cup white wine, 2 cloves of garlic and 2 twigs of fresh rosemary or 1 teaspoon powdered rosemary. Cook over low flame until a leaf can be removed from artichokes. Serve hot with sauce poured over artichokes.

Oyster plants (or salsify), beetroot and Jerusalem artichokes can be made appetising, though not delicate. They were planted each year, though one wondered why. The Jerusalem artichokes are redeemed by their agreeable substance. Oyster plants have no excuse for existing; they are long, too clean, have little flavour and are deservedly unpopular. Here the sauce justifies the time spent in preparing

OYSTER PLANT (SALSIFY) WITH WINE SAUCE

Melt 4 tablespoons butter in a casserole with a tight-fitting cover. Lightly brown in it 1 cup diced raw veal, 1 cup diced ham, 1 diced medium-sized carrot, ½ finely chopped medium-sized onion, 1 tablespoon finely chopped parsley, 1 of tarragon and 1 of chervil. Add ½ cup hot dry white wine and 1 cup hot *bouillon*. Bring to a boil. Add a pinch of powdered laurel and ¼ teaspoon pepper. Cover and cook gently for 2 hours. Clean and boil the oyster plant in salted water until nearly tender. Drain and tie in bunches like asparagus. Put in casserole and simmer for ½ hour. Add the juice of 1 lemon. Remove from flame and add 3 tablespoons butter in small pieces. Do not stir but tip casserole in all directions until butter is melted. Untie the oyster plants. Arrange neatly on preheated serving dish, pour the sauce over the oyster plants, and serve at once.

Celery root (celeriac) can be cooked in the same way. They will require not more than ¼ hour to boil and should, after being well drained, be cut in strips like potatoes for frying.

As for beetroots, their excuse for being is the fine colour they add to pale dishes. As a vegetable this recipe combines the decorative with the tasty.

PURÉE OF BEETROOT

Bake beetroots in oven till quite soft, peel and mash through strainer with a potato masher, add one-third their volume of thick cream sauce. Place over low heat in a casserole, add salt and pepper. When about to boil, add 1 tablespoon butter cut in small pieces to 2 cups *purée*. Do not allow to boil, do not stir but tip casserole in all directions. Serve in a mound on preheated dish. Sprinkle with chopped parsley. Or serve as a border around veal or pork roast.

Besides all the vegetables in the two gardens, there were the fruits and berries. Besides all the strawberries there were the raspberries which bore from the end of May all through the summer until December—the first snow did not discourage them. They were in a protected corner and were a lovely sight, growing as grape vines do in Lombardy. Attached to three rows of wire, each root was allowed six branches, three on either side. When one came upon them unexpectedly, one did not know what all the pendent clusters of colour could be. They never seemed real to me but a new and joyous surprise each morning. Every care they needed—and little enough did one pay for their beauty and for their incredible fertility—was more reward than labour. In spring the branches were tied on to the wires, and again later, so that the weight of the berries would not break the branches. Later still, there were new shoots from the root, and three or four of the healthiest were kept for the next year's bearing. The plants that were there when we came produced red berries. After we had secured a lease, we planted forty-eight white raspberries in the upper garden. They didn't thrive as well as the red, perhaps. As it was farther away from water and it was an exhausting effort to drag the hose so far, the upper garden had been chosen for the commoner vegetables—potatoes, pole beans and the marrow, squash and cucumber family. There was not room for more raspberries in the lower garden. The white ones were planted in lines near the currants, red, white and black, and the gooseberries. Unquestionably they felt they were not favoured, nor were they. They were not in the sun all day and never received the same attention as the red family below. The berries were much smaller but much sweeter. What a happy life it would be only to cultivate raspberries.

BLACK-CURRANT LIQUEUR

Wash and drain ½ lb. raspberries and 3 lbs. black currants. Mash them thoroughly. Cover with a cloth and put aside in a cool place for 24 hours. The next day add a handful of black-currant leaves that have been washed and dried, and 1 quart 90 per cent alcohol. Cover the bowl with a plate and put aside for 24 hours. On the third day place a sieve with a piece of fine linen over a bowl. Pour the fruit and the alcohol through, mashing with a heavy pestle or a potato masher. Put 3 lbs. sugar and ¾ quart water in an enameled saucepan. Stir until it commences to boil, over low heat. Boil for 5 minutes. Put aside until completely cold. Then add the syrup to the juice of the berries and the alcohol. Allow this to stand for several hours. Fit a filtering paper into a funnel and pour through it to fill the bottles. A filtering paper is bought at a good chemist's. This makes about 2¾ quarts.

This is not only served as a liqueur. In the Bugey it was poured into a glass filled with shaved ice. It was a very refreshing summer drink. A *mocha* (coffee) liqueur was also used for an iced drink. There were vulgarians who put whipped cream on top, and it was then called *à l'Américaine*—disparagingly, one is forced to acknowledge.

The gooseberries in France are four or five times larger than those grown in the United States, and very much sweeter. We grew a species that were raspberry coloured. They are cultivated like olive trees, the centre growths are removed as they appear—to give light and sun. Every year hornets would make a nest in the trunk of one of the bushes, and with a sharp knife I would have to cut it out. Wasps, hornets and bees rarely sting me, though my work with them has always been aggressive. Gertrude Stein did not care for any of them, nor for spiders, centipedes and bats. She had no violent feeling about them out of doors, but in the house she would call for aid. The instruments for getting rid of them were determination, newspapers, a broom and pincers. These were always effective.

A charming story of wifely and husbandly devotion was that of two of our friends. She did not wish her husband to be bored, annoyed or worried. When they were first married, she allowed him to believe that she was very much afraid of spiders. Whenever she saw him disturbed, she would call him with a wail, Darling, a spider; there, darling—don't you see it. He would come flying with a handkerchief, put it on the spot indicated, and, gathering up the imaginary spider would throw it into the garden. The wife would uncover her face and with a sigh say, How good and patient you are, dearest.

Rhubarb grew in the upper garden too. Two or three spring rhubarb tarts each year were not worth the space the rhubarb occupied, so they were rooted up and put on the compost heap. Melons too were not attempted after the first year. They required too much care, putting under glass and suppressing trailers and buds. In Paris we had a small room Gertrude Stein called the Salon des Refusés after the famous one at which the Impressionist painters showed their pictures the year when they had been refused admittance at the regular *salon*. Ours held the pictures Gertrude Stein refused—that is, pictures she had bought to find out what she felt about them and stored there when she found they did not interest her. In the garden it was simpler. When the *refusés* were rooted up and put on the compost heap, it caused no feeling from anyone involved.

Like all beans, pole beans flourish in French soil. In spite of reducing the number planted, there were always too many to gather. Then too they grew too high, nothing stopped them. Finally they were clipped at the top. To gather them was a problem not only because of the time it took but because of the narrow paths between rows. It wasn't practical to leave some steps out of doors, but by carefully balancing three very strong narrow wine cases one on top of the other and overlapping, the difficulty seemed overcome until one day we all came down in a heap dragging a pole and its garniture with us! A bruised leg put an end for a while to the beanstalk problem.

Fruits were neither as plentiful nor of so good a quality as the berries. When we came to Bilignin there was one pear, one plum and one apple tree in the garden, and all of them were old. With the landlord's permission we had the plum tree removed at once. Everything was done, but to no avail, to save the deep-rose-coloured pear tree. That left one excellent large apple tree. For an orchard it was not excessive—Gertrude Stein spoke of it as The Nucleus. We waited for three years until we secured a lease to plant apples, peaches, apricots and nectarines. The French like to plant fruit trees in the old-fashioned way, on the sunny side of the wall. There were only two such walls free, and a fine old laurel tree covered a part of one of them.

The laurel was a constant delight. There was a nameless mauve rose that cried for a border of laurel leaves. A bouquet of them was always in the bedroom of our young guests, writers and painters and occasionally musicians, as a symbol of a future wreath. None of them remarked the leaves.

The peaches, apricots and nectarines were not for long—they deteriorated in three or four years. It was not a soil or a climate that suited them. We were slow to learn this. As the apples were thriving, more of them replaced the fruits we were discarding. The famous Calville, of which the equally famous Calvados, an apple brandy, is not made, and the resembling Belles-Fleur Jaune, grew quickly and well. But fruit trees on a wall are not prolific. The Calvilles, sold by the piece in Paris, grow no more than forty to the tree. It was necessary to find a commoner, more hardy apple and to plant it in open ground—what the French, looking facts in the face, call open to the winds. And then we finally had an apple orchard. The forcing beds were returned to their sheltered home against the wall.

When autumn came, the last harvest was so occupying that one forgot that it meant leaving the garden for the return to Paris. Not only did the winter vegetables have to be gathered and placed to dry for a day before packing, but their roots and leaves had to be put on the compost heap with manure and leaves and packed down for the winter. The day the huge baskets were packed was my proudest in all the year. The cold sun would shine on the orange-coloured carrots, the green, yellow and white pumpkins and squash, the purple egg plants and a few last red tomatoes. They made for me more poignant colour than any post-Impressionist picture. Merely to look at them made all the rest of the year's pleasure insignificant. Gertrude Stein took a more practical attitude. She came out into the denuded wet cold garden and, looking at the number of baskets and crates, asked if they were all being sent to Paris, that if they were the *expressage* would ruin us. She thought that there were enough vegetables for an institution and reminded me that our household consisted of three people. There was no question that, looking at that harvest as an economic question, it was disastrous, but from the point of view of the satisfaction which work and aesthetic confer, it was sublime.

Our final, definite leaving of the gardens came one cold winter day, all too appropriate to our feelings and the state of the world. A sudden moment of sunshine peopled the gardens with all the friends and others who had passed through them. Ah, there would be another garden, the same friends, possibly, or no, probably new ones, and there would be other stories to tell and to hear. And so we left Bilignin, never to return.

And now it amuses me to remember that the only confidence I ever gave was given twice, in the upper garden to two friends. The first one gaily responded, How very amusing. The other asked with no little alarm, But, Alice, have you ever tried to write. As if a cook-book had anything to do with writing.

33

Summer Salad

MELISSA A. GOLDTHWAITE

On this morning of neglected pruning,
lopped and tumbling apple branches,
tiny green fists of fruit falling
to my feet, I breathe the air

thick with moisture, the scent
of just-mowed timothy
and clover rising, the throng
of mud-common chores crowding

my thoughts: more pruning, watering,
mowing, hauling. Last year's
wind-blown birch, cut and stacked,
still needs cover. The woodshed

nearly empty whispers dark
warnings of winter's freeze
and crunch, as certain as these
heat and swelter days of ripe

tomatoes and the sweet first ears of
corn. Skin sweat-slick, palms blister
red, I drop the pole pruner,
drag branches to the burn pile,

ache for the kitchen tile
cool balm underfoot, imagine
trading this plodding and pruning
for a dish of summer's abundance:

avocados wedged, kernels from the cob,
black beans, dice of tomato
and red onion with chopped parsley,
mixed and drizzled with a dressing

of whisked vinegar and oil, minced garlic,
a touch of cumin, salt and pepper all to taste,
to taste this living season: labor and heat
transformed in a bowl, beautiful and blue.

→ 34 ←

Reception

KATHY FAGAN

For the Romans, a barbarian
Was someone who wore trousers, had a beard, and ate butter.
Everyone else ate tomatoes.

From the Nahuatl *tomatl*, meaning *swelling*
Fruit, it must have reminded the Aztecs of the viscera
They witnessed at rituals of human sacrifice.

Nahuatl also gave us the names for chocolate, coyote, chili, and ocelet.
The tomato's Latin name, *Lycopersicon esculentum*, means
The edible wolf's peach.

Like all nightshades, the tomato contains poisonous alkaloids.
Grown strictly as an ornamental in England, a 1753 encyclopedia
Describes it as a fruit eaten only by "Spaniards,

Italians, and Jew families." An alternative name, *love apple*,
Is a probable misreading of the Italian name *pomodoro*.
Tomato is also recorded to mean *an attractive girl*.

For our wedding, we combined mouthful-sized
Chunks of heirloom tomato, roughly sliced Hungarian wax pepper,
Ribbons of purple onion,

Torn Italian basil, extra virgin
Olive oil, coarse kosher sea salt, and freshly ground pepper,
To make the family's *Insalata Pomodoro*,

A side dish for our guests. It was summer in Ohio;
Tomatoes were just coming on.
Four hundred miles southeast in 1789, Secretary of State

Thomas Jefferson had introduced the tomato
To the U.S. as part of a national nutrition program. The fruit
Wasn't commonly eaten, however, until decades later.

Our love salad was eaten by everyone in attendance.
Both children and adults sopped up the juices with fresh-baked bread;
They tilted the bowls to their wet mouths.

But before they were sliced and eaten,
The tomatoes had looked as livid as hearts,
And bore names like the roses I'd arranged at each table:

Brandy Wine, Black Prince, Ananas Noir,
Abraham Lincoln, Paul Robeson, Julia Child,
Lemon Boy, Flamme Orange, Green Zebra,

Marvel Stripe, Genovese Jewel, Chocolate Amazon,
Charlie's Mortgage Lifter, Buttery Azoychka, Gold-Shouldered Planet,
Purple Dog Creek, Bloody Butcher, Sweet Ocelot.

→ 35 ←

Potatoes and Love: Some Reflections

From *Heartburn*

NORA EPHRON

The Beginning

I have friends who begin with pasta, and friends who begin with rice, but whenever I fall in love, I begin with potatoes. Sometimes meat and potatoes and sometimes fish and potatoes, but always potatoes. I have made a lot of mistakes falling in love, and regretted most of them, but never the potatoes that went with them.

Not just any potato will do when it comes to love. There are people who go on about the virtues of plain potatoes—plain boiled new potatoes with a little parsley or dill, or plain baked potatoes with crackling skins—but my own feeling is that a taste for plain potatoes coincides with cultural antecedents I do not possess, and that in any case, the time for plain potatoes—if there is ever a time for plain potatoes—is never at the beginning of something. It is also, I should add, never at the end of something. Perhaps you can get away with plain potatoes in the middle, although I have never been able to.

All right, then: I am talking about crisp potatoes. Crisp potatoes require an immense amount of labor. It's not just the peeling, which is one of the few kitchen chores no electric device has been invented to alleviate; it's also that the potatoes, once peeled, must be cut into whatever shape you intend them to be, put into water to be systematically prevented from turning a loathsome shade of bluish-brownish-black, and then meticulously dried to ensure that they crisp properly. All this takes time, and time, as any fool can tell you, is what true romance is about. In fact, one of the main reasons why you must make crisp potatoes in the beginning is that if you don't make them in the beginning, you never will. I'm sorry to be so cynical about this, but that's the truth.

There are two kinds of crisp potatoes that I prefer above all others. The first are called Swiss potatoes, and they're essentially a large potato pancake of perfect hash browns; the flipping of the pancake is so wildly dramatic that the potatoes themselves are almost beside the point. The second are called potatoes Anna; they are thin circles of potato cooked in a shallow pan in the oven and then turned onto a plate in a darling mound of crunchy brownness. Potatoes Anna is a classic French recipe, but there is something so homely and old-fashioned about them that they can usually be passed off as either an ancient family recipe or something you just made up.

For Swiss potatoes: Peel 3 large (or 4 small) russet potatoes (or all-purpose if you can't get russets) and put them in cold water to cover. Start 4 tablespoons butter and 1 tablespoon cooking oil melting in a nice heavy large frying pan. Working quickly, dry the potatoes and grate them on a grating disk of the Cuisinart. Put them into a colander and squeeze out as much water as you can. Then dry them again on paper towels. You will need more paper towels to do this than you ever thought possible. Dump the potatoes into the frying pan, patting them down with a spatula, and cook over medium heat for about 15 minutes, until the bottom of the pancake is brown. Then, while someone is watching, loosen the pancake and, with one incredibly deft motion, flip it over. Salt it generously. Cook 5 minutes more. Serves two.

For potatoes Anna: Peel 3 large (or 4 small) russet potatoes (or Idahos if you can't get russets) and put them in water. Working quickly, dry each potato and slice into 1⁄16-inch rounds. Dry them with paper towels, round by round. Put 1 tablespoon clarified butter into a cast-iron skillet and line the skillet with overlapping potatoes. Dribble clarified butter and salt and pepper over them. Repeat twice. Put into a 425° oven for 45 minutes, pressing the potatoes down now and then. Then turn up the oven to 500° and cook 10 more minutes. Flip onto a round platter. Serves two.

The Middle (I)

One day the inevitable happens. I go to the potato drawer to make potatoes and discover that the little brown buggers I bought in a large sack a few weeks earlier have gotten soft and mushy and are sprouting long and quite uninteresting vines. In addition, one of them seems to have developed an odd brown leak, and the odd brown leak appears to be the cause of a terrible odor that in only a few seconds has permeated the entire kitchen. I throw out the potatoes and look in the cupboard for a box of pasta. This is the moment when the beginning ends and the middle begins.

The Middle (II)

Sometimes, when a loved one announces that he has decided to go on a low-carbohydrate, low-fat, low-salt diet (thus ruling out the possibility of potatoes, should you have been so inclined), he is signaling that the middle is ending and the end is beginning.

The End

In the end, I always want potatoes. Mashed potatoes. Nothing like mashed potatoes when you're feeling blue. Nothing like getting into bed with a bowl of hot mashed potatoes already loaded with butter, and methodically adding a thin cold slice of butter to every forkful. The problem with mashed potatoes, though, is that they require almost as much hard work as crisp potatoes, and when you're feeling blue the last thing you feel like is hard work. Of course, you can always get someone to make the mashed potatoes for you, but let's face it: the reason you're blue is that there isn't anyone to make them for you. As a result, most people do not have nearly enough mashed potatoes in their lives, and when they do, it's almost always at the wrong time.

(You can, of course, train children to mash potatoes, but you should know that Richard Nixon spent most of his childhood making mashed potatoes for his mother and was extremely methodical about getting the lumps out. A few lumps make mashed potatoes more authentic, if you ask me, but that's not the point. The point is that perhaps children should not be trained to mash potatoes.)

For mashed potatoes: Put 1 large (or 2 small) potatoes in a large pot of salted water and bring to a boil. Lower the heat and simmer for at least 20 minutes, until tender. Drain and place the potatoes back in the pot and shake over low heat to eliminate excess moisture. Peel. Put through a potato ricer and immediately add 1 tablespoon heavy cream and as much melted butter and salt and pepper as you feel like. Eat immediately. Serves one.

36

Repulsive Dinners: A Memoir

From *Home Cooking: A Writer in the Kitchen*

LAURIE COLWIN

There is something triumphant about a really disgusting meal. It lingers in the memory with a lurid glow just as something exalted is remembered with a kind of mellow brilliance. I am not thinking of kitchen disasters—chewy pasta, burnt brownies, curdled sauces: these can happen to anyone. I am thinking about meals that are positively loathsome from soup to nuts, although one is not usually fortunate enough to get either soup or nuts.

Bad food abounds in restaurants, but somehow a bad meal in a restaurant and a bad home-cooked meal are not the same: after all, the restaurant did not invite you to dinner.

My mother believes that people who can't cook should rely on filet mignon and boiled potatoes with parsley, and that they should be on excellent terms with an expensive bakery. But if everyone did that, there would be fewer horrible meals and the rich, complicated tapestry that is the human experience would be the poorer for it.

My life has been much enriched by ghastly meals, two of the awfulest of which took place in London. I am a great champion of English food, but what I was given at these dinners was neither English nor food so far as I could tell.

Once upon a time my old friend Richard Davies took me to a dinner party in Shepherd's Bush, a seedy part of town, at the flat of one of his oldest friends.

"What is he like?" I asked.

"He's a genius," Richard said. "He has vast powers of abstract thought." I did not think this was a good sign.

“How nice,” I said. “Can he cook?”

“I don’t know,” Richard said. “In all these years, I’ve never had a meal at his house. He’s a Scot, and they’re very mean.”

When the English say “mean,” they mean “cheap.”

Our host met us at the door. He was a glum, geniusy-looking person, and he led us into a large, bare room with a table set for six. There were no smells or sounds of anything being cooked. Two other guests sat in chairs, looking as if they wished there were an hors d’oeuvre. There was none.

“I don’t think there will be enough to go around,” our host said, as if we were responsible for being so many. Usually, this is not the sort of thing a guest likes to hear, but in the end we were grateful that it turned out to be true.

We drank some fairly crummy wine, and then when we were practically gnawing on each other’s arms, we were led to the table. The host placed a rather small casserole in the center. We peered at it hopefully. The host lifted the lid. “No peeking,” he said.

Usually when you lift the lid of a casserole that has come straight from the oven, some fragrant steam escapes. This did not happen, although it did not immediately occur to me that this casserole had not come straight from the oven, but had been sitting around outside the oven getting lukewarm and possibly breeding salmonella.

Here is what we had: the casserole contained a layer of partially cooked rice, a layer of pineapple rings and a layer of breakfast sausages, all of which was cooked in a liquid of some sort or other. Each person received one pineapple ring, one sausage and a large heap of crunchy rice. We ate in perfect silence, first in shock, then in amazement, and then in gratitude that not only was there not enough to go around, but that nothing else was forthcoming. That was the entire meal.

Later as Richard and I sat in the Pizza Express finishing off a second pie, I said: “Is that some sort of Scottish dish we had tonight?”

“No,” said Richard. “It is a genius dish.”

Several years later on another trip to London, Richard and I were invited to a dinner party in Hampstead. Our host and hostess lived in a beautiful old house, but they had taken out all the old fittings and the place had been redesigned in postindustrial futuristic.

At the door, our hostess spoke these dread words: "I'm trying this recipe out on you. I've never made it before. It's a medieval recipe. It looked very interesting."

Somehow I have never felt that "interesting" is an encouraging word when applied to food.

In the kitchen were two enormous and slightly crooked pies.

"How pretty," I said. "What kind are they?"

"They're medieval fish pies," she said. "A variation on starry gazey pie." Starry gazey pie is one in which the crust is slit so that the whole baked eels within can poke their nasty little heads out and look at the pie crust stars with which the top is supposed to be festooned.

"Oh," I said, swallowing hard. "In what way do they vary?"

"Well, I couldn't get eel," said my hostess. "So I got squid. It has squid, flounder, apples, onions, lots of cinnamon and something called gallingale. It's kind of like frankincense."

"I see," I said.

"It's from the twelfth or thirteenth century," she continued. "The crust is made of flour, water, salt and honey."

I do not like to think very often about that particular meal, but the third was worse.

It took place in suburban Connecticut on a beautiful summer evening. The season had been hot and lush, and the local markets were full of beautiful produce of all kinds. Some friends and I had been invited out to dinner.

"What will we have, do you think?" I asked.

"Our hostess said we weren't having anything special," my friends said. "She said something about an 'old-fashioned fish bake.'"

It is hard to imagine why those four innocent words sounded so ominous in combination.

For hors d'oeuvres we had something which I believe is called cheese food. It is not so much a food as a product. A few tired crackers were lying around with it. Then it was time for dinner.

The old-fashioned fish bake was a terrifying production. Someone in the family had gone fishing and had pulled up a number of smallish fish—no one was sure what kind. These were partially cleaned and not thoroughly scaled and then flung into a roasting pan. Perhaps to muffle their last screams, they were smothered in a thick blanket of sour cream and then pelted with raw chopped onion. As the coup de grâce, they were stuck in a hot oven for a brief period of time until their few juices ran out and the sour cream had a chance to become grainy. With this we were served boiled frozen peas and a salad with iceberg lettuce.

Iceberg lettuce is the cause of much controversy. Many people feel it is an abomination. Others have less intense feelings, but it did seem an odd thing to have when the market five minutes away contained at least five kinds of lettuce, including Oakleaf, Bibb and limestone.

For dessert we had a packaged cheesecake with iridescent cherries embedded in a topping of cerise gum and light tan coffee.

As appears to be traditional with me, a large pizza was the real end of this grisly experience.

But every once in a while, an execrable meal drags on way past the closing times of most pizzerias. You straggle home starving, exhausted, abused in body and spirit. You wonder why you have been given such a miserable dinner, a meal you would not serve to your worst enemy or a junkyard dog. You deserve something delicious to eat, but there is nothing much in the fridge.

You might have egg and toast, or a glass of hot milk, or toasted cheese, but you feel your spirit crying out for something more.

Here is the answer: rösti. Rösti is a Swiss grated potato dish. In reality it is an excuse for eating a quarter of a pound of butter. While your loved one is taking a hot shower or mixing a drink, you can get to work.

Take off your coat and plunge one large Idaho potato into boiling water. By the time you have gotten into your pajamas and hung up your clothes, it is time to take it out—seven minutes, tops. This seems to stabilize the starch.

Gently heat a large quantity (half a stick) of unsalted butter in a skillet. It should foam but not turn brown. Grate the potato on the shredder side of the grater, press into a cake and slip into the butter. Fry till golden brown on both sides.

The result is somewhat indigestible, but after all, you have already been subjected to the truly indigestible. You will feel better for it. You and your companion—or you yourself (this recipe makes two big cakes: if you are alone, you can have both all to yourself)—will begin to see the evening's desecrations as an amusement.

Because you *are* the better for your horrible meal: fortified, uplifted and ready to face the myriad surprises and challenges in this most interesting and amazing of all possible worlds.

37

The Demystification of Food

From *Vibration Cooking: Or, The Travel Notes of a Geechee Girl*

VERTAMAE SMART-GROSVENOR

In reading lots and lots of cookbooks written by white folks it occurred to me that people very casually say Spanish rice, French fries, Italian spaghetti, Chinese cabbage, Mexican beans, Swedish meatballs, Danish pastry, English muffins and Swiss cheese. And with the exception of black bottom pie and niggertoes, there is no reference to black people's contribution to the culinary arts. White folks act like they invented food and like there is some weird mystique surrounding it—something that only Julia and Jim can get to. There is no mystique. Food is food. Everybody eats!

And when I cook, I never measure or weigh anything. I cook by vibration. I can tell by the look and smell of it. Most of the ingredients in this book are approximate. Some of the recipes that people gave me list the amounts, but for my part, I just do it by vibration. Different strokes for different folks. Do your thing your way.

The amount of salt and pepper you want to use is your business. I don't like to get in people's business. I have made everything in here and found everything to be everything and everything came out very together. If you have any trouble, I would suggest that you check out your kitchen vibrations. *What kind of pots are you using?* Throw out all of them except the black ones. The cast-iron ones like your mother used to use. Can't no Teflon fry no fried chicken. I only use black pots and brown earthenware in the kitchen. White enamel is not what's happening.

I don't like fancy food. I like simple—plain—ordinary—call it what you choose. I like what is readily available. It is very easy to do special things. Like a cake you only make on your first cousin by your mother's second marriage's birthday. Or a ham you make for Sam's wedding anniversary every other February 29. I'm talking about being able to turn the daily ritual of cooking for your family into a beautiful everyday happening. Now, that's something else again.

The supermarket is full of exciting and interesting food. It doesn't really matter where you live. After a minute, there ain't but so many ways you can cook a sweet potato. I remember at a market on Rue Monge in Paris I saw some potatoes that looked very much in the sweet potato family. I asked and the lady said, "*C'est le pomme de terre douce.*" She said that they came from Madagascar. Just then a sister from Senegal came by. I asked her how they cooked them and where she came from and she said, "We make tarts . . ." (nothing but sweet potato pie); "We fry them in butter and sugar . . ." (nothing but candied sweet potatoes); "We roast them in the oven . . ." (nothing but baked sweet potatoes). It don't matter if it's Dakar or Savannah, you can cook exotic food any time you want. Just turn on the imagination, be wiling to change your style and let a little soul food in. Ayischia says you are what you eat and that's what I believe, too.

An evening with good food and good vibrations from the people with whom you're eating—that's the kind of evening that turns me on. I like men who enjoy food. Cooking for a man is a very feminine thing, and I can't understand how a woman can feed her man TV dinners. Food is sexy and you can tell a lot about people and where they're at by their food habits. People who eat food with pleasure and get pleasure from the different stirring of the senses that a well-prepared food experience can bring are my kind of people.

Like Archie says, "Eating is a very personal thing; you can't eat with everybody." Some people got such bad vibrations that to eat with them would give you indigestion. I would rather give such a person money to go to Horn & Hardart than to eat with 'em. God knows, I've had some good times eating with my friends. What times! Times, oh times! I often get nostalgia for the old days and old friends. Like those New Year's open houses I used to have and everyone I loved would come. Even Millie came from Germany one year. She arrived just in time for the black-eyes and rice. And that year I cooked the peas with beef neck bones instead of swine cause so many brothers and sisters have given up swine. I had ham hocks on the side for the others. You supposed to cook the whole hog head but I couldn't. I saw it hanging in the butcher store on Avenue D and I didn't dig it. I left the swine hanging right where he was.

If you eat black-eyed peas and rice (Hopping John) on New Year's Day, you supposed to have good luck for the coming year. Black people been eating that traditional New Year's Day dinner for years. That's why I'm not having no more open house on New Year's Day. I'm going to try something new. Like Kali says,

It's a New Kind of Day
It's a New Kind of Day
It's the love that make
a New kind of day

HOPPING JOHN

Cook black-eyed peas.
When they are almost done add rice.
Mix rice and peas together.
Season and—*voila!*—you got it.

And speaking of rice. I was sixteen years old before I knew that everyone didn't eat rice every day. Us being geechees, we had rice every day. When you said what you were eating for dinner, you always assumed that rice was there. That was one of my jobs too. To cook the rice. A source of pride to me was that I cooked rice like a grown person. I could cook it till every grain stood by itself. What you do is to rub it together in the palms of your hands and make sure you get all grains washed. Then you put it in a pot with cold water.

Use 1 part rice to 2 parts water. Always use cold water. Let it come to a boil and cover it with a tight cover. Soon as it comes to a boil you turn it to simmer and you cover with a tight cover. Let it cook for exactly 13 minutes and then cut it off. Let it stand for 12 minutes before eating.

38

How to Cook Moong Dal, Bengali Style

DEBORAH THOMPSON

. . . as told by Rajiv's Bengali mother
to his American wife
three years after his death

Again I will tell you. This time you will remember?

You need *moong dal,* which you have purchased from Indian grocery. You know moong dal? Means split moong beans without skin. Remember without skin.

What you have done with recipe that Raju had copied out? You have lost it? You must learn to cook Indian. It is not too late. Remember we are still your culture-in-law.

You need turmeric, dry red chilis, green chilis, onion, and vegetables—best if you can get bitter gourd, which you must purchase from Indian grocery, from Sardarji. Is good for digestion.

You remember bitter gourd? You have forgotten everything.

You must prepare *panchphoran*—Bengali panchphoran, which you cannot buy proper mix even in Indian grocery, which is equal amounts *kalonji, methi,* white cumin seeds, and fennel seeds. You must prepare yourself. Best to keep already mixed a tin of panchphoran. Remember this.

What you have done with all of Raju's spices? Do you still have? You must use. They do not last forever, remember.

Then? Heat oil in pot—just little bit oil, not like your American way, just little little. Add panchphoran; add dry red chilis. Fry until it splutters. Fry until smoke makes you cough, makes you cry.

Add onion and simmer until onion becomes translucent. Brown but translucent. Add dal, means beans. Without skin, remember. Add haldi, means turmeric. Add green chilis. Stir on low heat until they are little bit fried. Raju he preferred lot of chili, lot of turmeric.

If you use plastic stir spoons turmeric will not wash off. Raju left many spoons yellow, isn't it? Do you still have? Yellow stain is permanent.

Add water. Add more water.

Cover and simmer. Then? Take some rest.

What have you done with Raju's cooking books? You still have? What about rest of his books? So many books. You have given away? And his clothes? Now it is only remembering.

So. Cook beans until they split easily.

Now is time to add bitter gourd.

This time you will remember?

Remember without skin.

You must write it down.

39

Food and Belonging: At "Home" and in "Alien-Kitchens"

KETU H. KATRAK

Aromas at Amy Villa, 675 Parsi Colony (near Vadala Market), Dadar, Bombay 14. India. Dawn. The sun's first rays kiss the Arabian Sea. *Om jaye jagdish hare*. . . . Clanging sounds from the kitchen enter my waking body as mouth-watering aromas waft in—moist *chapatis, kando-papeto, kheechree-kadhi, papeta ma gosh*. These word-sounds in Gujarati, my mother tongue, carry the tastes and aromas that are lost in their English translations: *chapatis*, round flat wheat bread roasted on an iron griddle; *kando-papeto*, onions and potatoes spiced with pepper and ginger; *kheechree-kadhi*, spiced yoghurt sauce eaten with rice; *papeta ma gosh*, meat and potato stew. And their tastes and aromas are as different from English food as the sound of their names. Even after two hundred years in India, the British did not improve their cuisine.

Om jaye jagdish hare . . . is playing loudly in the living room, on Vividhbharati, our local Bombay radio station. *Om jaye jagdish hare*, Vividhbharati's signature tune is a popular hymn, a Sanskrit *bhajan* whose rounded notes mingle with the Avesta prayers being recited devoutly by my father. *Om jaye jagdish . . . yatha ahu vahiro, om jaye jagdish . . . kemna mazada, moveyte payum dada, yethma dregava*. Our Zoroastrian prayers are in the ancient Avesta and Pahlavi languages. Our mother tongue is Gujarati, adopted a long time ago when the Zoroastrians fled Persia and came to India around 1350.

All these sounds mingle with the aromatic spices wafting over my waking body. The sounds of prayer and smells of *chapatis* and vegetables weave into a pattern of belonging, of home-sounds and home-aromas. In Bombay, certain foods, such as bread and milk, are delivered to our door: tring tring: *paowalla* (fresh bread delivered to the door); tring tring: *doothwalla* (milkman); tring tring: *kerawalla* (banana-seller); tring tring: *tarkariwalli* (vegetable seller). Lots of traffic. No chance of lying quietly in bed! These words that simultaneously convey the food and a particular food-seller in a single musical sound lose their power when split into their English units. But worse even, *paowalla, doothwalla, kerawalla,* so familiar to me in India sound exotic in this, my American-alien-home context. How does one create the truth of one's life without slipping into outsiderness?

I love to shake out my half-sleep with a cup of hot tea, prepared with lemon grass and mint leaves, and it tastes even better when made by my mother. I keep lingering in that safe pace of being held in unspoken love. Waking up would be to leave it. Softly, like childhood.

As a child, I remember that the kitchen was expected to be my mother's domain though she was not happy inhabiting that space. She is a very fine and intuitive cook, but her spirit of accomplishment was often snuffed out by my father's critical palate. He was a Victorian man, born in 1902, authoritarian and domineering, certainly with a rigid sense of male and female roles and the sexual division of labor: he went to the office, and my mother cooked and took care of us at home. My father, the only son who lost his father when he was barely fourteen, was thrust into adult male responsibility, looking after his mother and two sisters. A highly motivated person, he put himself through school, determined to get an education and to raise his family's economic status. In the 1920s, his patriarchal status within his own family was never challenged, and with a college degree and an income, his male status was strengthened further. His doting mother spoiled him in terms of his expectations of food. Her identity and love were focused on making my father happy with varieties of homemade pickles, elaborate delicacies, and snacks. He began to regard such labor and such love as normative roles for women, especially within the parameters of home.

When my father got married, he expected the same kind of culinary performances from his wife. He expected my mother to embrace this role wholeheartedly. My mother, newly married, had to find a way to negotiate her own identity between the demanding personalities of a strong husband and a domineering mother-in-law who still wanted to play a role in her son's happiness at home. The classic scenario of an older woman oppressing her younger daughter-in-law was true in my family. Women in this patriarchal power structure gain power as mothers of sons; their seniority accords them the dubious privilege of dominating their young daughters-in-law in the joint family.

By the time I was growing up, being the last of five siblings, my parents had lived through two world wars, had moved from Calcutta to Nagpur, and finally had settled in Bombay. My memories of food as a child are filled with not tasting the food, with feeling tense and fearful about the conflicts between my parents that erupted inevitably around the dining table. My father, a fastidious connoisseur of food, often found something missing and would be vocal about it. He craved a delicate, subtle blending of flavors; he envisioned every meal as a work of art. So, with *kheechree-kadhi*, he had to have a *papad*, with *dhan-shak* (a heavily spiced Zoroastrian dish that combines five varieties of dals, or lentils, with vegetables), he had to have a particular kind of *kachumber* (a salad made of onions, tomatoes, fresh coriander leaves, and green chilies) and lime, and on and on. If some condiment, pickle, or appropriate chutney were missing, he would vent his distress, would enjoin my mother to leave the table, and gratify his needs. The table was the place where he expressed whatever frustrations he dealt with at work. He never talked about work at home, not that my mother was much interested.

My father's work—as chartered accountant for the Tata Steel Company—earned him considerable respect. The Tata, a multi-faceted industrialist company, played a key role in developing India's industrial base prior to and after independence from the British in 1947. The Tata companies shared a certain nationalist spirit that my father imbibed and practiced in his activist work during India's independence struggle. My father was a Gandhian and was so convinced of the Gandhian philosophy of supporting Indian-made versus European goods that he ran a modest Sarvodaya (homemade, indigenous goods) store in Bombay. The centerpiece of Gandhian philosophy was *khadi* (home-spun cotton), and my father imbibed the politics of *khadi* so integrally and devoutly that from the 1930s until his death in 1992, he wore *khadi*. This often distressed relatives abroad who were used to bringing back "phoren-made" clothes. I remember my father's stories about his involvement with Gandhi's Quit India movement in the 1940s, and the sheer exuberance of that midnight hour on August 15, 1947, when the country became independent.

As a child, I knew very little about my father's political activism as a Gandhian nationalist, nor did I understand his forthright manner, and at times stark honesty, in abiding by his convictions. My father was a distant and powerful influence, whose impact I realized only later in life, and I still retain some perhaps unfair memories of my father, all centered around the dining table, the site of conflicts between my parents.

Food was not pleasurable to me as a child. Thinking about this now as an adult, I can say that food was an overdetermined category for me; it tasted of the conflictual relationship my parents shared; it smelt of the heady tropical environment; it delineated who was in and out of favor with my father. I tasted anxiety in the onions fried a bit too brown and tension in the too many dark, burned spots on the roasted *papads*. One never knew what would be considered faulty at a particular meal, and the uncertainty overwhelmed any pleasure in what was eaten. The walls around our dining table must hold those memories of silent anxiety, of quiet fear, retaining those emotions even after the white-washing given them by painters every two years. My parents wanted that newness and freshness on the walls but underneath the layers of paint, long memories still throb.

As a child, I used to think that all this trouble of cooking was for naught, a waste of time, hours of chopping, grinding spices, stirring, sautéing, frying, boiling, and all consumed so quickly and without any appreciation or acknowledgement of the hard work. It was not customary for that generation to compliment the cook as it is common nowadays among my peers and with my sisters and their husbands. Perhaps because my mother's work was rendered so invisible and unrewarded, I did not want any part of it. It took me many years, and a long journey halfway around the world, from Bombay to the United States, before I understood the reasons behind my resistance. As a child and later as an adolescent, I had observed (though I can only now articulate this) that cooking did not give my mother any authority within the family hierarchy. I recall a deep sense of her powerlessness and invisibility—so much effort and so little acknowledgement. I was stopped short in my sadness for her. I could not enjoy the food, and I could not articulate why I felt distressed. Looking back now, her situation and my response seem to be dictated by the power structure within a joint family's hierarchy. Since the greatest authority was enjoyed by my father, I identified with him rather than with my mother.

The conflicts that seeped into our meals around the dining table filled me with unexpressed rage against my father. At that age, I did not have the vocabulary or the intellectual tools to speak up for my mother. Usually, she acquiesced quietly. That was her role. No argument. Period. Later in her own life, in her seventies, I have been fascinated at my mother's own growing feminism. She began to resist by simply refusing to comply with certain demands. Although she never abandoned her responsibilities, she began to express the limits of what she would do.

My mother cooked because she had to. That was not her passion. But she handled this chore so efficiently, and despite the invisibility of her labor, with love. She would rise very early and labor to complete the cooking for the entire day. At home, the afternoon meal is a hot cooked meal quite unlike the cold sandwich that is so common in Western cultures. (When my mother visited me in the States, and when she spent time with my brothers in Australia, she said that she'd take a serious break from sandwiches when she returned to India!) At home, we had a large, cylindrical cooker, about three feet tall with a coal *sagdi* (heater). The coals would be lit and crackling very early in the morning, and the *sagdi*'s smoky smell mingled with the spices as they were fried in order to be added to the vegetables, the rice, and on certain days, the meat before all the various pots were placed into the cooker. All the aluminum pots were stacked up—beginning with meat at the bottom, closest to the highest heat—and four to five different dishes cooked at once.

Most of our cooking began with chopping and frying onions. As my father remarked jokingly to me, "However much you study, and however highly educated you are, ultimately you will always have to chop onions." He did not mean to be unsupportive about my education and career; in fact, he encouraged and provided emotional and material support for not only my brothers' but also my sisters' higher studies. It is thanks to him that I am in the United States today. Nonetheless, for him, all such intellectual labor had to be balanced for women by our culinary abilities.

My mother had help in chopping the onion, garlic, ginger—the staples for most of our cooking. At times, our *bai* would grind the spices such as cumin, coriander, roasted peanuts, and many other varieties of spices in seed form that I am unable to translate on a grindstone with a heavy grinder that looked like a thick, stone rolling pin. This was in the days before grinders became common. And I recall our *bai* being very upset when my sister returned from her studies in France with a mixer/blender.

My sister thought that it would ease the hard work; our *bai* was worried that this gadget would make her dispensable.

As a young girl, I helped my mother—chopping onions, observing, and soaking the flavors almost through the pores of my skin where those memories were held intact. Years later, I tapped into those early remembrances that seem to be held as lovingly in my body as in my mind.

My mother longed to complete her cooking chores and would prepare all the food in the morning for the entire day. In some other communities in India, women are enjoined to prepare each meal just before it is eaten, and as a result spend most of their day inside the kitchen walls, but my mother was always very clear about not doing that. She'd often complete all the cooking by the time my father left for his office, around 8:30 a.m. Then she would be free for the rest of the day to spend time with her most beloved activity—painting on fabric, on sarees, scarves, and runners, creating magic in color, an activity that she enjoys to this day in her eighty-fifth year. I remember my mother most at peace with herself when engrossed at her painting table. My mother painted forget-me-nots, daffodils, poppies, flowers that I had never seen in Bombay. I wonder now why my mother always painted foreign flowers, not our own bougainvilleas, shoeflowers, *gulmohur*. She used to go to an art class at the J. J. Institute of Art in Bombay during the thirties and forties where, I guess, they taught her as part of our colonial heritage that foreign flowers were better. Ironically, they became more real to her than the ones in our own backyard.

Growing up in an atmosphere of unspoken love, I never recognized my mother's incredible creativity, not just in her obvious talents as a painter, but in her artistry in the activities of daily living, particularly in her inventiveness in creating new recipes without taking any credit; her practical creativity in creating my lunch-packets to take to college. Putting together meals from minimal ingredients, knowing how to replace one missing ingredient with another, not complaining, and accomplishing delightful feasts.

My own memory banks about food overflowed only after I left India to come to the United States as a graduate student. The disinterest in food that I had felt during my childhood years was transformed into a new kind of need for that food as an essential connection with home. I longed for my native food as I dealt with my dislocation from the throbbing Bombay metropolis with its dust; crowded public buses and trains; the prevalence of so many languages on the street, Hindi, Gujarati, Marathi; and to this strange new world in the quiet insularity of Bryn Mawr College with its academic-towerish atmosphere, where I was one of few foreigners, exotic and exoticized. English language only. American food only. Language, languish, anguish of belonging. Institutional cafeteria food in the graduate dorm. As cafeteria food goes, I suppose that it was decent, but suddenly, I was so bereft, longing for those early morning aromas of spices mingling with the igniting coals. I kept a packet of garam masala in my dorm room and would often close my eyes and take a long whiff in order to be transported to my tropical home in Bombay.

Cafeteria food and a new geography mingled in alienness. There were new trees and flowers, new and shiny trains, and everything was so orderly and quiet that the silence rang out to my ears that were used to the bustle of crowds, the chaos and shouting of the Bombay locals. My spirit inhabited a new sky, and new air getting crisper as fall slid into winter and I encountered snow for the first time in my life. The alienness deepened as a white landscape replaced a perpetually green one at home.

Moving from the dorm into apartment living—and learning an American-style independence—I began to cook Indian food, to invent several recipes, creating from memory, from observing my mother, following the trail of appropriate tastes and smells—add some turmeric, pop the mustard seeds (the black ones) in hot oil (careful not to burn them), add cumin seeds, fry in the basmati rice and add water. Bring to a boil and as the aromas waft in, be transported into other skies. My Amherst friends call this "Yellow rice."

A recipe has so many different hands and minds in its history—I cannot recall who taught me what, and what parts I invented. That is the boundaryless pleasure of cooking: no one authorship. What counts is the final taste. *Rye na Papeta,* which my friends call "Ketu's potatoes." Yes, today, I cook this dish, but many hands and minds are part of its history and its success.

Today, homesickness often drives me (sometimes for miles depending on where I am) in search of a samosa, or *masala chai,* a spiced tea, or *masala dosa,* the paper-thin pancakes made of different dals and filled with spiced potatoes, or sweet *lassi,* a sweetened yoghurt drink. The fullness and varied nature of Indian cuisine, so regionally diverse, was very much a part of my life in Bombay, a cosmopolitan community of Gujaratis,

Tamilians, Maharashtrians, and Zoroastrians among other communities, each with its own special flavors in spicing and cooking. Luckily, even in the United States, I've never had to live in a place where I would panic about running out of coriander or cumin and not being able to find these in a specialty store. It's part of a pilgrimage "home" for me to visit the Indian grocery stores wherever there is a sizeable South Asian presence—as India Food and Spices in Cambridge, Massachusetts, my savior when I'm in Amherst, or Bharat Bazar in Los Angeles.

Food and home. Returning home through the tastebuds, through the aromas. Now, having homes in so many locations, different foods also provide a kind of anchor for my wandering spirit—the reliable predictability of eating at our corner Greek restaurant after sharing a yoga class with my close friends in Northampton, breathing in unison, and eating in unity, falafel, souvlakia, salad and tzaziki sauce. Breathing consciously for our hour-and-a-half yoga class connects us with our bodies, renews our bodily location, connects mind and body, integrates body, soul, and spirit. Here, accepting this body as home, I often try to rest and stop my frantic search for another home. From that space of belonging, touched at times fleetingly, at other times deeply as in intense meditation, I can touch the limits of my being often in turmoil in alien-homes.

Sitting cross-legged in lotus position, eyes closed, breathing in and breathing out—yogic practice brings me home to myself, takes me home to India, brings me home into my body. My body. As a child, I used to observe my father practicing yoga—he usually did the headstand. I was too fearful then. Now as an adult, and living in this foreign home, I discover the ancient principles of yoga, simple and profound. Yoga in Northampton—a sort of West meets East, the United States and India, at times a polarity, at other times a harmonious weaving together of many colored strands of values, music, languages, rhythms. Chanting Sanskrit *slokas* (religious words and syllables) with many-flavored accents in America; relaxing to the sounds of New Age rhythms. Mind and body integrating, the many public and private selves weaving together in a harmonious tapestry. Like a vast ocean, joyously exuberant and incredibly calming. Yoga's symmetry and asanas center my wandering spirit.

The body is home. This writing is home. The body into which we put food is our first and most inescapable home. As basic as breathing in and breathing out, as the breath consciously washes over the body, it calls up the mind, finding that space of rich silence, a kind of emptiness that is very full with a vibrant peacefulness. From that space of wholeness there is a language that is similar to the language of food—the tongue that speaks and the tongue that tastes. This is the speaking of my mother tongue Gujarati, but I also claim this alien English tongue that speaks and tastes. As the poet Kamala Das puts it, "I speak three languages, write in / Two, dream in one. Don't write in English they said, / English is not your mother-tongue. Why not leave / Me alone, critics, friends. . . . / The language I speak / Becomes mine." This body that breathes, that craves breath, water, and food is home. And this body finds new language-homes and new food-homes sharing and mingling spices and friendships. This body is home. This writing is home. Its labyrinthine journeys weave soul, sinew, and mind into union.

KETU'S RICE

1 cup rice, preferably basmati
2 cups water
1 tablespoon vegetable oil
½ teaspoon each black mustard seeds, turmeric, and cumin seeds
¼ teaspoon salt (an important ingredient, use unless you have a dietary restriction)

1. Wash rice and soak in cold water for at least 10 minutes.
2. Heat oil in heavy bottom pot with tight fitting lid. Add mustard seeds when oil is hot enough to pop seeds. When you think it has reached the right temperature, drop in one seed. If it pops immediately, the oil is ready. Cover pot immediately, reduce heat, and shake pot as if making popcorn until you no longer hear the seeds popping.
3. Lower heat and add turmeric, cumin seeds, and salt. Cook for a minute or two, stirring at all times.
4. Add thoroughly drained rice and stir until grains are well coated with oil and spices.
5. Add water, raise heat to high, and bring to a boil. Reduce heat to low, cover pot, and cook for 25 minutes. Rice will be fragrant and beautiful yellow color. Serves 4.

YELLOW POTATOES

4 white potatoes
¼ cup vegetable oil
1 green chili (or to taste), finely diced
1 teaspoon each mustard seeds, turmeric, and chopped ginger
juice of one lime
a few strings of cilantro, chopped
salt to taste

1. Peel and cut potatoes into small (¼ inch) dice.
2. Heat oil in heavy bottom pot with lid and add mustard seeds when oil is hot enough to pop them. When you think the oil has reached the right temperature, drop in one seed. If it pops immediately the oil is ready. Cover pot immediately, reduce heat, and shake pot as if making popcorn until you no longer hear the seeds popping.
3. Lower heat and add the potatoes, stir well. Cover pot and cook for about 10 minutes, until the potatoes are half-cooked.
4. Add chopped chili, ginger, turmeric, and salt, stirring until potatoes are coated with spices. Cover and cook for about 15 minutes or until potatoes are cooked, stirring often and adding more oil if potatoes stick to pan.
5. When potatoes are done add lime juice and cilantro. Serves 4.

PART VI

Desserts

The final course of a meal—dessert—may consist of a sweet dish, such as pie, pudding, cake, cookies, or ice cream; cheese and fruit; or even nuts. Ancient peoples enjoyed fruits and nuts (sometimes rolled in honey) at the end of their meals. As technology changed—especially with the manufacturing of cane sugar granules in the Middle Ages—options for desserts expanded across Europe. In the Renaissance, as sugar became more available to the middle classes, dessert courses—confusingly called "banquets"—became marks of household distinction, including cakes, tarts, candied fruits and vegetables, and elaborate "marchpane" (or marzipan) sculptures akin to the ornate and multi-tiered structures of contemporary wedding cakes. In the mid-sixteenth century, Elizabeth I is said to have been presented with marchpanes in shapes as varied as a chessboard, a castle tower replete with soldiers and artillery, and even a replica of St. Paul's church.[1]

Many of the desserts we are familiar with today were also prepared early in America's history. For example, Amelia Simmons, in her 1796 *American Cookery*, offered directions for making a variety of puddings, tarts, custards, cakes, and cookies—from rice pudding to gingerbread. A century later, similar desserts were popular, but others, especially ones served cold, also found a place in cookbooks. Fannie Merritt Farmer, in her *Boston Cooking-School Cook Book*, includes an entire chapter on ices, ice creams, and other frozen desserts.

The twentieth century brought increased manufacturing, which also affected the widespread availability of desserts—from candy bars to various desserts prepared from canned foods. In the beginning of the twentieth century, Hershey's chocolate bars were introduced and became an important ingredient in the newly developed Devil's Food Cake—a chocolate version of the already popular Angel Food Cake. In the 1930s, cookbook chapters on desserts looked similar to earlier American cookbooks but with one notable difference: the incorporation of canned foods. Irma Rombauer, in her 1931 *Joy of Cooking*, provided directions for freezing a can of fruit and serving slices of the frozen fruit and juice with whipped cream.

In this section, we include Kate Moses's "Baking for Sylvia"—an essay largely about the poet Sylvia Plath, who was an avid baker and, ironically, committed suicide by breathing in gas from her oven. The recipe Moses includes is one that Plath used for tomato soup cake, which includes canned soup. Moses characterizes the recipe as "a Depression-era holdover, like putting corn flakes in a meatloaf"—practices that might surprise, even repulse, some modern cooks but that provide convenience and economy for others. Although the idea of cake that includes canned tomato soup does not appeal to Moses, she observes, "It gave Sylvia Plath comfort, and for that reason alone I would be willing to make it."

As the twentieth century continued, technology further affected desserts—and advice for cooking—with the rise of prepackaged foods and the ubiquity of microwave ovens. In the one-hundredth-anniversary edition of *The Fannie Farmer Cookbook* published in 1996, editor Marion Cunningham reminds readers that they should not try to bake cakes, cookies, or pies in the microwave, even as she states that it is "like unearthing a collection of old treasures to discover the goodness of the simple desserts that families loved in the last century" and that they are more "delicious than commercially packaged desserts."[2] Alice Waters echoes such a sentiment in her choice of dessert recipes for her 2007 *The Art of Simple Food,* which includes recipes for both winter and summer fruit compotes (made from fresh fruits, not canned), candied citrus peel, and candied nuts—showing that the kinds of desserts enjoyed centuries ago, such as the Renaissance penchant for candied fruits, can still be enjoyed in the twenty-first century.

Within this section, we have chosen recipes for literal desserts as well as ones that take into account metaphorical uses of the word *dessert.* Originally from the Latin *dis + servir,* meaning "to remove what has just been served," that is, to clear the table, *dessert* is now sometimes associated with the phrase *just deserts,* also from the root *servir,* which has come to refer to those who get what they deserve—although it is not something pleasant or delicious. CrimethInc. Ex-Workers' Collective provides a recipe for serving up precisely this kind of "just desserts." They dictate two essential ingredients in their essay "Pie Throwing": a deserving target as well as crazed, pie-slinging assailant(s).

In turn, in "The Assurance of Caramel Cake," Maya Angelou offers both a literal recipe for a dessert as well as a narrative that shows someone also getting her "just desserts." When Angelou was a child, traumatized by sexual assault, she stopped talking. One of her teachers, in an attempt to force the young girl to speak, slapped Maya across the face. When Angelou's grandmother found out, she marched down to the school and slapped the teacher across the face—in front of a classroom of children. When Maya arrived home from school that day, she found that her grandmother, known as "Momma," had baked a caramel cake for her. As Angelou's uncle states, "This cake can't pay you for being slapped in the face. Momma made it just to tell you how much we love you and how precious you are."

Yet usually Americans think of "desserts" as rewards, not punishments—as sweets for the sweet. From sweet memories of preparing dessert with a parent, as we see in Cheryl Quimba's poem "Suman sa Ibos," to a fairy tale that links hunger to erotic desire, as we see in Caitlin Newcomer's short story "All the Old Tales Are Tales of Hunger"; from a solitary pie baker feeling as if she is "handmaiden to a miracle," as Judith Moore describes herself in "Pie," to a community comforting and caring for the bereaved by bringing lemon chess pie or lemon bars, as Michael Lee West writes about in "Funeral Food"—this chapter offers a range of both literal and metaphorical desserts and considers the many roles they can play in individual lives and in our larger culture.

The cookbook we have chosen to begin this final part of our collection could very well have been chosen for the first chapter. In this selection from *Chez Panisse Menu Cookbook*, Alice Waters provides guidance for composing a menu. We hope, though, that in reading the entire book (if, indeed, one chooses to read it—and eat it—from starters to desserts) there is a hunger to reread, to experiment, to revision and reassemble—and in doing so, one may feel prepared to compose an intimate, unique, and personal menu: a menu composing the perfect literary and literal meal.

NOTES

1. Andrew Dalby, *The Shakespeare Cookbook* (London: British Museum Press, 2012).
2. Marion Cunningham, in *The Fannie Farmer Cookbook: Celebrating the 100th Anniversary of America's Great Classic* (New York: Knopf, 1996), 588, 608, 634, 667.

→ 40 ←

From *Chez Panisse Menu Cookbook*

ALICE WATERS

Composing a Menu: How to Use the Menus in This Book

Marrying the elements of a meal correctly so as to achieve that elusive equilibrium requires an understanding of each separate course and its importance within the overall structure of the menu. To succeed, first consider what foods are at their peak that particular day. Second, consider the factors that affect the meal's reception: the guests and their gastronomic idiosyncrasies; the time of year, and the temperature; and most important, what you feel like cooking and eating yourself.

Bread

My criterion for good bread is that it be good all by itself with just the addition of some sweet butter. But wonderful homemade bread can take over a dinner so completely that by the time the entrée arrives your guests have filled up on delicious bread! It is splendid to serve bread alone as a lunch—bread, olive oil, garlic, and a glass of wine—but I believe that one food should never be allowed to overpower a meal of which it is merely a part, however important. At the restaurant we try to use bread as an integral part of the various courses rather than serve an unlimited quantity of it on the dining-room tables. We may make little croutons to dip in the olive oil of a salad or we may serve a walnut bread with the cheese.

Hors d'Oeuvres—First Course

The first food tasted in a meal should be enticing. This course should never be heavy and filling. It could be a savory dish such as roasted red peppers and anchovies, or a goat cheese soufflé with thyme, or cold oysters and hot spicy sausages—something to get the juices flowing. Awaken and energize the palate, but don't stun it into unconsciousness.

Soup

It is very difficult to integrate soup into a menu successfully because soups can easily assume the same role as an overwhelming quantity of bread—too much of one food at one time. I like rich, one-course dinners with soup as the main course, such as bouillabaisse with perhaps just a little *mesclun* salad before, and a bit of sherbet afterward. However, as a part of a more complicated menu, the type and amount of soup become critical issues. For that reason, the soups included in this book are generally light vegetable or fish broths or purées with a minimum of cream or stock. Often the garnishes are intended to offset any richness, such as in the addition of lemon thyme in the squash soup or black pepper on a cream of leek soup.

Fish Course

Fish is wonderfully flexible; it can appear on a menu in a garlicky salt cod hors d'oeuvre, in a fish soup, or as a grilled entrée with a red wine sauce. In the menus at Chez Panisse, we often use fish instead of soup courses; for our purposes, a fish course looks lighter and less filling.

Entrée

I do not really believe in entrées in the American sense of lots of meat, potatoes, and vegetables in the center of a menu. This may be appropriate when the main dish is a suckling pig or some large bird, but I generally prefer to give a number of courses equal weight and importance. The small courses of a French service are appealing to me, and I am fascinated by the kind of menu composition found in Japanese or Chinese meals that have recurring themes, no main dish, and hot, spicy foods at the end of the meal.

I personally cannot eat massive quantities of food, so to me, heaped-up plates are truly offensive. A heavily laden plate allows one course to dominate, and the risk is that it will overwhelm the entire framework of the meal. I do like platters of food in the middle of the table, family style; a more appealing presentation can be made and those at the table can help themselves to precisely the amount they want. This encourages everyone's involvement with the food, eases serving complications in the kitchen, and evokes a communal sense about dining.

Salad

I am often asked whether to serve salads before or after the main course. This depends on the particular menu you have composed. Because I do serve a number of salad-like first courses at the restaurant, I tend to eliminate the salad after the entrée. My personal preference at this point in a meal, particularly after a very rich entrée, is for some little course that's refreshing; this serves the purpose of cleansing and piquing the palate before the cheese and the dessert.

I find that many people do not understand or appreciate two salads in one meal. I don't mind, particularly if they are considerably different in looks, texture, and taste. I like serving a salad to begin a meal, regardless of whether there is to be one after the entrée, because it is nice to have the tart pungency of a good vinaigrette to pick up your palate and awaken the senses the way the right hors d'oeuvre should. You can then proceed with the dinner and perhaps have a cheese course after the entrée, especially if you are drinking wine with the meal and don't wish to interrupt the flow of the wine with an incompatible vinegar-based dressing.

Cheese

Because cheese is one of those simple, straightforward commodities, it can be enormously appealing as a course all by itself with red wine or as the ending to a meal. When the cheese is truly at its peak, it can be a marvelous experience; but cheeses are often badly stored, or they arrive from Europe underripe and uncorrectable or overripe and ammoniated. Therefore, tasting and discrimination are essential, and so is the cultivation of your local cheese merchant.

The simple earthiness of cheese appeals to me, and its facility for making a good wine taste even better endears it to me. When I am in France I am always fascinated by the choice of cheeses, and have even had the wonderfully instructive experience of tasting a cheese in all its various stages of development and age. I like serving more than one type of cheese at a time, for the opportunity for comparison right there at the dining-room table is interesting. So is comparing and contrasting several cheeses of the same type—three or four different blue cheeses, for example.

Desserts

Where I have listed a dessert suggestion for each menu in this cookbook, I have not always included the recipe; I have often found, when testing these menus, that I did not really wish to have a dessert at the meal's end. My desire is frequently for an unexpected taste and texture—a refreshing sherbet, or a wonderfully ripe piece of fruit accompanied by some cheese, a glass of lovely Sauternes, some nuts sautéed in olive oil served hot, or a little glass of anisette.

There should be an ending to a meal, but it need not be a rich and sweet traditional dessert. When I finish a meal, I want to feel *just* satisfied, not stuffed. That stuffed feeling is anathema to me, so my inclination is for something light. At a recent meal I was treated to goat cheese and sage flowers in lieu of dessert, and was intrigued by the fact that this pairing had the very same effect a good dessert should have; it was very refreshing and seemed to aid the digestion more than a heavy dessert ever could have. Too often, dessert is a sugar fix rather than a little touch of sweetness as a change from the savory, the salty, or the piquant. This final course could also be a very dramatic change in look such as a fruit salad, not necessarily sweet, that you could conceive having had at the meal's beginning. A dish that is very hot or very cold can be highly effective: a dramatic change in temperature is quite refreshing.

Wine

Combining wine with food to achieve a perfect balance requires thought, knowledge, and experience. Occasionally a combination of food and wine will result in an almost transcendental balance, a whole greater than the sum of its parts. This is difficult to achieve because there are so many variables. You may think about a certain dish and plan on a certain wine to accompany it, but when you actually cook the dish you may find that it has taken on an entirely different character from what you expected; the wine, too, because it is a living, breathing commodity, may reveal an unexpected aspect—perhaps it is fruitier or drier than you anticipated.

When you achieve that perfect pairing, you stand in awe and never forget. A recent memory is of a St. Péray, a Côtes-du-Rhône, which, when paired with a leek and goat cheese tart, produced such a wonderful combination of flavors that it took me by surprise. On another occasion, I found that a young Château Suduiraut, accompanied by a lightly smoked salmon, made a lovely lunch. A special combination, charcoal-grilled salmon and a 1966 Château Léoville-Las-Cases, made me realize that the oily, smoky salmon needed the charming elegance of an older Bordeaux. My favorite wines are those that are never mistaken for any other. A Joseph Swan Zinfandel will always be a Joseph Swan Zinfandel, and will always jump up from the wine glass to grab my senses when I taste it. Great wines, like those from Domaine Tempier in Bandol, should have an elusive character and breed that the winemaker is able to capture in each and every vintage. I am striving to bring the same energy and dedication to my cooking.

How to Use the Menus in This Book

After most of the menus you will find recipes for all the courses; but sometimes no recipe is given. This may be because I've thought of a dish as an optional course, more an afterthought than an integral part of the meal; or it may be that the missing recipe would have been redundant or self-evident. In either case, the entry is marked with an asterisk. In the same way, the wine suggestions are usually offered as a general idea of some appropriate wines; but sometimes I've listed a wine more specifically because it's a proven success with the menu.

The point is that if you use these menus, you, too, can be more or less specific. To execute any menu in this book will be to re-compose it; to cook any recipe will be to re-invent it. In the end, it will be your character and your taste that determine the outcome.

LINDA'S CHOCOLATE CUPS

About thirty cups
8 ounces Swiss bittersweet chocolate

YOU WILL NEED:
¾-inch new pastry brush
Small paper bonbon cups
Cookie sheet or muffin tin
Instant-reading thermometer

First temper the chocolate by alternately heating and cooling it; this will prevent cocoa butter from rising to the surface and leaving white streaks on the finished chocolate. To do this, grate the chocolate and place it in a double boiler over hot water at 140°F. Stir frequently to ensure that it remains well-blended and that it melts more quickly. Use the thermometer to monitor the temperature of the chocolate; *never* allow it to rise over 100°F. The chocolate should be completely melted at approximately 96°F; remove the double boiler from the heat, replace the hot water with cool water, and replace the chocolate over the water.

Stirring constantly, allow the chocolate temperature to fall to 80°F. Remove the top of the double boiler, replace the cool water with warm water at between 120° and 130°F, and put the chocolate over the warm water. Stirring constantly and checking the temperature frequently, raise the temperature of the chocolate to 89°F, exactly. Remove the chocolate from over the warm water. It may be necessary during the molding of the cups to replace the chocolate over warm water to melt it slightly, but never allow it to rise over 89°F. Add hot water or replace water in the lower half of the double boiler as needed to maintain the chocolate at 86°F to 89°F; stir the chocolate frequently.

Take a small stack of bonbon cups and loosen the top cup. Put this cup back on the stack. Using the pastry brush, paint the inside of the top cup with the melted chocolate, keeping the coating of the chocolate as even as possible. (The paper will be removed after the chocolate cools and hardens, so the cup must be strong enough to hold its shape unaided.) Carefully remove the top cup from the stack and place it on a cookie sheet or muffin tin.

When you have used all the melted chocolate, place the cookie sheet or muffin tin in the refrigerator. It is not necessary or desirable to leave the cups in the refrigerator for a long period of time, just until the chocolate has hardened (about 10 minutes). When they are hard, remove a few cups at a time from the refrigerator.

Carefully peel away the paper cup on the outside of the chocolate. Chocolate cups made with any dark chocolate will keep indefinitely if stored in a closed container in a cool place (but not in the refrigerator). They may then be used as needed. Eight ounces of chocolate, properly tempered, will yield approximately thirty chocolate cups, depending upon the thickness of the chocolate coating.

When you are ready to serve after-dinner espresso, place the chocolate cups on a tray and carefully fill them with heavy cream, then let each person drop a cream-filled chocolate cup into his or her coffee cup.

⊸ 41 ⊷

All the Old Tales Are Tales of Hunger

CAITLIN NEWCOMER

Say there was an apple. A basket. A red cloak. A forest thick with trees. Say there was a wolf. And a path. And a girl. Say there is the threat of coming darkness.

Say peel one, core two. Whisk and let settle. Shake and shake and shake.

There are wolves in the forest. So many wolves. Watch them glide through the trees like mist. They have big eyes. They have slow jaws. They have claws to rip flesh from white, white bones. Are these wolves men or dogs? This is always the question. Are wolves a metaphor for sexual predator, for threats to virginity, for dirty hands and impure thoughts? Or is this about the threat of wolfish nature, hot breath and yellow teeth, a thirst for hot-running blood? Or is this magic, sorcery of the arboreal, men who, under the spell of a powerful Circe, lose their minds and grow thick fur? What wolves are they who stalk out there—waiting, watching, hungry for a little girl?

Peel one, core two. Whisk and let settle. Sift white flour with small white hands.

Mother is the one who passes the instructions down. How to kill a chicken, mend a stocking, make a dish to help the dying forget their sickness in a spoon. Take four apples. Slice them. Soften butter in the sun. Butter, good for cooking, fattening, keeping soft, smooth hands. Take enough butter to fill one-third of a wooden cup. White flour, one-half cup's worth. Scoop it from the barrel with quick hands. Do not spill it. Do not be careless, heedless, as Mother says this girl so often is.

Add brown sugar, three-quarters cup. Mix with the butter and flour in a wooden bowl. Mix until it clings in clusters. (How the tongue yearns for it. How the heart beats—a taste, a taste.) Add in oats, one-half cup. Add a teaspoon of cinnamon. A dash of nutmeg. Sweet spices that bring the sun into rooms gone dark with sickness. Then, layer the apples in a pan. Pour the batter over the apples from the mixing bowl. Bake in a hot oven until it browns and bubbles, crisp and sweet. The little girl, she will take it to her grandmother, sick in her cottage on the far edge of the forest. Why she lives out there, no one will ever know. Out with the shadows and the howling wolves. Out of sense and out of mind. There, the little girl will take the apples, small shoulders wrapped in a red woolen cloak. Red as the sky on the day she was born. Red as curses, red as blood.

Mother is the one who tells the girl to stop her dreaming. Words can't put bread in a stomach, and wolves are wolves, not men. Don't trust pretty talkers, child. Child, always carry a long, sharp knife.

Peel one, core two. Whisk and let settle. Take the warm dish into the cold forest with trembling hands.

But oh, the wolves. Kings of the forest. Or rather, he is king. Massive as thick boulders piled up in a cairn. Coal-black coat and dark-globed eyes. Red mouth curving over fangs. White teeth, red mouth. Snow white, rose red. Cursed or blessed with the power of human speech. A man once? Should it be so? A man punished by a forest god, perhaps. Yes, punished for seeing what should not be seen: now-white nakedness chilled in winter air. Bright limbs resettled into ragged haunch, into high-pricked ears to hear you with, into sharp eyes to see.

Oh, how he howls at the moon. The sound cuts like bone on bone.

Peel one, core two. Whisk and let settle. Clutch fingers white against reddened, cold-chapped hands.

In the forest, the girl's heart hops and thuds, a rabbit in its snare of ribs. She prefers the open fields around her mother's house, space to run, to hide in the tall, damp grass. She already knows her feet will not go undetected down this path, no matter how soft she sets her small boots on the frozen ground. This is the way of the story. The dark silk of the forest settles on her with the weight of iron chains.

Yet how easy it would be to say she is brave. Or stupid. Heedless like her mother and the storybooks all said. But this girl knows more than enough to feel afraid. She is aware of what is quiet among the forest's trees. This girl is not soft innocence. She has seen the stable boy with the dairymaid, rutting like pigs in a muddied field. She has seen her grandfather's lungs go still. She is aware of how fragile the human animal can be. She has felt skin rip like Mother tearing stitches out of cloth. She has a curving scar along her shin. She has seen the ease with which bones can puncture skin.

And soon, she hears that he is there—a rustle, sleek and low among the browning leaves. Slow, dogged speech. *Little girl, don't be afraid.* His voice is the old voice of hunger. A voice slick with butter, with the choicest cuts of meat. Rasped with wheat, oatcakes, the strike of bone on teeth. *Such a small girl,* the voice says, making the girl's heart skitter and freeze, the blind panic of the rabbit who knows it has been sighted. *Such a sweet red cloak and hood. Out in the woods all alone.*

Peel one, core two. Feel his breath through the trees, hot air along cold skin.

Wolf or man, wolf or man? Does this need to be decided for her? Whatever he is, he is dangerous. Whatever he is, he makes her want. If only she were safe back in Mother's house slicing apples, the barnyard kitten on her knee. But the path did not lead that way. It never does. And still, she wants to see the wolf—she peers fast through the trees, seeking a swish of tail or claw, the rising mist of ragged breath—to see him would be to see story shaped into skeleton, frozen into the truth of bone. She is so hungry to see. If she can see him, she will touch her fingers to this tale. Then words will taste like sugar on her tongue.

Beside her, the wolf stalks through the leaves. In all the old stories, it is his hunger that matters most. His animal lust. His curved teeth. Yet the wolf, too, is aware of dangers. He whispers the lines he is supposed to utter, the ones that have been waiting for him. *The better to taste you with, my dear.* But he can smell the want on her. He has lured many children from the path—cloaked in all colors, trailing back through many years. Some have fought, and other have gone limp and quiet. Some have sought him out, looking for meat in dead of winter, hoping to cut down a threat to their sheep. None have come back. But they have wanted only his fat, his muscle. To them he is not myth but meat. To this girl, he is story turned flesh. She hungers for him. If he lets her, how much will she take? Cloak, hands, lips—all red as blood.

Peel one, core two. One, two hearts beat in the forest, a twinned rhythm.

A story is a recipe for hunger. To bake it properly, you must peel the skin from the apple, and find the beast within a little girl. Shake sounds from a dream. Press a man into a wolf until you don't know which way to see. Make the path long and hard to follow. File your pen to a sharp point. *The better to see you with, my dear.* Make the oven hot.

Peel one, core two. Drop their skins along the path for birds to find.

The path ends. Lost in listening, locked in the rhythm of heartbeat and footfall, girl and wolf do not realize the distance they have traveled. Yet there is Grandmother's cottage, gray through dead leaves. There is her chimney's plume of smoke. There is the fork in the path: one to Grandmother's door, one to the village, its dark houses snug in a treeless hill. The trees in the forest thin.

The wolf steps out from among the wide-spaced trees. He says nothing. He stands on the path facing the girl. Black as shadows, as rain-slicked rock. The girl lets her red hood slip down past her shoulders. *I have been waiting for you,* she says.

Peel the red skin from the apple. Coil it around your finger. Let the skin drop.

In this tale, the girl follows the wolf into the forest. First, she fulfills her errand, unlatching the door of Grandmother's house with care, calling out kindly as she steps inside. She wipes sweat from the old woman's face with a damp cloth, says a prayer with her, speaks softly as she feeds her grandmother the apples baked in sugared sunlight. She settles the quilts back around Grandmother's chin. As she steps outside, she pulls the door tight.

In the shadow of the tall trees, the girl lays her hands on the wolf. He stands, still as the crags above the village, and lets her feed from him, slipping her hands along his tapered muzzle, the silk of his pointed ears, his thick neck and slender limbs. The girl closes her eyes. Behind her lids, she sees wolf change into man, sees the sinews stretch and lengthen, the fur recede, until all that remains the same are the dark depths of his shadowed eyes. He has slow hands. He has soft skin. He can make the most delicate wounds. She sees words spin themselves around him like a second skin. In the forest, the girl twists her fingers into the wolf's dank fur.

Peel skin from the apple. Touch its silk with your tongue. Now let the skin drop.

42

Baking for Sylvia

KATE MOSES

It was the week of my fortieth birthday, an august event I had celebrated with half of a leftover burrito, heated in the microwave and taken up to my tiny study, shambling in my husband's faded bathrobe and coughing; I shut the door to the sound of my family coughing around the dinner table downstairs, cat hair matted on every textured surface in the house. The deadline—extended—to turn in the manuscript for my novel about Sylvia Plath was six weeks away, and by my birthday I still had to write a third of the outlined forty-one chapters. I'd been writing solidly for two and a half years. My husband and two children were getting used to my conspicuous absence or my thousand-mile stare when I was physically present; I had taken to shouting things such as "Go away! Go turn on the TV!" or "Can we just order pizza?" through the sliding pocket door of my study. My five-year-old was sometimes heard muttering in the hallway, "Mommy's behind *the door*."

But on the day I'm thinking of, during my fortieth birthday week, I was not writing and shouting but doing the other thing that I did every day, *every* day, feverishly and obsessively: I was in my kitchen, baking. I was in my kitchen baking my way into and out of Sylvia Plath's head, as if my life depended on it. On that day, I was baking a hot milk sponge cake with caramel icing because I didn't have the focus to confect Paul Prudhomme's three-layer spiced pecan cake, which I'd been making for my own birthday each year since I was twenty, and I was sick of chocolate chip cookies, and I can make the hot milk caramel cake with my eyes closed. Chapter 29 was cooling on a rack, the hot milk cake was already in the oven, and I was getting ready to muscle up to Chapter 30. That's when the mail hurtled through the slot into our front hall, and I, always eager for catalogs or some other unexpected bit of magnetically distracting detail, lurched down the hallway to gather the slumping bundle off the floor. There was a small envelope from one of my closest friends. I ripped it open; inside was a retro-style birthday card depicting a kewpie girl in two pieces and attached with a metal band so that she could bend back and forth at the waist, lifting a birthday cake out of the oven. Except that in the postal trajectory between Baltimore and San Francisco, the kewpie girl had bent so far forward that not only was the cake in the oven, but so were her head and shoulders, right up to her dimpled elbows.

Is it okay to have a sense of humor about this stuff? —*Peel off the napkin / O my enemy. / Do I terrify?*—Is it okay to even talk about this?

She died with her head in the oven, her cheek resting on a folded dishcloth. This is the shuddering, horrible truth of Sylvia Plath's self-inflicted death forty years ago, on a frigid February morning, a truth of such excruciating magnitude that it has overshadowed her poetry, her astonishing virtuoso artistry, and how we understand the relationship between this particular writer's art and her life. It has permitted reductivist theorizing about the death itself—its inevitability, say—as well as about Plath's sexual politics: her violent rejection of the traditional female role, some would have it embodied by her last, successful act in her kitchen. But the writer's death is not the writer's life, or her work, despite, in Plath's case, the people who would consider them one and the same.

"I would live a life of conflict," she wrote in 1956, just prior to meeting her future husband, "of balancing children, sonnets, love and dirty dishes." She was doing just that in the fall of 1962—nursing in rural isolation her anguish over her failed marriage, writing what we know as the Ariel poems at four a.m. every morning before her two tiny children awoke and sent her into the daily spin of dirty dishes and dirty laundry. Knowing how Plath's acute sensitivities transformed the stuff of her life into art, it seems appropriate that her 1962 daily calendar tells us that she had lamb on her grocery list the day before she wrote "Mary's Song," on a Monday morning: *The Sunday lamb cracks in its fat. / . . . It is a heart, / This holocaust I walk in, / O golden child the world will kill and eat.*

Is it really such a surprise, then, to learn that she made custard and banana bread on the day she wrote "Medusa," the scathing indictment of her relationship with her mother; or lemon pudding cake while she was composing "Lady Lazarus"; or custard, banana bread, applesauce, and apple cake on the same day as "Fever 103"; or tomato soup cake, one of her specialties, on the day she wrote "Death & Co."? Maybe it's more surprising that she logged her daily baking plans while never noting what she wrote—the poems that made her, as she well knew, a genius of a writer.

For Plath, cooking and baking and reading cookbooks was therapeutic and consoling, a means to reconnect to the life of the body for someone who spent so much time engaged with the vivid anxieties of the life of the mind. In Plath's breathless letters to her mother during the early days of her enthralled courtship with Ted Hughes in Cambridge, she described the myriad ways in which she found in Hughes the perfect match of intellect, creativity, and passionate living, how they would "romp" through the words of Shakespeare and Dylan Thomas and how she cooked salmon roes and Shrimp Newburg on her single gas ring, Hughes pulling fresh trout out of his pockets. Just two weeks into the relationship, Plath pleaded with her mother to mail her copy of *The Joy of Cooking,* what she referred to more than once as her "blessed Rombauer, the one book I really miss." Later, settled permanently in England, she begged a subscription to *Ladies' Home Journal,* not just because it and the *New Yorker* were the two magazines she most wanted to be published in but also for the *Journal*'s American recipes that she was homesick for. During her pregnancies with her two children, Plath prepared for their home births by baking in volume—sand tarts, tollhouse cookies, apple pies—and stocking the goods away in her American-style icebox. By Nicholas's birth in 1962, she considered the gift of her family-recipe carrot cake her "traditional" gift for her midwives.

But Plath did not cook in a vacuum. She was acutely aware of the tension between her domestic consolations and her artistic ambition. "I was getting worried about becoming too stodgily practical," she wrote in her journal in 1957, a few months after her marriage to Hughes. "Instead of studying Locke, for instance, or writing—I go make an apple pie, or study the *Joy of Cooking,* reading it like a rare novel. Whoa, I said to myself. You will escape into domesticity & stifle yourself by falling headfirst into a bowl of cookie batter. And just now I pick up the blessed diary of Virginia Woolf. . . . And she works off her depression over rejections from *Harper's* . . . by cleaning out the kitchen. And cooks haddock & sausage. Bless her."

"I have my four-hour morning ahead, whole as a pie," she wrote with telling metaphoric significance in the summer of 1958, finally freed of the deadening Ivy League teaching job that had kept her from writing for a year. It must have been especially galling, then, that after quitting her job in order to write full-time, she spent much of the following year in a state of creative paralysis in Boston, noodling with various stories and counting the rejections for her poetry collection while concocting dinners for neighbors such as Robert Lowell and Elizabeth Hardwick.

In the spring of 1959, as she and Hughes were budgeting for their permanent removal to England, Plath sold her first essay to the *Christian Science Monitor*, which "opened a vista of $50 checks." In that essay, titled "Kitchen of the Fig Tree," she recalls the trio of kitchens in which she had cooked since her marriage: the Spanish kitchen of her honeymoon, which had a fig tree studded with ripening fruit right outside; the Kitchen of Doors in Cambridge, which was dim and primitive but had a tiny back garden with an apple tree and an old rose bush; and her current Beacon Hill kitchen with a panoramic sixth-floor view and every imaginable electric convenience. What Plath inadvertently reveals in this reminiscence about her desire for "a kitchen with a view" is how that desire and those views fed her imagination. From her Boston kitchen, she imagines herself not "an aproned housewife at a stove" but a passenger on a plane looking down at the mysteries of familiar streets. In Spain, a new bride bursting with the dream of juggling "books and babies and beef stews," she watched the village women shelling green almonds outside a room that was piled literally to the ceiling with the summer's harvest. That same spring, when her essay of the domestic churned her fantasy of writerly success, she was actively fretting over her biological fertility as well, wanting to be a writer and a mother, a good wife and a good daughter, not knowing yet how she could accommodate all of these roles.

> When I am quiet at my cooking I feel it looking, I feel it thinking
>
> "Is this the one I am to appear for,
> Is this the elect one, the one with black eye-pits and a scar?
>
> Measuring the flour, cutting off the surplus,
> Adhering to rules, to rules, to rules. . . ."

I know this juggling act intimately: How *do* you pull yourself back into the world of dirty dishes and children when the work that is your blood-jet has started? *Once one has seen god,* Plath wrote in "Mystic," *what is the remedy?*

I have a niece who called me "Kake" when she was a toddler. Cake has been my remedy of choice since I was nine years old: cake, cookies, pies. It is mathematical and precise, baking; it requires full conscription to rules and chemistry before one is ready to charge off on one's own soaking raisins in bourbon instead of orange juice or substituting honey for dark molasses. It compels its own containment even as it encourages fancy and elaboration. I baked all through my miserable adolescence, notorious for ferociously preventing my brothers from eating what I made. I baked my way though my unfortunate first marriage, though by then even I had no appetite; the marriage finally sizzled out, and I remember sitting at the table with a nearly warm chocolate layer cake in front of me when our dog, who was the size of a baby goat, set his chin on the table top and began to lick the frosting off. I sat watching him, unable to react, as he choked down the entire cake, to the last crumb. And I baked my way through writing the last months of the life of Sylvia Plath.

It was not a conscious decision, at first, my baking for Sylvia; later, it wasn't so much a conscious decision as a compulsion I was conscious of: I *had* to. Like Plath, I had always baked to relax; sometimes I baked to avoid the things I ought to be doing (like writing); sometimes I baked because it was orderly when the rest of my life felt like chaos. Plath knew this about baking, too; in her earnest journal notes for a misbegotten short story called "The Day of the Twenty-Four Cakes," Plath's heroine, a disaffected wife and mother, has "lost sense of order in universe / all meaningless / loss of hopes" after a quarrel with her husband. As an antidote to "wavering between running away and committing suicide," the heroine begins methodically to bake cakes, one an hour from midnight to midnight. It's the process of creating order that saves her, cinched in Plath's unintentionally hilarious, feeble denouement: "Husband comes home: new understanding."

From the start of my baking-between-chapters habit, order and relaxation were the themes *du jour*. Turning out a batch of cupcakes or a lemon tart was akin to a palate-cleansing sorbet between dinner courses: it didn't take much to do the job, and I emerged refreshed for the next fictional push. But I did notice a corollary spike in my baking whenever there were extenuating circumstances related to the creation of the novel: if a chapter was going badly, I baked more; if Sylvia was in a particularly terrible state in a chapter, I baked more; if I had to cope with other household issues that infringed on my writing time (the transmission going out, sick children, a homework impasse), I baked a lot more, though you wouldn't think I had the time.

I thought, then, that the tension between my baking and my writing about Plath was a surface tension: it was no different than my baking and everything else I did, nothing more than a quirk of personality. But something shifted in my awareness of that tension around the midpoint of the novel. I was ecstatic about the fact that I had gotten halfway to the goal of completion, and yet I felt oddly conflicted about finishing those last twenty chapters. It wasn't simply a premature nostalgia for the experience of writing my first novel. The real tension, I had begun to sense, was between the true story of Plath's life, the end of which is all too well known, and the story I was creating for my fictional Sylvia, who in the end would be spared the final, terrible knowledge of her ultimate fate.

I had known from the start that I would not write about Plath's death; I was only interested in writing about her struggle to stay alive in those last frantic weeks. And yet her real, nonnegotiable death weighed heavily upon me like a stone. At some point during the final months holed up with my novel, as I inched toward the foregone, desperate conclusion from which I was sheltering my fictional Sylvia, I realized I was ending every day of writing in my kitchen. Every day. I baked while my family was at school or at work, mostly, or while they were asleep; while I stood at the stove or at my mixer I thought about where I'd just been with my made-up Sylvia, and where I was taking her next, even closer to an ending. Baking was our lifeline; it was a way for me to keep us, my character and me, connected to the tangible things in this world, and to stave off a truth I had no power over. While I was baking, I was able to give us both a morning whole as a pie.

Months after I finished the manuscript of *Wintering*, I was sorting through my files, which had gotten completely disarrayed in the final scramble toward my deadline. I came across an article by Plath's daughter, Frieda Hughes, from the *London Times* magazine, sent to me by a friend in 2000 when Sylvia Plath had been granted a commemorative blue plaque by the Royal Society of Arts in England. It was Frieda Hughes who had asked that the plaque not be placed at 23 Fitzroy Road in London, where Plath had lived with her mother and infant brother for a few weeks and where her mother had committed suicide; Hughes had asked that the plaque be placed on the house a couple of blocks away at Chalcot Square, where her parents had lived for two years and where Plath had written *The Bell Jar* and published her first poetry collection, *The Colossus*. Frieda Hughes had been born at that house on Chalcot Square and knew better than anyone that it had been a place of happiness and promise for her mother, a far more fitting site for honoring her achievements than the place of her final misery. What struck me most about Hughes's article, though, was how she participated in that commemorative ceremony for her mother: she baked. For the champagne reception at the neighborhood library, Hughes and her husband baked spanakopita and quiches and baklava and smoked-salmon-and-gruyere-cheese pies. Frieda Hughes had been two years old when her mother died, going behind the door forever. "I got carried away," Hughes wrote about baking for the reception, "because I felt I was doing this for my mother."

I've thought since, often, about making tomato soup cake for Sylvia, even though it sounds more than unlikely, a Depression-era holdover, like putting corn flakes in a meatloaf. Plath loved it, and she made it over and over; she wrote to her mother to inquire about the size of tomato soup cans in America, because the first cake she made in England was "a bit wet." I have trouble imagining it, how the savory flavor of tomato soup could transform itself into something else, with sweetness and complexity. But it gave Sylvia Plath comfort, and for that reason alone I would be willing to make it. Already I can taste the salt in my mouth.

TOMATO SOUP CAKE À LA SYLVIA PLATH

2 cups sifted cake flour
1 tbsp baking powder
½ tsp baking soda
½ tsp ground cloves
½ tsp ground cinnamon
½ tsp ground nutmeg
1 cup seedless raisins
½ cup butter
1 cup sugar
2 large eggs
1 can (about 11 ounces) condensed tomato soup
½ cup chopped walnuts, optional

Preheat oven to 375°. Grease and flour two 8-inch cake pans.

Sift the flour, baking powder, baking soda, and spices together. Toss the raisins with about ¼ cup of the flour mixture in a separate bowl and set aside. Cream the butter and sugar in a mixing bowl until light. Beat in the eggs until thoroughly mixed. To the creamed sugar/butter mixture, add the flour alternately with the soup by thirds. Fold in the raisins and the walnuts, if using. Divide evenly between the cake pans and bake about 35 minutes, until a toothpick inserted in the center comes out clean. Allow to cool in the pans for 5 minutes before removing to a cake rack to cool thoroughly. Frost with cream cheese frosting.

CREAM CHEESE FROSTING

1 pound (16 oz.) cream cheese, at room temperature
½ cup butter, at room temperature
2 tsps vanilla
pinch of salt
5 cups confectioners' sugar

Combine the cream cheese and butter in a mixing bowl and beat until creamy and uniform. Add vanilla and salt. Gradually add the confectioners' sugar, beating until smooth.

→ 43 ←

Suman sa Ibos

CHERYL QUIMBA

4 cups
of rice

and she only wanted
me to sit there in the kitchen that

same black hair skimming
at the neck

4 cups of rice
washed and soaked   until it swelled

how to smell it was to know it

already as if we were always forever
eating

mother-expert joining 2 cups of coconut milk with

4 cups of rice—I tossed
salt—   how else do we work

with those pads of our fingers

the outdoors merely
outdoors just past

her shoulder we could push against it but

here were banana leaves to fill   4 cups now

fattened

portioned into the leaves wrapped with string and

dropped
into a pot of boiling water at the stove

how to watch and
how to wait

then sugar on top

then a mango on the side

→ 44 ←

Pie

From *Never Eat Your Heart Out*

JUDITH MOORE

> I have simply wanted to show that whenever life seeks to shelter, protect, cover, or hide itself, the imagination sympathizes with the being that inhabits the protected space.
>
> —Rilke

> As far back in time as we can go, the gastronomic value has always been more highly prized than the nutritive value.
>
> —Bachelard

Its filling sequestered beneath a canopy of top crust, hidden from the eye (if not the nose), a pie (not unlike the body) offers itself for reverie on the enigma of inside and out.

Even when I was a child, a pre-school toddler, I adored concocting for my dolls mud-crust pies in doll-size pie tins. I filled them with pansies or nasturtiums or marigolds or yellow chinaberries picked off bushes that grew along the back alley, or with pea gravel culled from our driveway. With Belinda, my rag doll, snuggled in the crook of my arm, I would curl up in bed at naptime or at night, engrossed—transported, really—in figuring out what ingredients I could fill pies with next. In my mind I would roll out mud circles, and more daintily in thought than ever in fact I would tuck these crusts in pans. In my mind's eye I would see myself, in passionate imitation of adult pie-makers. Layering in flowers or pebbles, dribbling over them my sandbox sand for sugar, and adding daubs of wet mud butter. Then, carefully, with an enormous sigh of satisfaction that comes as one nears a task's completion, I spread a top crust over my pie's filling, and with the stubby dimpled fingers I see now in my photographs at that age, I pinched together, around the pie's entire circumference, the edges of the top and bottom mud crusts. What was in the pie was a secret only I knew.

I so heartily believed in my mud and sand ingredients that falling asleep I smelled my pie baking (it would be a doubled make-believe, because I did not smell mud, I smelled apples, cherries, apricots). While my body gave off that last shudder as tensed muscle let go, I began to arrange in my mind's eye all the dolls on chairs around my playhouse table, even incontinent Betsy-Wetsy, who left wet spots wherever she sat, the cloth rabbit, the woolen Pooh bear come across the ocean from what my father called "war-torn England."

Next to pie, what pleasure cake offers, whether looked at or eaten, seems meager. To wonder about a cake's interior, given a well-made cake's unvarying, uniform web and constant all-chocolate or all-"white" taste (even when lemon or raspberry filling or dark chocolate glistens silkily between its layers) is to have the mind taken nowhere. The simplest breakfast muffin, aclutter with plump raisins and walnuts, seems more a marvel, inciting curiosity in the mind, bonanza for the mouth.

Another person might see this pie-cake distinction in an entirely opposite fashion, and consider cake, leavened as it is by baking powder and by the air-retaining foam of whipped egg whites or whole eggs and baking powder—which means that its volume is significantly increased by internal gas expansion—as far more the miracle. But it seems to me that mere chemistry can explain what makes a cake, while pie demands metaphysics. The opposition between a pie's inside and out, the dialectic, if you will, between crust and filling, can't but set minds wondering. As children and as adults we never lose interest in it. Confronted with turtle or snail shell, high fence, blank wall, lid, door, veil, or wrapping past which the eye cannot go (think of egg rolls, turnovers, pocket bread), the mind proceeds at once to ask, "What's in there?" or, more suspiciously, "What is being hidden?" and, of course, "Why?" If one is in an elegiac mood, this consideration of outside and in may steer one to certain qualities of innerness: tenderness, vulnerability. One may find oneself filled with emotions similar to the poet Rilke's, in which "the imagination sympathizes with the being that inhabits the protected space."

In my mud-pie days I had a tiny wooden rolling pin equipped with handles lacquered bright red. I had to ask permission, but once having done so, I was allowed to dust the wide lower step of the back stoop with sand from my sandbox and then I'd plop down my mud mix on top of the sand, pat my mud flat, and roll out my crusts on the concrete.

How did I bake my mud pies? Next to my sandbox I built an oven from red bricks left over from some project of my father's. Four bricks made the oven floor, four bricks stood on end made its sides, and for the oven roof I used a piece of corrugated tin. I had more bricks that I stood up against the oven for its door. As my pies (I could fit two in the oven) baked, I would conjure drawings in my mind like the ones in my picture books: pies cooling on wide wooden windowsills, steam rising up out of vents cut in the pies' top crusts and floating in chimney-smoke whorls across blue skies about fairy-tale villages, and I could work myself up into a fret of fear by imagining that the sweet fruity aroma drifting off my pie had attracted a sharp-toothed wolf. I would remember the nursery rhyme that began:

Sing a song of sixpence,
A pocket full of rye;
Four and twenty blackbirds,
Baked in a pie.

I asked permission to use the back stoop for my mud-pie making from Black Mary, so called to distinguish her from my father's aunt, whom, I guess, we would have called White Mary, had things been equal. Black Mary lived with us, kept our house, washed and ironed our clothes, and cooked our food. She had raised my father and his younger brother from the day they were born, and after their mother died, when my father was six, she became all the mother my father had left. He adored her. Black Mary had what my father called a Queen Mary bosom, by which he meant a breastline carried well forward, like a ship's prow. She was better to me than anybody, better than my maternal grandmother or paternal stepgrandmother, better than my mother, and better even than my father, if only because she, unlike my father and mother, was always home. I loved to bury my nose deep down in the cleft between her breasts, where her smooth skin gave off the fragrance of spices and breakfast bacon and furniture oil and the flowery talcum she dusted her brown skin with, spotting it white. I loved to lay my cheek along the bodice of Mary's print dresses and hear her heart beat. Its thump reverberated through her huge body into my ear, her flesh quivered and hummed, and I would begin to breathe with her. I felt lulled and narcotized, and I wondered if, like Sleeping Beauty or Rip Van Winkle, I might not fall asleep there forever.

I remember a springtime afternoon when a storm came up; bright lightning strokes and a series of thunderclaps—not rolling thunder, but sharp, harsh cracks—woke me from my nap. It was not long after lunch, but outside, the sky looked dark as evening. My mother was at school and my father at work. Mary set me at the kitchen table. Our dog, a black Scottie like president Roosevelt's Fala, lay under the table and whimpered every time another thunderbolt crashed. Mary had her little Bakelite radio turned on to one of her stories about romance, which did not interest me. I touched the dog with my bare toes, and he growled.

My father loved Mary's chicken pie, and she was fixing us one for dinner. To make the pie she had to start by stewing what she called an old hen. I remember old hens coming to us (but don't remember from where, or how they got to the kitchen). The hens arrived headless and plucked, with their skinny yellow scaly legs and feet still attached.

That afternoon Mary stood by the stove and held the old hen over a gas flame, singeing off bluish pinfeathers that poked out from the hen's naked body the same way my father's weekend beard poked from his chin. The remains of the hen's broken neck drooped downward, and a long empty sleeve of loose skin hung off it, bobbing. Every time a flame caught at a pinfeather, the burning feather set off a *psst* sound. The feathers burning smelled the same as hair burning.

The storm didn't let up and rain came down so hard onto our roof that I couldn't even hear the voices on Mary's radio anymore. Mary had water boiling by then in her black iron stew pot and had put the hen in the bubbling water and then turned down the flame and covered the pot with a lid. Right away, the glass in the kitchen windows began to steam up, and soon I couldn't see out the window, and then my father called from his office to make sure we were all right in the storm. Mary let me talk to him for a minute. He said if I couldn't see out the kitchen windows I should get in the dining-room window seat and watch the storm from there, and then the line crackled, and I could barely hear him and gave the phone back to Mary.

I knelt on the window-seat cushions, which were covered with rough monk's cloth and scratched my bare knees. I pulled back the curtain and looked through the glass Mary kept spotless with ammonia, out into the unnaturally dark side yard. Lightning flared across the sky, leaving behind the eerie radiance. Rain hit the grass and beat yellow blossoms off the forsythia canes and knocked petals off the red Darwin tulips. Low spots in the yard were drowning.

In no time rain turned to hail, and Mary came and stood by me, hand on my shoulder and dog whimpering right behind her, and Mary said that with so much hail hitting the roof so hard she felt as if we were stuck inside a drum that was being rat-a-tat-tatted with about a hundred drumsticks. She said she hoped the hail didn't ruin our roof or break her windshield, which had happened before, or beat down the lettuce and spinach that had been up just a few weeks out in the garden.

Mary said come along into the kitchen, which by then was hot and smelled of good chicken steam. I helped by shelling peas while Mary chopped onion and carrot and potato to go into the chicken pie. The dog went to sleep, and when I had all the peas shelled and a bowl on the table half full of bright green peas and a pan heaped up with empty pods, I looked up and the storm was over. Sun was shining down in a twinkly brightness onto the yard. I squinted because I had gotten used to the dark. Mary brushed flour off her hands, which had made them all white, and helped me into my shoes and tied them and, telling me not to fall on slick grass or get in puddles, allowed me out the back door to go play.

Right away of course I went out to the sidewalk to see if my friend Janet from across the street was out, but she wasn't. I started looking around to see what had happened in the storm. Hailstones, big as mothballs and as white, littered the lawn, and my father's spinach and lettuce had been beaten down in the rows he'd planted them in, and dirt was on the lettuce leaves. The poplars that stood in a line between our lot and the one next door had their leaves knocked off, and the apple trees along the back fence, too. My foot touched something soft, and I looked down. My foot had touched a dead baby robin.

Maybe wind had blown the bird from its nest; maybe rain had drowned the bird in its nest, or maybe hailstones had killed it. It had no real feathers yet, only fuzzy down, and the down was soaked. Its bluish-pink skin was wrinkled all over its body, and its wings had hardly formed and were more like flippers. Its feet were needle-like and not strong enough to have held it up if it had tried to stand. Its head looked too big for its body and its eyes too big for its head. Its beak was halfway open, as if maybe it had struggled for breath. There was no life left in it.

I wasn't supposed to touch it, and I knew I wasn't. It was cold to touch. I felt voracious guilt, the quality of which returns to me even now. I was disobeying Mary and my parents—"Do not touch wild birds; they're dirty, crawling with filthy diseases and nasty lice."

I knew what I should do. I should call for Mary and say, "Come quick, there's a dead baby bird out here." Against my better judgment, against what I knew was right, I felt my will move the other way. I felt myself slide down into the desire to make this dead bird into a pretend-chicken pie. I ran to the door and knocked, and Mary stuck out her head. The smell of chicken pie baking came out. Mary looked up in the sky and wondered out loud if I needed my sweater, and I said no and asked permission to make mud pies and got it, as long as I didn't come in and out and track her clean linoleum. She said soon my father and mother would be home.

So I gathered my pots and pans and used water from a puddle and dug with my old tablespoon in the back flower bed, where my father let me dig, and I got two mud balls, one for the top crust and one for the bottom, just right, not too wet and not too dry, and I put some sand on the stoop and took the red lacquered handles of the rolling pin, one handle in each hand, and rolled and rolled the mud balls out flat, and I fitted the bottom crust into the little pie pan and then looked up at the kitchen window with its blue-checkered curtains and the window in the back door to see if Mary was looking out and she wasn't, and I hurried over with my pie pan to the fruit trees where the bird was lying with its beak half open and its feet up in the air and I picked it up and tucked it on its side in the pie shell and it just fit and then I carried the pie pan back to the back stoop and when I looked up Mary was still not looking out, her big face wasn't smiling in the window, so I put the pie pan down on the stoop and carefully picked up the top crust and laid it over the leaves and pinched the two crusts together all around and carried it to my oven and put it in and pulled up the bricks and sat down on the corner of my sandbox to wait for it to be done. I never told anyone this until now.

Of course I knew I couldn't feed the pie to my dolls, because it didn't seem right, and I wasn't happy, sitting there, with all the robins by then singing and out in the yard pulling worms from the wet ground, and I thought that one of them was the one whose baby was dead and she would fly up to her nest and her nest would be empty. I undid the door bricks and took the pie out of the oven and walked to the far corner of the garden and gently turned the pie over at the back of a flower bed and tipped all of it on to the ground and covered it up with the dead leaves that my father stacked there in the fall.

By the time I got my mess cleaned up off the stoop, my mother and father were home. My father first thing checked his garden for damage, and Mary let the dog out, and he yipped and ran in circles around my father and got muddy paw prints on his trousers. My father and mother asked Mary and me if we'd been scared during the storm, and we said no. For dinner, we had the chicken pie, served in the high-sided Pyrex pie pan in which Mary had baked it. I am sure that it tasted as it always did and does not when I make it: chunks of white breast meat, green peas, squares of potato, carrot, celery, the rich chicken gravy, which, mixed together, is like tasting an old-fashioned farm landscape. But I didn't eat much, and Mary said maybe I was tired because the storm woke me from my nap.

After that I didn't make mud pies anymore. Not for a long time, or not for what seemed, at that age, like a long time, probably only a week or two. And then I went to nursery school, and then my parents broke up, and then we moved, and I started grade school. All that was a long time ago. But it stayed with me.

As a child rolling out mud crusts I felt much as I feel now, wearing an apron in my kitchen—that making a pie I'm handmaiden to a miracle. I will begin, let's say, with pale green and ruby rhubarb stalks, sour red pie cherries, McIntosh apples, butter, sugar, flour, salt, and shortening. I peel the coarse strings off the outer blades of the rhubarb, pit cherries, peel and core apples. I spoon the raw fruit into the bottom pie shell, daub the fruit with chunks of butter, dribble sugar and strew flour, the latter for thickening. I sprinkle all this with no more cinnamon than will lightly freckle the fruit. I fold the second round of pie dough in half and gently lift it onto the heaped high fruit with the fold in the pie's center. One half of the pie's fruit, then, is covered. Last, ever so painstakingly, I unfold the top crust across the pie's other half and crimp the edges of the top and bottom crusts together. With a fork I prick the top crust in several places so that while the pie bakes steam can escape.

A transformation that is almost sorcery begins when the pie is set on a middle rack in the heated oven. While I wash the bowl and knives and dust flour off the pastry board, the baking fruit's aroma begins to perfume the house. Thirty, forty minutes later, I open the oven door a few inches and peer in. The oven's radiating heat rises around the pie in indistinct waves, like the contours of a dream. The heat is insinuating itself into the pie's interior, creating between the sealed crusts its own steamy, primordial climate, a site (to use the French postman-philosopher Gaston Bachelard's translated-into-English words) of "thermal sympathy" and "calorific happiness," in which apple and rhubarb and cherry cell walls break down and sugar crystals alter and butter melts.

Another half hour passes and I lean over, open the oven door. Heat rushes out onto my cheeks. What I take out from the oven (my hands protected by potholders) seems precisely like those childhood pies: born rather than made.

If the weather's right I'll set the pie to cool on the windowsill. I have no trouble, all these years later, imagining that heat floats off the pie's browned crust out the window and sails in stylized whorls out into the courtyard and over the fence into the neighborhood. If I happen to be anxious, I may fear that the pie's aroma may tempt a distant wolf. The wolf will appear decidedly older, leaner, and more vicious than the wolves from my childhood.

As a child with mud and as an adult with crust and apples, in the moment before the first cut is taken into a pie, I often have felt uncomfortable, as if I were about to violate a taboo. Someone has suggested to me that cutting into a pie is not all that different from cutting into a body. So I think it is good to make something of a ceremony of cutting a pie. The table can be laid with a pretty cloth and napkins and the best silver and your favorite plates.

Once the pie is brought to the table, I like to take a moment to admire it. I like to give the pie a chance to wet the mouth with anticipation of its tastes (the mouth's imagination at work). I like to contemplate the lustrous lightly browned crust. I like to think one more time about inside and out.

Because the moment the pie is cut, outside will have no more meaning. A new dimension, the dimension of this pie's delectable interiority, opens up.

Gathered around the table, those about to eat will say "Ahhh" and "Mmmmm, doesn't that look delicious." They will lean forward, noses alert. Sometimes you can hear them breathing in.

The first bite rises toward the opening mouth. The sentinel nose having anticipated pie's arrival, a tide of saliva crests in the mouth, pools in the tongue's center, washes over the several thousand taste buds. The teeth bite through flaky, slightly salty crust and then into tart cherries and rhubarb and apple. The fruits' sweet and buttery juices, in a total immersion baptism of the mouth, flood tongue, teeth, cheeks. There is no more outside. Everything is in.

→ 45 ←

Funeral Food

From *Consuming Passions: A Food-Obsessed Life*

MICHAEL LEE WEST

Live and learn. Die and get food. That's the Southern way.
—anonymous casserole enthusiast, on her way to the
mayor's funeral, Cookeville, Tennessee, 1995

In small towns, after a death, it is traditional to bring covered dishes to the family. When words fail us, we offer food. A platter of fried chicken says, *I'm sorry for your loss.* A chocolate layer cake whispers, *I know you feel that life has soured, so here is something sweet.*

In church lingo it is called "food for the bereaved." Southern churches have traditionally provided the meal after the funeral; it can be grand or pathetic. And you can't go by a church's size, either—even though church kitchens are built to feed the multitudes. Nowadays they are professionally outfitted with six-burner stoves (electric, most likely), convection ovens, and walk-in pantries. When it comes to good funeral food, it all depends on how many good cooks are in the congregation.

Even the funeral home anticipates the culinary hodgepodge. The undertakers thoughtfully provide the family with a little booklet, a food log to jot down the donor's name, offering, and description of the plate. They even provide gummed stickers to affix to the bottom of dishes, so each one can be returned to its proper owner. All funeral food is acknowledged with a thank-you note. The dishes are washed and promptly returned to the donor (although I know a family in Texas who received so much food it took them eight months to return all the bowls). My mama says the returning of dishes forces widows and orphans to get dressed and crawl out of their shells; after a spell of grieving, it is therapeutic to visit with friends.

Taking food to the bereaved always throws me into a panic—what to prepare? Food lore suggests that eggplant helps the grieving soul come to terms with endings. Zucchini is also a comfort food, and poppy seeds are said to induce sleep. Other cultures literally bring food to the dead. In Mexico, the deceased's favorite foods are brought to the cemetery and left on the grave. A burning candle sheds light on the feast, leading the recently departed to his earthly delights.

Funeral food has a few unwritten rules. It must transport with ease and be reheatable. Spicy foods should be avoided. Choose dishes that comfort the broken-hearted, entice blunted appetites, and satisfy the nongrieving relatives—distant kin who, for various reasons, always seem to gather at funerals. They come in four types: the curious, the dutiful, the greedy, and the reluctant. This last group consists of children and preteenagers who have been dragged to the event. One thing never changes: they all want food, and plenty of it.

After a death, fried chicken is usually the first dish to appear on the bereaved's table. I've often thought it would be interesting to do a comparative study of funeral chicken. Some crusts are flaky and crisp, the color of mahogany; others are pale brown and damp, with the consistency of wet toilet paper. Still others clearly come from KFC. My friend John Myers recently lamented the passing of good church food. At a family funeral, his mother's church brought fried chicken from Hardee's. John was aghast, especially since this was the Deep South, and for decades, his mother had been supplying the church with jugs of sun tea, baked hams, and potato salad. In her basement was a whole set of funeral dishes, with her name scrawled in laundry ink on the bottom of each pan.

In addition to fried chicken, typical funeral fare ranges from baked ham to rump roast to pit barbecue. Other dishes include deviled eggs, potato salad, coleslaw, cheese grits, macaroni and cheese. Large quantities of sweet tea are usually available. Crock-Pots always show up at a funeral, usually filled with green beans or a roast. A dozen Jell-O salads will materialize, spread out on the table like quivering jewels. Some are sweet, with marshmallows, nuts, and canned fruit; others are savory, with mayonnaise, chopped celery, and olives.

The casserole will make an appearance at every funeral dinner. Hot chicken salad topped with crushed potato chips is a perpetual favorite, along with a broccoli-and-chicken concoction. Chicken and dumplings fall under the category of old-fashioned funeral food, but it takes time and effort to prepare. Chicken pot pie is another funeral dish that's fallen out of favor probably because it's best eaten the same day it's cooked, otherwise the crust suffers.

If the death occurs in the summer, when gardens are producing, someone is bound to bring a platter of sliced tomatoes. Squash casserole is a favorite dish, along with simple bowls of peas, snap beans, and fried corn. Any time of year, a platter of sandwiches is appealing: egg salad, tuna, ham, chicken, roast beef. For breakfast, a pan of sweet rolls, with a sprinkling of pecans, can soothe an anguished heart. Every church usually has a home baker who supplies yeast rolls, sausage and biscuits, and corn bread (although I have begun to see an influx of store-bought rolls).

At the home of any bereaved soul, you will find extravagant desserts, mostly pies and layer cakes. This is a time when home cooks bring their specialties. The pies are typical Southern holiday fare: lemon icebox, chocolate, coconut, pecan. In the South chess pie is also known as funeral pie:

Lemon Chess Pie

Yield: One 9-inch pie

PREPARATION

1½ cups sugar

1 stick unsalted butter, melted

4 eggs, beaten

1 teaspoon vanilla

2 teaspoons fresh lemon juice

Preheat the oven to 325 degrees. Cream together the sugar and the butter. Add the eggs and blend well. Add the other ingredients. Pour into a 9-inch unbaked pie shell. Bake 40 to 50 minutes, until set. Test by inserting a knife toward the pie's center; if it emerges clean, the pie is ready. This basic recipe cries out for tinkering. If you want to make a chess coconut pie, add 3½ ounces flaked coconut. If you dislike lemony pies, substitute 1½ teaspoons vinegar. For buttermilk pie, omit the lemon juice and add 1 teaspoon all-purpose flour and a 1½ cups buttermilk. If anyone asks why it's called chess pie, explain that old Southern cooks used to keep their pies in a chest, or safe. The doors of the chest were made of perforated tin to allow air circulation.

Pound cakes and sheet cakes are also popular offerings. They are quick to bake and easy to transport. Sometimes the simplest desserts are the most pleasing: a yellow Bundt cake with a plain confectioners' glaze is a soothing thing to feed a child. Banana pudding, usually made in a round Pyrex bowl and topped with two inches of meringue, is an eternal favorite. Lemon squares, piled up on a cut-glass plate, will make you smile—they are cheerful and soul-lifting, the culinary equivalent of spending time on a sunporch. My mother used to say that a lemon square, served with a cup of hot tea, revives the spirit. It's a recipe that requires a little effort, but it pays you back tenfold.

LEMON SQUARES

Yield: 16 bars

TO MAKE THE CRUST

1 cup all-purpose flour
1 cup confectioners' sugar
⅛ teaspoon salt
1 stick unsalted butter, cut up

Preheat the oven to 350 degrees. In a large bowl, sift together the flour, sugar, and salt. Using a pastry blender (or two knives), cut the butter into the mixture until it is crumbly. Press the dough into a greased 9-inch square pan. Bake 15 to 20 minutes. The crust should be lightly browned.

TO MAKE THE FILLING

3 large eggs
1 cup granulated sugar
1 tablespoon lemon zest, finely chopped
4 tablespoons fresh lemon juice
2 tablespoons all-purpose flour
½ teaspoon baking powder
⅛ teaspoon salt

In a large bowl, beat the eggs until blended. Add the sugar and blend. Add the zest. Gradually stir in the lemon juice. Sift the flour, baking powder, and salt into the egg mixture and blend until smooth. Pour the mixture over the crust. Bake 25 minutes. Cool on a rack—do not remove from the pan.

TO MAKE THE TOPPING

1½ cups confectioners' sugar

3 tablespoons lemon juice

Mix sugar and lemon juice. Spread over cooled filling. When the icing sets, cut into squares.

Some food is inappropriate for the bereaved. This is not the time to bring Better Than Sex Cake or Death by Chocolate. And it's never a good idea to use uncooked eggs in funeral food. For instance, butter-cream frosting is easy to make and outrageously delicious, but it calls for raw egg yolk. This can be dangerous for the very young and the elderly, or anyone suffering from immunosuppression. If your famous chicken salad recipe calls for homemade mayonnaise, you might want to substitute a commercial brand.

It is wise to consider the effects of grief on the gastrointestinal system. During times of stress, the body is delicate. Also, depending on the geographical region, it's probably not wise to bring a platter of stuffed jalapeños or *anacuchos*. Even something as ubiquitous as chili might throw the digestive system into a tizzy. Personally, I think a tongue-burning salsa would be a welcome distraction from mourning, but in sensitive souls, the jalapeños might produce reflux, better known as indigestion, which feels like a powerful heartache. A stressed-out person might confuse the pain with angina, resulting in an unnecessary trip to the emergency room.

Another improper funeral dish is baked beans. At first glance, this classic food seems to fulfill the criteria of bereavement cuisine: it's easy to make, easy to transport, and feeds a throng of guests. But this dish is traditionally hard on the gut. Unless you lay in a supply of Beano, flatulence will most certainly result, and this condition is not welcome in closed-up houses and funeral parlors. The results have been known to incite bitter family quarrels.

I myself have never seen appetizers at a funeral. And I have yet to see chicken soup. You'd think it would be just the thing to take the edge off grief: it serves a crowd, it's a snap to reheat, and it possesses amazing powers to console and cure. However, it sloshes while being transported. Unless you bring it in a huge Tupperware bowl, the poor widow, who is already distracted by grief and guests, will have to find a great big pot to reheat the soup. Unless a kind neighbor is pulling kitchen duty, the widow has two pans to wash—yours and hers.

Mashed potatoes is the ultimate comfort food, but no one ever shows up with it at wakes. For all its virtues meat loaf hits the wrong notes; but I'm sure it has been offered—and devoured. I have never seen beef stew, liver and onions, or hamburgers brought to the bereaved—but I'm sure it's been done. Many years ago, I brought a piña colada cake to grieving teetotalers, with my name carefully taped on the bottom of the pan, and my cousin Lula once brought bourbon balls to a deacon's widow.

For those of us who can't think of anything appropriate to say or cook, my mother suggests bringing paper plates. After a funeral, or in the days preceding one, someone is always eating, and the last thing a widow needs is dishpan hands. It is also a good idea to provide plastic forks, knives, and cups. Napkins are thoughtful. A pound of freshly ground coffee beans will be put to good use, along with Styrofoam cups, sugar cubes, packets of Sweet'n Low, and a jar of Coffee-mate. My mother once said that coffee seems to be the beverage of choice after a death. I have never seen wine or beer brought to the bereaved's house, although on some occasions a tiny nip of something stout, like Jack Daniel's or Wild Turkey, might be just the thing.

When you bring food to a neighbor or a friend, you are wisely letting the food fill in the gaps. Sometimes we say all the wrong things, but food knows all languages. It says, I know you are inconsolable. I know you are fragile right now. And I am so sorry for your loss. I am here if you need me. The bringing of food has no denomination and no race. It is concern and sympathy in a Pyrex bowl. In the kindest sort of way, it reminds us that life continues, that we must sustain and nourish it. Funeral cuisine may be an old custom, but it is the ultimate joining of community and food—it is humanity at its finest.

46

Pie Throwing

From *Recipes for Disaster: An Anarchist Cookbook*

CRIMETHINC. EX-WORKERS' COLLECTIVE

Ingredients

Deserving Target
Crazed, Pie-Slinging Assailant(s)
Pie—*see below for recipe and packaging options, and factors to consider in choosing*

Optional Ingredients

Diversions
Witnesses
Photographers
Scouts
Getaway Driver

Instructions

Pieing, like property destruction, demystifies and undermines the power structures of our society by showing that icons and idols are not unassailable or above ridicule. It's like burning someone in effigy, only better, because it reveals how, in this media-addled society, public figureheads are nothing more than effigies of themselves, ripe for the roasting.

First Things First . . .

Choose a worthy target. It could be a specialist, CEO, or head of state—pie terrorists have already hit all of these on various occasions to great effect—or a less obvious quarry who nonetheless represents social forces imbued with a seriousness that must be undercut. Hitting a reporter during a live media event, for example, could send an important message.

The other question is when and where. Striking while your target is onstage giving a speech delivers the maximum shock and awe; on the other hand, it also involves the maximum danger of being caught, so if you're not eager to go to court and perhaps jail, you could try striking somewhere between the chauffeured car and the red-carpeted doorway and then making a break for it. Be on the lookout for perfect opportunities; don't force things, they'll present themselves sooner or later. As you balance risk versus audience and humiliation potential, factor in local legal precedents, the prevailing political climate, and the competence of your lawyer. Don't expect justice, but don't let the police state keep you down.

Dress the Part

It doesn't take an economist or espionage expert to figure out that if you try to enter a meeting of the pretentious and portentous with metal spikes in your nose and pie-stains on your t-shirt, you may not be admitted. Shave, put on a suit, wear an American flag pin, keep your hair short—you'll be able to go anywhere! More important than the accessories, however, is the vibe you project: you should radiate confidence, comfort, and a sense of purpose, as if you not only belong there but serve an important organizational role. It can be shockingly easy to sneak into high-security events: a few weeks ago, my student friends got in free to a top dollar fundraiser at which the Vice President was speaking, simply by introducing themselves at the door as the local Young Republicans group. They would have been able to stay for the whole event, had the Young Republicans themselves not eventually shown up . . . !

As for the pie, carry it in a bowling ball bag, or keep it in a container with a plastic lid and carry it in a nondescript briefcase or top-secret spy satchel under your coat. The type of pie will dictate the details of concealment and delivery, while the environment will dictate your subterfuge; at a press conference, you might want to smuggle it in inside a smart attaché case or large notebook, while on the street you could carry it in a pizza box. . . .

The Meringue Is the Message

The experienced pie assassins of the Biotic Baking Brigade use whipped cream on paper plates whenever possible: whipped cream makes a dramatic mess, and paper plates are harmless projectiles. On the other hand, if your target is surrounded by security personnel, you probably won't be safe stopping to fill a plate with whipped cream at the last moment; in such a situation, something with enough internal coherence to be kept sidewise until the moment of truth, such as a tofu cream pie, will serve better. Old-fashioned apple or cherry pies have a certain nostalgia value that can sometimes outweigh their unwieldiness.

Try not to do anything that will actually injure your target—your goal is to humiliate, not hospitalize, or else you'd be using a crowbar. If your target is wearing glasses, unless you are indeed using whipped cream on a paper plate or something similarly fluffy, try to hit from the side, avoiding the eye area. As for ingredients, staying away from animal products is not only eco-friendly, but also saves you the trouble of researching whether your quarry is lactose intolerant. Some pie fillings can look like blood on the recipient's face, so stay away from those unless that's the image you want the world to see.

Launch

Should you throw your missile, or mash it right in the victim's face? The former is less certain to succeed, but safer for the target, and more breathtaking to behold when it works; the latter is harder to carry off in the midst of high security, especially if you're hoping to escape. If you may indeed have to throw the pie, make sure you get plenty of practice in advance.

If there are armed guards present, try to make it clear at the last instant that your weapon is a pie and nothing more: hold it high and move with steadiness and confidence—no desperate lunges! You want to retain just enough of the element of surprise to hit your object without getting shot full of bullets as a result. It never hurts to have a clever quip prepared, either: "It's a good day to pie," et cetera.

How many assailants is enough? Having several ready can increase the odds that one will succeed, but it might be easier to stay inconspicuous if only one or two people are sneaking around where they shouldn't be. If a diversion draws everyone's attention in one direction, the lone pie-slinger can approach from the other side. Again, the terrain will determine what works; if you have to cover a broad area and don't know where your quarry will show himself, a dozen groups of three might fan out to be sure one could do the job.

Pies on Prime Time

A funny, dramatic photo and a witty press release . . . will get you a long way, whether your intention is to get coverage in the corporate press or just inspire your fellow radicals through underground reports. To this end, having your own photographers on hand can be a good idea—if you do succeed in acting with the element of surprise, they'll probably be the only ones ready to snap the pictures at the big moment, unless you've interrupted a photo session to make your hit. A good image of a successful pieing can make it into commercial outlets that would otherwise never publish anything compromising the dignity of dignitaries. If you're set on making this happen, get your image and press release out the instant the event takes place, and have a press liaison ready to answer questions immediately about why anyone would want to pie your chosen target. Even if you're trying to get media attention, don't rely on those deceit-spewing mercenaries—make sure you're putting the necessary energy into supporting independent media networks that are ready to tell the truth for its own sake.

Account

A Pie Never Thrown

The President of the United States was running for re-election, and showed up at a city in our territory for a fundraising luncheon. Quite a few of the state's wealthiest and most conservative businessmen came to pay thousands of dollars a plate to hear him speak, a far greater number of angry protesters showed up to boo him, and the city brought in massive numbers of police to assist the Secret Service in protecting our Campaigner in Chief. The stage was set for something to happen—but what?

The character of the pre-protest rally was dictated by the "opposition" party, which was as repugnant as the incumbent himself. None of us had made it out in advance to beautify the terrain, and though there were some radicals present, there was no framework for militant action organized, either. Things only got a little interesting when everyone converged around the convention center at the end of the luncheon; finally, there was a little noise and spirit. The police had us lined up behind a metal fence on one side of the building, however, and it was still one of those disempowering, demoralizing situations where the best you can hope for is to perform your posed discontent for a camera crew.

I ran around to survey the area and figured out which route the President's motorcade would be using to leave. The police had blocked all access to it except for an alley that could be reached by passing through a hotel parking garage. I slipped back to the main group and let the drummers know about this; they proceeded there to see the motorcade off. I was about to join them, when I spied a small group of men in expensive business suits. They were walking down the street in the opposite direction, right past the protesters and away from the police lines, receiving attention from no one. In twos and threes behind them, more such groups were leaving the building and walking out of the area, presumably back to their cars. These were the men who had paid to attend the fundraiser. I decided to let the drummers handle the going-away part and investigate.

I accosted the next pair of businessmen, looked deep into their eyes, and raised my fingers in their faces in an insulting gesture. This did little to advance the struggle for social liberation, though it did prompt the Muslim minister who had been the only even vaguely radical speaker at the pre-protest rally to point me out to his friends and give me his card. I took a different tact with the next capitalist who came along—I fell in beside him and began interrogating him about his social role and political goals. Well-practiced as his kind have to be in evasiveness and prevarication, he was nearly a match for me in the rhetoric department, and I hadn't quite finished converting him to anarchism by the time he got to his car.

At that point, we were quite far from the protest and the police—looking around the empty streets, I saw only a few figures, all of them other bourgeois pigs leaving the luncheon! Christ, I realized, this is where the action could have been, if only we'd prepared. Fuck the big guy, with his millions of dollars of security—he only has power because these people pay so much to come to his luncheons, and here they are totally unprotected! If we had come in small groups with cameras and pies, we could have provided a persuasive deterrent to these folks showing up to future such events, and quite probably gotten away with it, too. I guess there's always next time—and yes, kids, if there's ever a noxious political fundraiser in your area, please do try this at home!

47

Burn

JENNIFER COGNARD-BLACK

The night Edith set Morton's house on fire, she stood far back in the wrecked wheat field that doubled as his lawn, her face smooth as stone, petrol hands in her pockets, and she whispered his name with such force that even the fire now moving from the main room to the sun porch couldn't match the heat of her words. The ground shone with frost. Mitou, the heartbeat at her feet, barked and jumped. Edith's lungs ached as if yanked by breath.

"Morton Fullerton, Morton Fullerton," she said, wanting it to sound like a chant, like the name of a devil. "Morton Fullerton," she repeated, but too soft—the *t*'s more kisses than curse.

The fire had been hard to set, though Edith had thought it would be easy. When stateside rather than a Parisian expat, Morton lived a mile from any neighbor, right in the middle of Berkshire farmland. His family's old house was antediluvian, ill kept, built at the middle of the last century when every floor and doorjamb was hewn of solid oak. Edith knew Morton and his current companion, Miss Luna, had gone to the city for the weekend, and what with the cans of turpentine and all the books, Edith was sure the house would go up fast. At the cinema, arsonists never had any trouble—flames ate up everything, woosh, in a moment. A smoldering cigarette or a tipped candle could consume a curtain, a room, a whole house in nothing but a few seconds. Yet even though Edith's first petrol bomb had swallowed Morton's dresser in glorious orange, after scorching the bedroom wall, the fire had fizzled. She simply didn't understand. She'd followed Wintringham's recipe to the letter: a jam jar filled with fuel, part of a blanket wrapped over the mouth and tied with string, a petrol-soaked end hanging down, ready for the light. Perhaps the wick had been dry, the petrol thin. Until tonight, Edith had never even lit a bonfire.

Or maybe it had been her pause. After shattering the windowpane, instead of igniting and launching her firebomb, Edith had paused, the room framed like a painting. She hadn't seen the Massachusetts bedroom for almost three years, hadn't been in the Parisian one for nearly two—not since her discovery of Morton's passion for Luna, the betrayal, all of it. It had taken more than a little sleuthing, but when she'd finally found a love letter addressed to "My dear little moon," Edith had already come to know about Morton's clandestine wedding to the French *chanteuse*, his ongoing amour with the Ranee of Sarawak, his liaison with the Paris landlady—even his dalliance with that dandy English sculptor. Dear Henry had put the point on it in one of his novels, how Morton, only five-foot-six with sky-blue eyes, a round chin, a waxed moustache, and fresh-fresh flowers in his daily buttonhole, ever looked "vague without looking weak—idle without looking empty." An *homme de coeur*, his past hazy, nothing clear or sharp, tantalizingly impressionistic, both intelligent and mysterious. Precisely the kind of man who let himself be loved.

Yet Morton could love back, surely. After their first night together—in this very house, this very room, in fact—Morton had written to her, a letter unlike any other. That next morning, Edith had been avoiding her husband Teddy (or, as Morton persisted in calling him, "Mr. Wharton"), skipping breakfast and sitting up in her bed at the Mount, her dogs, Mitou and Nicette, the bedwarmers against her feet. Pretending to catch up on correspondence, she'd written in her diary, "I know now all that I have never known before, the interfusion of spirit & sense, the double nearness, the mingled communion of touch & thought." Her heart drummed terror and rapture, her lips sore, her cheeks rough from Morton's mustache. Then came his note—as beautiful on the silver tray as a winter lamp garlanding an avenue in Paris. "I want this with you," he wrote, his handwriting large and looped. "I want you to know, my dearest dear, that I find you engulfing and beautiful and lovely and womanly and very sensual. Very animal magnetism."

After that, Edith had met him at his old farmhouse as much as she could before he sailed for France, and yet, later, when she tried to recall the details of the place—the walls and floors etched by sweat and breath—what she remembered most were his history books piled against every wall, stacked like lean-tos, more on the coffee table, the desk, even piled next to the bathtub. His nightstand was all but invisible, merely a scaffolding to support all of his books about war and agriculture and law and slavery in between the novels Edith had given him, the ones she'd written (two of them) as well as the ones by Henry (all of them). So, now, pausing at his bedroom window, Edith expected to see a room built of books. She expected, too, to see her own Christmas gift of a Civil War tintype, an unknown soldier winking silver in the moonlight, which should have been on top of an antique toolbox holding, among other trinkets, a ring Edith had found for Morton's fortieth. Above his bed should have been a painting—some bovine landscape savoring a bit too much of larder and manger that she'd talked him into buying on the one stolen afternoon they'd managed to motor into the city. And then there was the old shirtwaist that should have hung in the closet, what she'd worn their first night together—a shirt Morton had insisted on keeping, to hold her smell, he said, when she left.

After making love, he would hold her from behind, would ask "What are you thinking?" and while sometimes Edith thought about whether he loved her, more often she considered her small gifts—the photograph, the ring, the novels—how they hummed for him when she couldn't be there, when she was writing or entertaining or taking care of Teddy's bouts of melancholy. As if the gifts sang to Morton a small, quiet song without words, the loving, tender tune a mother hums to a child fighting sleep.

When Edith had first met Miss Luna, she'd seemed like a child herself—more like a figure out of a children's book than a grown woman, and one who fit her name: whittled as a waning moon, a bit chilly. Quite out of the blue, Teddy had invited Luna to the Mount for dinner, along with Morton and Henry and the rest. Teddy had said that he found her both "odd and amusing" when they'd met at Brigham's Oyster House, a local place—one where Luna herself had recently finished two murals: a group of wine bottles circled by a grapevine and another with a cluster of lemons next to dead fowl and bowls of pasta. Teddy said the murals reminded him of eighteenth-century trompe l'oeil, and much later, when Edith created the opportunity to sip wine and eat oysters under Luna's nests of pasta, she had to admit that the paintings were precisely detailed, so careful with light and shadow they looked like windows—as if the viewer could reach his hand past the sill and pick a lemon or pheasant off the plate.

Yet even before Teddy admitted to having invited this lady painter to dinner, Edith was dreading the meal. Morton had written her a brief note from Paris, explaining about the request to speak at Bryn Mawr on the subject of the New York edition of Henry's novels and asking if he could make a visit—but by the time Edith received it off the steamer, Morton had already arrived. All that past summer and autumn, Edith had been haunted by his silence. From moments of such nearness, when the last shadow of separateness would melt, back into a complete *néant* of silence, of not hearing, not knowing—it was as if she didn't exist. Before Morton left, he'd written like a lover, but then for six months he treated her like an acquaintance. She finally telegraphed him, writing only, "I don't know what you want, or what I am," and still—nothing. The ocean silent as snow.

Such inconsistencies stood out as bas-relief against the memories of their few months together, first at Morton's farmhouse, then the following spring in Paris when Teddy took the Vanderbilt apartment at the Rue de Varenne with the charming old furniture—all those fine bronzes and Chinese porcelains. Months—half a year—later, and still Edith would pass by a dear, old, crooked New England church and relive and relive and relive every moment, every phrase, every look from a happy hour spent with Morton in Notre Dame, where history and romance forged a glad upward rush under her ribcage. Or, too, she would recall the moments when Morton would bark a harsh laugh, tell her something hard or brittle, such as, "You'll write better for this experience of loving," and she would imagine then that his sentimental mood had cooled, that he'd found a younger, comelier woman of wit and wealth. When she felt her most desperate, she'd lock her bedroom door and reread his old letters—the "Darling" and the "Cher amié" and the "I am mad about you, Dear Heart"—and refuse to believe that the man who wrote them did not feel them.

And, then, after six months apart, here Morton was coming to dinner, and so Edith consulted all day with the staff, closely monitoring what evolved into an antique menu. Edith took the risk of being thought a parvenu, bringing back the nostalgic table she recalled from her childhood in old New York, what with a heavy roast, both canvasback and terrapin, two soups, two sweets, and a Roman punch in the middle. She even ordered greenhouse roses and had the menu hand-printed on gilt-edged cards. The meal would allow for wearing a vintage costume of short sleeves and full décolletage—a Victorian look that flattered her thicker waist and ample bosom, what Morton had once called his "delight."

The guests had found the Roman punch agreeably quaint. Henry had declared the syrupy, old-fashioned drink—consisting of six cups lemonade, the juice of two oranges, and equal parts rum and champagne—"a time-honored frozen slush of a happy ending." Everyone had laughed and raised their glasses, save Miss Luna, who had gazed at the punch bowl and held her glass without drinking.

Edith had leaned towards her then, had said, "You may be the only bona fide female painter I have ever met." Luna had a boyish body, wishbone thin, clearly corsetless, and this evening she was sporting a man's tie, her blouse buttoned to the neck. "What made you make such a choice? The life of an artist."

"Oh, I don't know why I paint," Luna had said with a small laugh, turning her glass between delicate hands, etched like fossils. "Neither does anyone else, I imagine. No one really cares, in any case. Do they?" Luna's large, pale eyes bounced light rather than owned it.

"Perhaps," said Edith. "And yet if I didn't write, I believe I would die." She glanced towards Morton, hoping he would hear her emphasis on "die." Apart from a stilted greeting in front of Teddy, one in which she'd felt ripples of flame all over, she and Morton hadn't spoken all evening, although she'd noticed every flick of his blue eyes round the table—how they paused every so often at Miss Luna.

"I doubt I would die if I wasn't able to paint," said Luna, laughing again.

"I would die if I dined alone!" said another woman, a Miss Jones who had come as the Captain's guest, her waterfall of Gibson Girl curls forever bouncing, bouncing.

From his end of the table, Henry said, "But women never dine alone," in his steadiest, deepest, most pedagogical voice. "When they are alone, they don't dine."

At this, the group cheered themselves again with a toast, though this time Morton was the one to still his glass, looking hard at Luna. His look held all Edith already knew of him and his women—how in Paris they lived with their lovers in apartments with the rooms all on one floor. For Morton, Luna would be a veritable George Sand. Like a scene from French fiction, Edith could already imagine their first tryst.

When Morton left that evening, Edith did not even show him to the door. The thank-you note he sent the following morning contained nothing but the requisite "I am obliged" and "so very good to see you." Years ago, when he'd sent her what she now thought of as his first love letter, the cordial formality of his "thank you" for dinner at the Mount was belied by an enclosed sprig of witch hazel—a wet bloom he'd unexpectedly found motoring home across the snowy roads.

But, now, pausing and peering into Morton's farmhouse bedroom, her feet cold against the foundation, Edith remembered every word of yet another note, the one she'd found to Luna, Morton's handwriting still looping and open as if sincere. "The letters survive, and everything survives," he wrote at the close. "All the ghosts of the old kisses come back, my dearest dear, and live again in the one I send you tonight."

It had taken Edith two full weeks to find that note, evidence of what she already knew was true. Edith—a "lady of talent," as Teddy called her—had spent plenty of time in Paris salons and English garden parties, and so she knew something of artists. She knew, for instance, that they kept odd hours, that they were often impulsive and vain, and that they were forever trying to capture a fugitive moment—how light dapples the inside of one's eyelids or the look of lace across a windowpane. So Edith had decided to show up, unannounced, at Luna's Boston studio.

On the long drive with her chauffeur, Edith had written fragments in her working journal, notes of what she most remembered during the long silence, ever waiting and waiting for Morton to send word across the pond, even a single sentence, a single word. Returning to the Mount after that spring together in Paris—when Teddy went off to the Boston sanatorium for his nerves and the big house creaked for want of voices—Edith had unpacked her own trunk, refusing help. Pulling her dresses out one by one, she'd spread them on the bed, the sofa, the easy chair. Cloaks, too, as well as hats and tea gowns: all that she had worn in America and France for the six months of her *affaire de coeur*. Of the black dress she wore the first time they went to the Sorbonne, she wrote, "Would he like me in it? I wondered and wondered." Then how many of the other dresses gave her the same thought—how when he noticed an *ensemble*, or praised it, *quelle joie*! All of the frocks and gowns, all of their excursions to Herblay . . . Mountfort L'Amaury . . . Provins . . . Beauvais . . . Montmorency . . . Senlis . . . Meudon. What dear, sweet, crowding memories. The grey tea gown she'd worn the first night they had dined alone. The aubergine dress she'd put on the day they went to Herblay, when, in a small church, for the briefest moment, she'd first felt complete happiness.

For her surprise visit to Luna, Edith had once again dressed with care—a semi-princess design made of ruby-red *crepe de chine* with bands of pink silk at the waist and hem. The style emphasized all that made her womanly, what in polite circles a gentleman might call "flattering." Yet when Luna opened her own door wearing a paint-splattered man's shirt and a startling pair of cuffed trousers, Edith felt like a pink flamingo.

"Oh, would you like a slice of cake?" Luna asked by way of a greeting. "I've tried something and made it with pickled mangoes."

Edith didn't know quite what to say other than she would be interested to see such a cake.

It turned out that the cake was a light orange color, sloped, placed right on top of numerous drawings of squares and circles that littered a table. Having never baked a cake entirely by herself—only assisting her childhood cook now and then—Edith was surprised at how crude it looked, like a hunk of clay before molding.

"You made it yourself," Edith said, not a question.

"Of course, of course," said Luna. "My nephew Martin's fifth birthday is soon, and I said I would bake him any cake he wished. He asked for mango. Mango! So exotic, I thought I'd better practice."

Above the cake there were several other sketches pinned to the wall of even more squares and circles—this time arranged as if the circles inhabited the squares—as well as another drawing of a table, a steaming cup of coffee at its center. It looked like an exercise in perspective, with straight lines radiating from cup to corners, a kind of precision Edith equated with Morton, all those fussy collars and ties. Beyond was another room—a bedroom, Edith assumed, given the rumple of bedclothes she could just glimpse through the doorway (seemingly Luna's rooms were all on one floor)—with a bicycle tire, a baseball bat, and a rugby ball crowded together along the baseboard.

"Martin's equipment," said Luna, waving her hand as if saying goodbye. "He believes he is a bandit, wears a bandana up over his nose most of the time. The bicycle tire, the bat—well, I'm not sure what they have to do with thievery, but something."

"I imagine he will find it hard to enjoy his cake through a bandana," said Edith.

Luna laughed again, asking if Edith wanted a cup of tea with her cake. Luna almost always spoke with a laugh.

"Thank you, yes," said Edith. "May I peruse your paintings for a moment?"

Luna agreed and disappeared, and Edith moved to the other side of the large room, which consisted of the upper part of an old storage building. Allowing for quantities of liquid light, the two main windows were enormous—giant, blank eyes. Following the arrangement of modern New York galleries, the paintings and photographs were interspersed together on the walls. Morton himself had written of the Photo-Secessionists for a *Times* article, and so Edith knew of their desire for dialogue across artists of all ranks and types.

"Are all of the paintings yours?" Edith called, her voice too high. "Did you paint them?"

"The ones of food," Luna called back. "The food—the food is all mine!"

The paintings were colossal. A mammoth melon shaped like a giant's green head, an ice cream sundae heaped as high as a cumulous cloud, a joint of Brobdingnagian meat, a bottle of wine as big as an Elizabethan headboard. "Have you yet painted a mango?" asked Edith, though too quietly for Luna to hear, imagining a citrus circle to eclipse the sun—which is when she glanced down and spied an envelope on the floor of the bedroom, next to the bicycle tire. Edith's skin turned to ice. Morton's writing paper, she was sure.

Edith couldn't see Luna in whatever rough space served as the kitchen, and so she moved quickly. "I have drunk the wine of life, my dear little moon," it began, "and I have been warmed through." In one of Edith's own letters—left at Morton's Paris apartment with a servant and a bottle of Burgundy—she had written to him, "I have drunk the wine of life at last, I have known the thing best worth knowing, I have been warmed through & through, never to grow quite cold again till the end." That had been towards the end of Edith's time at the Rue de Varenne, when she had believed that the compass of their two hearts had turned into one, a miracle.

Though Edith ate every bite of her slice of mango cake and dutifully asked after the receipt, the remainder of her afternoon was a locked door on a bitter night.

"Four eggs," said Luna, "beaten until quite fluffy, then tip in one and a half cups of sugar. I poured in a half cup of melted butter and a whole cup of honey slowly—slowly, slowly—into the bowl." At this Luna laughed yet again, this time for long enough that it sounded a bit like crying. "Then, let me see, two cups of cake flour, dashes of cinnamon, nutmeg, some cut-up bits of orange and lemon rind, a few walnuts, a couple of pinches of yeast powder, a fistful of raisins—well, and, of course, two of the pickled mangoes, diced small."

"And the frosting?" asked Edith, who was wondering if Morton had crossed this very threshold, had sat in this very chair, had tried his own bit of mango cake. Morton Fullerton—who had split Edith's heart, an apple to a cutting board.

"A basic frosting," Luna said. "Butter, sugar. A little orange juice."

A novelist knows how to design a plot, and from the moment she left Luna's studio, Edith's planning had been precise. She'd waited ten days—until Teddy was back in Boston, Morton in New York. That evening, she'd retired early, claiming a headache to the servants, then had woken promptly at one o'clock in the morning. With speed and care, she had dressed in clothes worthy of Luna—men's marauding garb: black trousers, a dark shirt and an even darker jacket, black socks and shoes, finished with a stable boy's hat and coat and gloves. After double-checking the petrol level in the motorcar, Edith had made sure she had the two firebombs, the rubbish sack, and her change of clothing. She brought Mitou along, for company and nerve. Even the weather cooperated: cold and dry, but with a brilliant moon.

Usually her chauffeur, Cook, drove, but Edith remained confident with the wheel, her grip solid and sure. Once—only once—Edith and Morton had driven without Cook, a dear half hour coming back from St. Cloud. It had been snowing—the first snow of that Berkshire winter—and the flakes had frozen on the windows, shutting them in, shutting everything else out. Edith had felt Morton's dearest side then, the side that she always thought of as simple and sensitive and true. In that moment, their breath visible, mingling their words, so warm and so cold, Edith had wished to be like a touch of wings brushing by him in the darkness or like the scent of an invisible garden that he would pass on an unknown road at night. She wanted to be his comfort—not a momentary sympathy but the very threads that would weave the fabric of his heart. When she'd finally confided in Henry—she simply had to tell someone; it was impossible to contain her joy—he had looked at her under that beetle brow of his and had said that while Morton was beautiful and tender and intelligent, he was not kind. "He's not kind, Puss. There it is." Henry had pulled down the front of his waistcoat like an exclamation mark. "Fullerton is not kind." With Mitou curled on the car seat next to her, Edith had repeated, "Fullerton is not kind. Morton Fullerton is not kind."

When finally she had arrived at his farmhouse, even never having smashed anything on purpose—not one wine glass or china plate—she had no trouble finding a concrete baseball from his crumbling foundation, throwing it hard, and smashing Morton's pane of glass on the very first try.

But then, then—instead of lighting the wick and hurling her homemade firebomb into the room, grabbing Mitou, and finding a safe distance to make sure that the whole house would burn—she'd paused. Edith had paused and looked for herself in the room, lit by moonlight. The toolbox was gone, as was the tintype. Replacing the bovine landscape, above the bed was what had to be a self-portrait of Luna walking away from her own canvas, her brittle back naked, another scandalous pair of man's trousers slung low, a shoe hooked on each thumb. Tossed in the corners were her painting smocks, a pair of earrings and an amber pendant lay tangled on the dresser, her bloomers looped the floor. Even the books on the nightstand layered Luna's over Morton's, like a kid's game of stacking hands: his history books beneath her shilling shockers. This room wasn't a painting, fixed and still. It was a moving, thrumming room, one in which two people slept and dressed and read and talked and fought and laughed and, yes, made love.

It was then that Edith had told Mitou to get back, lit the blanket's wick and quickly broke her first bomb against the dresser—against that honey-colored pendant given, she was sure, as a gift from Morton. As Edith's face grew warm, she'd thought of all these humming objects, the songs they sang, and wondered if the pendant's little tune would start to scream.

But the fire had died almost as soon as it started, the blue-orange light and moonlit shadows transforming the room into something beautiful and strange. If Edith could paint, she'd thought, she wouldn't paint pasta or mangoes—she would paint this: a shock of lantern light moving across a bedroom wall at night, wells of darkness crowding old corners. She would paint the mystery of looking: how a short, not particularly handsome man could transform into something gorgeous or a woman with no bosom and a boy's straight hips could become, under this man's body, as greenish-blue fresh as a fish just landed, slapping and quivering on a rock, waiting to be slit open.

The second time, Edith had lit her firebomb more carefully, aiming for Morton's books, that tinderbox of cherished paper. The explosion was tactile, dazzling.

Feeling sore in her shoulders and wrists as if she'd just fought in hand-to-hand combat, Edith had called to Mitou, springing from side to side as if caged, and they'd walked the mile or so between the house and where she'd left the motorcar. There, she'd turned back once towards the fire, watching as the sunporch glowed yellow.

"Morton Fullerton, Morton Fullerton," she'd whispered.

Now, turning away, she took off every piece of men's clothing, one by one, folding each neatly into a rubbish bag. When she went back to the Mount, she would drop the whole down an unused well. She was momentarily naked and outdoors—something Edith had never experienced before and never would again. The wind burned. Would Morton like this gown, she wondered, this particular drape of skin? Then she dressed again in her sober driving gown and called to Mitou.

The roof collapsed. Even at this distance, Edith felt singed. The heat was a push, a hot hand propelling her backwards.

"Come on," she said to Mitou, who'd barked himself raw. "Come on. Come on, now," she said, opening the back and front door of the motorcar together, letting them both in at once.

Driving down the dirt road, fields as empty as her heart on either side, the burning farmhouse was an exploding star behind her.

Edith said, "Goodbye, my dearest dear," and her words were both heard and seen, formed whole from the steam of her mouth.

48

The Assurance of Caramel Cake

From *Hallelujah! The Welcome Table: A Lifetime of Memories with Recipes*

MAYA ANGELOU

Quilting bees were eagerly anticipated by southern black women. They offered the only nonlabor, nonreligious occasions where women could gather and exchange all the communities' good and bad news. The women planned for weeks. Then they selected and cooked their favorite dessert dishes and brought them to the gathering. The bees were always held in the back of the store, which meant that Bailey and I could look forward to some delicious cakes and pies and, if the event took place in the summer, some luscious hand-cranked strawberry ice cream. Usually cranked by us.

Mrs. Sneed, the pastor's wife, would bring sweet potato pie, warm and a little too sweet for Momma's taste but perfect to Bailey and me. Mrs. Mille's coconut cake and Mrs. Kendrick's chocolate fudge were what Adam and Eve ate in the Garden just before the Fall. But the most divine dessert of all was Momma's Caramel Cake.

Momma would labor prayerfully over her selection because she knew but would never admit that she and all the women were in hot competition over whose culinary masterpiece was the finest.

Momma could bake all the other women's dishes and often made them for the family, but not one of the other cooks would even dare the Caramel Cake (always to be spoken of in capital letters). Since she didn't have brown sugar, she had to make her own caramel syrup. Making her caramel cake took four to five hours, but the result was worthy of the labor. The salty sweetness of the caramel frosting along with the richness of the batter made the dessert soften and liquefy on the tongue and slip quietly down the throat almost without notice. Save that it left a memory of heaven itself in the mouth.

Of course Bailey and I were a little biased in Momma's favor, but who could have resisted the bighearted woman who was taller and bigger than most men yet who spoke in a voice a little above a whisper? Her hands were so large one could span my entire head, but they were so gentle that when she rubbed my legs and arms and face with blue-seal Vaseline every morning, I felt as if an angel had just approved of me.

I not only loved her, I liked her. So I followed her around. People began calling me her shadow.

"Hello, Sister Henderson, I see you got your shadow with you as usual." She would smile and answer, "I guess you got that right. If I go, she goes. If I stop, she stops. Yes, sir, I have me two shadows. Well, three by rights. My own and my two grandbabies."

I only saw Momma's anger become physical once. The incident alarmed me, but at the same time it assured me that I had great protection. Because of a horrible sexual violence I experienced when I was seven, I stopped talking to everyone but Bailey.

All teachers who came to Stamps to work at Lafayette County Training School had to find room and board with black families, for there were no boardinghouses where they could gain admittance.

All renting families acted as individual chambers of commerce for the newcomers. Each teacher was told of the churches and the preachers, of the hairdressers and barbers, of the white store downtown and the Wm. Johnson General Merchandise Store where they were likely to get accounts to tide them over between paychecks. The new teachers were also alerted to Mrs. Henderson's mute granddaughter and her grandson who stuttered seriously.

Summer was over, and we returned to school with all the other children. I looked forward to meeting the new teacher of the fourth-, fifth-, and sixth-grade classes. I was really happy because for the first time Bailey and I were in the same classroom.

Miss Williams was small and perky. She reminded me of a young chicken pecking in the yard. Her voice was high-pitched. She separated the classes by row. Sixth-graders sat near the windows, fifth-graders were in the middle rows, and fourth-graders were near the door.

Miss Williams said she wanted each student to stand up and say his or her name and what grades they received at the end of the last semester.

She started with the sixth-graders. I looked at Bailey when he stood and said, "Bailey Johnson, Jr." At home he would make me fall out laughing when he said what he wished his whole name was: "Bailey James Jester Jonathan Johnson, Jr."

Because I didn't talk I had developed a pattern of behavior in classrooms. Whenever I was questioned, I wrote my answer on the blackboard. I had reached the blackboard in Miss Williams's room when the teacher approached me. We were nearly the same height.

She said, "Go back to your seat. Go on."

Bailey stood up over by the window.

He said, "She's going to write her name and grade on the blackboard."

Miss Williams said to me, "I've heard about you. You can talk, but you just *won't* talk."

The students, who usually teased me relentlessly, were on my side. They began explaining, "She never talks, Miss Williams, never." Bailey was nervous. He began to stutter, "My . . . Maya can't talk."

Miss Williams said, "You will talk in my classroom. Yes, you will." I didn't know what to do. Bailey and the other children were trying to persuade her to allow me to write on the blackboard. I did not resist as she took the chalk out of my hand. "I know you can talk. And I will not stand for your silliness in my classroom." I watched her as she made herself angry. "You will not be treated differently just because your people own a store."

"Speak, speak." She was fairly shouting. Her hand came up unexpectedly, and she slapped me. Truly, I had not known what to do when she was winding herself up to hit me, but I knew what I had to do the second her hand landed on my cheek. I ran. I ran out of the classroom with Bailey following shouting, "Wait, My, wait." I couldn't wait. I was running to Momma. He caught up with me on the porch of the store.

Momma, hearing the noise, opened the screen door.

"What happened? Why aren't you in school? Sister, why are you crying?"

Bailey tried to answer her, but his brain moved faster than his tongue could form the words.

I took my notebook and pencil and wrote, "Miss Williams slapped me because I wouldn't talk."

"She slapped you? Slapped? Where?"

Bailey said, "Fa . . . fa . . . fa . . . face."

Momma told Bailey to go back to school. She said she and I would be coming soon.

Momma's calm voice and unhurried manner helped Bailey to settle down enough to speak.

"You want me to tell Miss Williams that you are coming?"

Momma answered, "I want you to go back to school and get your lesson." He looked at me once, saw that I had stopped crying, so he nodded and jumped off the porch and headed back up the hill.

"Sister, go to the well and put some fresh water on your face." I went around behind the store to the well.

When I returned to the porch Momma had put on one of her huge freshly washed, starched, sun-dried, and ironed aprons. In her hand she had the board that was slipped into pockets closing off the front door. We had a similar plank for the store, which we used every night to let customers know we were closed. I don't remember there being a lock for the house or the store.

Momma dropped the board into the slots, and in a second she was striding up the hill to the school.

I hurried beside, hoping to read her intentions in her face.

She looked as she always looked, serene, quiet. If she planned something unusual it did not register in her face.

She walked into the school building and turned around to me.

"Sister, show me your classroom."

I guided her to Miss Williams's room. She opened the door and Miss Williams walked up to Momma.

She asked, "Yes? May I help you?"

My grandmother asked, "Are you Miss Williams?"

Miss Williams said, "I am."

Momma asked, "Are you somebody's grandbaby?"

Miss Williams answered, "I am someone's granddaughter."

Momma said, "Well, this child here is my grandbaby." Then she slapped her. Not full force but hard enough for the sound to go around the room and to elicit gasps from the students.

"Now, Sister, nobody has the right to hit nobody in the face. So I am wrong this time, but I'm teaching a lesson." She looked at me. "Now find yourself a seat and sit down and get your lesson."

Momma left the room, and it was suddenly empty and very quiet.

Miss Williams left the room for a few minutes. Not a word was spoken.

Miss Williams reentered and said, "Students, turn to lesson one on page one."

I looked at Bailey, and he gave me the smallest nod. I turned to page one, lesson one.

No one spoke of the incident on the way home, and when I returned to the store Momma and Uncle Willie were sitting on the porch.

Uncle Willie said, "Sister, there's something on the kitchen table. Bring it out here please."

I went into the kitchen and on the chopping table stood the most wondrous Caramel Cake looking like paradise, oozing sweetness.

Carefully I brought it back to the porch, and it was nearly worth being slapped just to hear Bailey gasp.

Uncle Willie said, "This cake can't pay you for being slapped in the face. Momma made it just to tell you how much we love you and how precious you are."

CARAMEL CAKE

Serves 8

8 tablespoons (1 stick) butter
1¼ cups sugar
¼ cup Caramel Syrup (recipe follows)
2 cups sifted all-purpose flour
2 teaspoons baking powder
½ teaspoon salt
1 cup milk
2 large eggs
Caramel Frosting (recipe follows)

Preheat oven to 375°F. Line two 8-inch layer cake pans with greased wax paper.

In large mixing bowl, beat butter, and add 1 cup sugar gradually until light and fluffy. Beat in syrup.

In medium mixing bowl, sift flour, baking powder, and salt together. Add sifted ingredients to creamed mixture, alternating with milk.

In separate medium mixing bowl, beat eggs about 3 minutes, until foamy. Add remaining sugar, and beat until there is a fine spongy foam. Stir into cake batter until blended.

Divide batter between cake pans. Bake for about 25 minutes. Remove pans from oven. Gently press center of cake with forefinger. Cake should spring back when finger is removed. If it doesn't return to oven for 10 minutes. Cool in pans for 10 minutes. Turn out onto rack, and remove wax paper. Let cakes cool to room temperature before frosting.

To assemble: Center one cooled cake layer on cake plate. Cover top and sides with generous helping of frosting. Place second layer evenly on frosted layer. Repeat frosting procedure. Make certain that sides are completely frosted. Cool in refrigerator until ready to serve.

CARAMEL SYRUP

1 cup white sugar
1 cup boiling water

Heat sugar in heavy skillet over medium-low heat. Stir constantly until melted to a brown liquid. When it bubbles over entire surface, remove from heat. Slowly add boiling water, stirring constantly. Pour into container and cool.

CARAMEL FROSTING

6 tablespoons (¾ stick) butter
One 8-ounce package confectioners' sugar
4 tablespoons heavy cream
1½ teaspoons vanilla extract
Pinch of salt

Brown butter in heavy pot over medium heat—be vigilant or it will burn. Allow butter to cool. In large mixing bowl, add confectioners' sugar, cream, vanilla extract, and salt to the butter, and beat until smooth. If frosting is too stiff, add tablespoon of half-and-half or full cream to thin.

A Toast

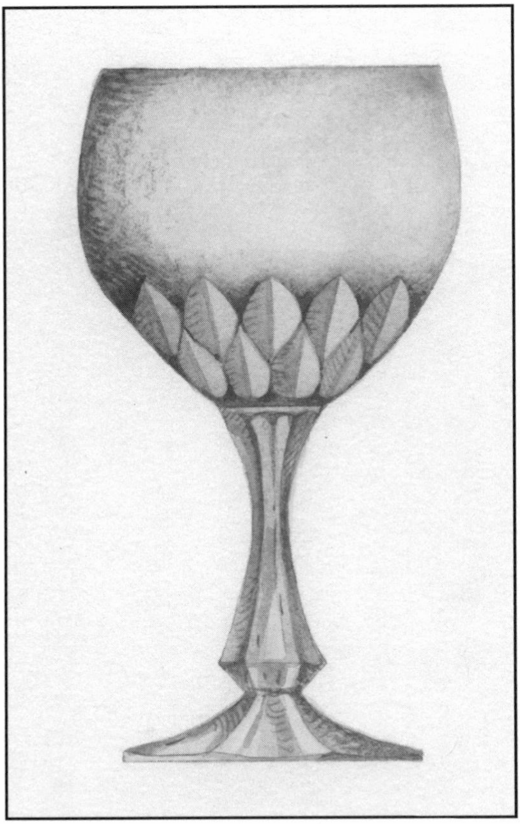

49

How to Make Rhubarb Wine

TED KOOSER

Go to the patch some afternoon
in early summer, fuzzy with beer
and sunlight, and pick a sack
of rhubarb (red or green will do)
and God knows watch for rattlesnakes
or better, listen: they make a sound
like an old lawnmower rolled downhill.
Wear a hat. A straw hat's best
for the heat but lets the gnats in.
Bunch up the stalks and chop the leaves off
with a buck-knife and be careful.
You need ten pounds; a grocery bag
packed full will do it. Then go home
and sit barefooted in the shade
behind the house with a can of beer.
Spread out the rhubarb in the grass
and wash it with cold water
from the garden hose, washing
your feet as well. Then take a nap.
That evening, dice the rhubarb up
and put it in a crock. Then pour
eight quarts of boiling water in,
cover it up with a checkered cloth
to keep the fruit flies out of it,
and let it stand five days or so.
Take time each day to think of it.

When the time is up, dip out the pulp
with your hands for strainers; leave the juice.
Stir in five pounds of sugar
and an envelope of Red Star yeast.
Ferment ten days, under the cloth,
sniffing of it from time to time,
then siphon it off, swallowing some,
and bottle it. Sit back and watch
the liquid clear to honey-yellow,
bottled and ready for the years,
and smile. You've done it awfully well.

CONTRIBUTORS

SHERMAN ALEXIE is a poet and fiction writer best known for his books *The Lone Ranger and Tonto Fistfight in Heaven* and *War Dances.* Alexie is the recipient of the PEN/Faulkner Award for Fiction, and his newest collection of short stories, *Blasphemy,* won the National Book Award.

KAREN LEONA ANDERSON is Associate Professor at St. Mary's College of Maryland and the author of *Punish Honey,* a collection of poetry. Anderson's work has appeared in such places as *ecopoetics, jubilat, Verse, Indiana Review, Fence, Volt,* and *The Best American Poetry 2012.*

MAYA ANGELOU—poet, playwright, activist, filmmaker, essayist, and memoirist—is the Reynolds Professor of American Studies at Wake Forest University. Her autobiography *I Know Why the Caged Bird Sings* was the first book to portray the coming-of-age experiences of an African American woman and is now widely taught in public schools and universities. At Bill Clinton's first inauguration, Angelou recited her poem "On the Pulse of the Morning."

THOMAS FOX AVERILL, who is Writer-in-Residence and Professor of English at Washburn University, is the author of four books of fiction: the novels *Secrets of the Tsil Café, Rode,* and *The Slow Air of Ewan MacPherson* as well as the short-story collection *Ordinary Genius.*

JAMES BEARD, a professional chef and food writer, authored more than thirty books on culinary culture during his lifetime, including *The James Beard Cookbook, James Beard's American Cookery, Beard on Bread, Beard on Pasta, James Beard's Simple Foods,* and many others.

JULIA CHILD and her husband, Paul, moved to France after World War II; there Child studied French cuisine at the Cordon Bleu and taught cooking lessons with SIMONE BECK and LOUISETTE BERTHOLLE. Their collaboration resulted in the 1961 cookbook classic *Mastering the Art of French Cooking*. The book's success led to Child's popular TV series *The French Chef*, which made her the first celebrity chef in America.

LYDIA MARIA CHILD published more than two dozen books, including the novel *Hobomok: A Tale of Early Times* as well as *The First Settlers of New England, The Indian Wife, The Family Nurse,* and *Fact and Fiction*. Her manual on good housekeeping, *The American Frugal Housewife,* was a bestseller in nineteenth-century America.

DAVID CITINO, poet and Professor of English at The Ohio State University for over three decades, was the author of ten books of poetry, including *The Weight of the Heart, Broken Symmetry, The News and Other Poems,* and *A History of Hands*.

JENNIFER COGNARD-BLACK is Professor of English at St. Mary's College of Maryland, where she teaches creative writing, women's literature, and the novel. The author of *Narrative in the Professional Age* as well as the coeditor of *Kindred Hands: Letters on Writing* and *Advancing Rhetoric,* Cognard-Black also publishes short fiction under the pseudonym J. Annie MacLeod.

LAURIE COLWIN was a fiction writer and essayist who published across a number of venues, from the *New Yorker* to *Mademoiselle* to *Playboy*. The author of ten books, Colwin is widely known for works *Home Cooking* and *More Home Cooking*. Under the title *Ask Me Again,* PBS aired an adaptation of one of her pieces of short fiction, "An Old-Fashioned Story."

CRIMETHINC. EX-WORKERS' COLLECTIVE (CWC) is a nonprofit anarchist group—composed of many autonomous cells—that organizes and records protests against democracy, capitalism, and globalization. In addition to *Recipes for Disaster: An Anarchist Cookbook,* the CWC has published such texts as *Contradictionary, Work,* and *Expect Resistance*.

TENAYA DARLINGTON blogs about cheese under the moniker "Madame Fromage." Her most recent book is *The Di Bruno Bros. House of Cheese: A*

Guide to Wedges, Recipes, and Pairings. She is also the author of a novel, *Maybe Baby*, and a poetry collection, *Madame Deluxe*.

HOWARD DININ is a writer, photographer, and educator (having taught courses in design, marketing, advertising, photography, and the history of art). He is the author of *Same Difference: Life in France / Peter Mayle Got Some of It Right*.

DAVID JAMES DUNCAN—essayist and novelist, fly fisher and father, and a self-dubbed "compassion-activist"—is the author of *The Brothers K*, *The River Why*, and *My Story as Told by Water*, among other books. His work has received three Pushcart Prizes and has been included in the *Best American Essays* as well as the *Best American Spiritual Writing*.

PETER ELBLING is a writer, director, actor, and songwriter. He is the author of a number of books, including *The Food Taster*, *Aria*, *The 80s: A Look Back*, and *The 90s: A Look Back*.

NORA EPHRON was a journalist, humorist, playwright, and screenwriter, made famous by her films *When Harry Met Sally*, *Sleepless in Seattle*, *You've Got Mail*, and *Julie & Julia*. Her screenplays were nominated for an Academy Award three times. Ephron's novel *Heartburn*, which includes recipes, was made into a movie starring Jack Nicholson and Meryl Streep.

KATHY FAGAN is the author of four collections of poems, most recently *Lip*. She is Professor of English at The Ohio State University, where she also serves as Poetry Editor of the OSU Press.

FANNIE MERRITT FARMER published seven books between 1896 and 1913. Best known for her *Boston Cooking-School Cook Book*, she also wrote *Chafing Dish Possibilities*, *Food and Cookery for the Sick and Convalescent*, *What to Have for Dinner*, *Catering for Special Occasions*, and *A New Book of Cookery*. In addition, she edited *The Priscilla Cook Book for Everyday Housekeepers*.

M. F. K. FISHER wrote more than thirty books, most of them about food and set in either France or California. Some of her best-known titles include *Serve It Forth, How to Cook a Wolf, The Gastronomical Me, An Alphabet for Gourmets, The Art of Eating,* and *With Bold Knife and Fork.* Fisher also translated Jean Anthelme Brillat-Savarin's *The Physiology of Taste* into English.

FANNIE FLAGG (born Patricia Neal) is an author and actress. Her novel *Fried Green Tomatoes at the Whistle Stop Cafe* was adapted into a movie in 1991 starring Kathy Bates, Jessica Tandy, Mary Stuart Masterson, and Mary-Louise Parker, and the film was nominated for two Academy Awards. Her other books include *Daisy Fay and the Miracle Man, Welcome to the World, Baby Girl!, Standing in the Rainbow, A Redbird Christmas,* and *I Still Dream about You: A Novel.*

MICHAEL S. GLASER has published seven collections of poetry and edited three anthologies, including *The Collected Poems of Lucille Clifton.* He served as Poet Laureate of Maryland from 2004 to 2009 and spent thirty-eight years at St. Mary's College of Maryland as a teacher and administrator.

MELISSA A. GOLDTHWAITE is Professor of English at Saint Joseph's University, where she teaches writing. Her books include *The Norton Reader, The St. Martin's Guide to Teaching Writing, The Norton Pocket Book of Writing by Students,* and *Surveying the Literary Landscapes of Terry Tempest Williams.*

CAROLINE M. GRANT is a writer and editor. She directs the Sustainable Arts Foundation, is Editor in Chief of *Literary Mama,* and writes about food and family. Her books include the coedited volumes *Mama PhD* and *The Cassoulet Saved Our Marriage.* She lives in San Francisco with her husband and sons.

PAUL HANSTEDT is Professor of English and Writing at Roanoke College in Virginia. In addition to articles and essays in various journals and magazines, he is the author of two books: *General Education Essentials: A Guide for College Faculty* and *Hong Konged,* a memoir of a year in Asia with three kids under the age of ten.

SUE JOHNSON is Professor of Art at St. Mary's College of Maryland. Her work pays homage to the genre of still life and *vanitas*, exploring the role of artist naturalists as well as collectors from the eighteenth century to the present and engaging the intersections of science, art, and popular culture. Johnson has had over thirty solo exhibitions of her work at venues such as the Rosenbach Museum and Library in Philadelphia, the University of Richmond, and the Pitt Rivers Museum in Oxford, England.

KETU H. KATRAK is Professor of Drama at the University of California, Irvine. The author of *Wole Soyinka and Modern Tragedy* as well as *Politics of the Female Body*, Katrak received a Fulbright to India and has served as dramaturg for the Oregon Shakespeare Festival. Her forthcoming book is titled *Contemporary Choreography in Indian Dance*.

BILL KLOEFKORN was the author of several collections of poetry as well as a collection of children's Christmas stories, two short-story collections, and four memoirs, most recently *Breathing in the Fullness of Time*. Kloefkorn was the Nebraska State Poet from 1982 until his death in 2011 and taught at Nebraska Wesleyan University for forty years.

TED KOOSER is a former United States Poet Laureate and the editor of a weekly newspaper column, "American Life in Poetry." He has published a dozen poetry collections, a number of nonfiction books, and stories for children, including *Delights and Shadows* (poetry), *The Poetry Home Repair Manual* (nonfiction), and the forthcoming *The Bell in the Bridge* (for children). Kooser is Presidential Professor at the University of Nebraska, Lincoln.

E. J. LEVY teaches at Colorado State University and has published the short-story collection *Love, in Theory* as well as the memoir *Amazons: A Love Story*. Levy also edited *Tasting Life Twice: Literary Lesbian Fiction by New American Writers*, winner of the Lambda Literary Award.

SHIRLEY GEOK-LIN LIM is a writer of fiction, nonfiction, poetry, and literary criticism. Her memoir, *Among the White Moon Faces*, received an American Book Award, while her poetry and fiction books include

Crossing the Peninsula, What the Fortune Teller Didn't Say, Walking Backwards: New Poems, Two Dreams: New and Selected Stories, and the recent novel *Joss and Gold.* Lim is Professor Emeritus at the University of California, Santa Barbara.

APRIL LINDNER is the author of two poetry collections—*Skin* and *This Bed Our Bodies Shaped*—as well as two young-adult novels based on novels by the Brontë sisters, *Jane* and *Catherine.* Lindner is Professor of English at Saint Joseph's University in Philadelphia.

TERESA LUST is a professional cook, best known as the author of the cookbook memoir *Pass the Polenta and Other Writings from the Kitchen.* In addition to having worked in restaurants from the Pacific Northwest to New England, she also translated the novel *The Librarians of Alexandria: A Tale of Two Sisters* by Alessandra Lavagnino from the Italian.

ELLEN MELOY was a nature writer and environmentalist vitally interested in charting a "deep map of place." Her books include *Raven's Exile, The Last Cheater's Waltz, Eating Stone,* and *The Anthropology of Turquoise,* which was nominated for the Pulitzer Prize. Established to honor her memory, the Ellen Meloy Fund for Desert Writers supports authors whose work reflects the "spirit and passions" found in Meloy's own writings.

JUDITH MOORE was a writer and reviewer best known for her book *Fat Girl: A True Story.* The author of the culinary memoir *Never Eat Your Heart Out,* Moore spent most of her career as an editor and feature writer for the *San Diego Reader.*

KATE MOSES is the author of *Mothers Who Think,* an anthology that won the American Book Award, and the subsequent collection *Because I Said So.* She has also written *Wintering: A Novel of Sylvia Plath* and the memoir *Cakewalk* about her love of stories and sugar.

MARION NESTLE is Paulette Goddard Professor in the Department of Nutrition, Food Studies, and Public Health at New York University as well as Professor of Sociology at NYU and Visiting Professor of Nutritional Sciences at Cornell. Nestle is the author of three prize-winning books, including *Food Politics: How the Food Industry Influences Nutrition and Health, Safe Food: The Politics of Food Safety,* and *What to Eat.*

CAITLIN NEWCOMER is a doctoral candidate in twentieth-century literature at Florida State University, with an MFA in fiction from The Ohio State University. Her fiction and poetry has appeared in *Hayden's Ferry Review,* the *Cincinnati Review, Nimrod,* and the *Laurel Review* and was nominated for *The Best American Nonrequired Reading* in 2009.

SHARON OLDS teaches creative writing at New York University. She has published twelve collections of poetry, most recently *One Secret Thing* and *Stag's Leap*. Her poetry collection *The Dead and the Living* won the National Book Critics Circle Award.

CHERYL QUIMBA is a graduate of the MFA program in creative writing at Purdue University. Her poems have appeared in *Dusie, Phoebe, Tinfish, Everyday Genius,* and *1913*. Quimba's forthcoming chapbook, *Scattered Trees Grow in Some Tundra,* will be published by the University of Toledo Press.

SARA ROAHEN is a food writer, whose books include *Gumbo Tales: Finding My Place at the New Orleans Table* and the coauthored *The Southern Foodways Alliance Community Cookbook*. Her essays have appeared in *Food & Wine, Tin House,* and *Oxford American.*

IRMA S. ROMBAUER self-published her famous cookbook *The Joy of Cooking* in 1931. The original book was illustrated by Rombauer's daughter Marion Rombauer Becker, who edited the popular 1975 edition after her mother's death. In 1936, the book was published by the Bobbs-Merrill Company, and it has been in print continuously—in different versions—since that first commercial publication. A facsimile of the 1931 version has been available since 1998.

NTOZAKE SHANGE writes plays, poetry, novels, children's books, and nonfiction. She is the author of more than forty books, including the food-related essay collection *If I Can Cook / You Know God Can*. Her poetic play *For Colored Girls Who Have Considered Suicide / When the Rainbow Is*

Enuf was nominated for a Tony, a Grammy, and an Emmy Award and was subsequently made into a movie.

RAVI SHANKAR is the editor of *Drunken Boat,* an online journal of the arts, and is Poet-in-Residence and Associate Professor of English at Central Connecticut State University. His first book of poetry, *Instrumentality,* was a finalist for a Connecticut Book Award.

AMELIA SIMMONS wrote *American Cookery* in 1796, the first cookbook produced by an American author. *American Cookery* is her only known publication.

VERTAMAE SMART-GROSVENOR is a culinary anthropologist, poet, and actress who has served as a commentator on National Public Radio. The author of the celebrated memoir-cookbook *Vibration Cooking: Or, The Travel Notes of a Geechee Girl,* she has also written *Vertamae Cooks in the Americas' Family Kitchen, Vertamae Cooks Again,* and *Thursdays and Every Other Sunday Off.*

GARY SNYDER is a lecturer, essayist, and environmental activist as well as a poet who won the Pulitzer Prize for his collection *Turtle Island.* Professor Emeritus of English at the University of California–Davis, Snyder is a member of the American Academy of Arts and Letters and is the subject of a recent documentary titled *The Practice of the Wild.*

DEBORAH THOMPSON teaches classes in cultural studies, literary criticism, and modern drama at Colorado State University, where she is Associate Professor of English. Her essays on gender, race, and sexuality have appeared in journals such as *MELUS, African American Review,* and *Theatre Journal,* and her creative nonfiction has received a Pushcart Prize.

ALICE B. TOKLAS—a member of the early twentieth-century avant-garde expatriates in Paris—published her memoir with recipes, *The Alice B. Toklas Cook Book,* in 1954. Initially known as Gertrude Stein's amanuensis, lover, and cook, with her book's popularity, Toklas became recognized as a writer in her own right. Her most famous recipe is for marijuana brownies, or "Haschich Fudge," which are known as "Alice B. Toklas brownies."

ALICE WATERS is a chef, cookbook writer, and food activist who opened her Chez Panisse restaurant in San Francisco in 1971: the first American restaurant to offer a local-seasonal menu with ingredients "foraged" at farmers' markets. Waters's subsequent Chez Panisse Foundation now supports the Edible Schoolyard program across the United States, in which children are taught sustainable gardening and eat their own produce as part of school lunches. Waters's most recent books are *The Art of Simple Food* and *In the Green Kitchen*.

MICHAEL LEE WEST is a self-styled "accidental gourmet" and the author of nine books, including *A Teeny Bit of Trouble, Crazy Ladies, American Pie, She Flew the Coop,* and *Gone with a Handsomer Man*. Her culinary memoir *Consuming Passions: A Food-Obsessed Life* is based on her experiences growing up on the Gulf Coast with a "wild tribe" of southern cooks.

TERRY TEMPEST WILLIAMS, a writer and environmental activist, is the author of *Pieces of White Shell, Refuge: An Unnatural History of Family and Place, Coyote's Canyon, An Unspoken Hunger: Stories from the Field, Desert Quartet: An Erotic Landscape, Red: Passion and Patience in the Desert, Finding Beauty in a Broken World, When Women Were Birds, Leap,* and several other books.

Some selections from this book were previously published. The editors gratefully acknowledge permission to reprint the following material:

Excerpts from *American Cookery, or the Art of Dressing Viands, Fish, Poultry, and Vegetables, and the Best Modes of Making Pastes, Puffs, Pies, Tarts, Puddings, Custards and Preserves, and All Kinds of Cakes, from the Imperial Plumb to Plain Cake. Adapted to This Country, and All Grades of Life,* by Amelia Simmons (Hartford, CT: Hudson & Goodwin, 1796).

Excerpt from *Delights and Prejudices* by James Beard, copyright © 1964 by James Beard. Used by permission of The Blumer Literary Agency Inc.

"Puffballs: Finding the Inside," from *Secrets of the Tsil Café* by Thomas Fox Averill. Copyright © 2012 University of New Mexico Press.

"To Cèpe, with Love (or, The Alchemy of Longing)" by E. J. Levy appeared in *Salmagundi* in spring 2011. Published by permission of E. J. Levy.

"An Unspoken Hunger," from *An Unspoken Hunger: Stories from the Field* by Terry Tempest Williams, copyright © 1994 by Pantheon.

Excerpts from *The American Frugal Housewife: Dedicated to Those Who Are Not Ashamed of Economy* by Lydia Maria Child (1829; Boston: Carter & Hendee, 1832).

"Whistle Stop, Alabama" and "Sipsey's Buttermilk Biscuits," from *Fried Green Tomatoes at the Whistle Stop Cafe* by Fannie Flagg, copyright © 1987 by Fannie Flagg. Used by permission of Random House, Inc. Any third party use of this material, outside of this publication, is prohibited. Interested parties must apply directly to Random House, Inc. for permission.

"Bread," from *The Dead & the Living* by Sharon Olds, copyright © 1987 by Sharon Olds. Used by permission of Alfred A. Knopf, an imprint of the Knopf Doubleday Publishing Group, a division of Random House LLC. All rights reserved.

Excerpts from *The Food Taster* by Peter Elbling, copyright © 2002 by The Permanent Press.

Excerpts from *Boston Cooking-School Cookbook* by Fannie Merritt Farmer (Boston: Little, Brown, 1896).

"H Is for Happy," from *The Art of Eating: 50th Anniversary Edition* by M. F. K. Fisher and Joan Reardon. Copyright © 2004 by M. F. K. Fisher. Reproduced with permission of John Wiley & Sons, Inc.

"All It Took Was a Road / Surprises of Urban Renewal," from *If I Can Cook, You Know God Can* by Ntozake Shange. Copyright © 1998 by Ntozake Shange. Reprinted by permission of Beacon Press, Boston.

Excerpts from *The Joy of Cooking* reprinted with the permission of Scribner, a Division of Simon & Schuster, Inc., from *The Joy of Cooking 1931 Facsimile Edition: A Facsimile of the First Edition 1931* by Irma S. Rombauer. Copyright © 1931 by Simon & Schuster, Inc. Copyright renewed © 1959 by Simon & Schuster, Inc. Foreword to the Facsimile Edition copyright © 1998 by Edgar R. Rombauer. All rights reserved.

"American Liver Mush" by Ravi Shankar was published online in *AGNI Magazine*. Reprinted by permission of Ravi Shankar.

"Eat Your Pets" by Ellen Meloy. Reprinted by permission of SLL/Sterling Lord Literistic, Inc. Copyright © by Mark Meloy. "Eat Your Pets" was previously published in *Northern Lights*.

"How to Make Stew in the Pinacate Desert: Recipe for Locke & Drum" by Gary Snyder, from *The Back Country*, copyright © 1968 by Gary Snyder. Reprinted by permission of New Directions Publishing Corp.

"Spirit-Fried No-Name River Brown Trout" published in *My Story as Told by Water* by David James Duncan. Copyright © 2001 by David James Duncan. Reprinted by permission of Sierra Club Books.

"The Poet in the Kitchen" and "The Poem of Chicken Breast with Fettuccine," from *Paperwork* by David Citino, copyright © 2003 by Kent State University Press. This piece first appeared in the *Columbus Dispatch*. Reprinted by permission of Mary Citino.

"A Good Roast Chicken," from *Pass the Polenta: And Other Writings from the Kitchen* by Teresa Lust, copyright © 1998 by Teresa Lust. Reprinted by permission of Steerforth Press.

"Turkey Bone Gumbo," from *Gumbo Tales* by Sara Roahen. Copyright © 2008 by Sara Roahen. Used by permission of W. W. Norton & Company, Inc.

"Boiled Chicken Feet and Hundred-Year-Old Eggs" by Shirley Geok-Lin Lim, from *Through the Kitchen Window: Women Explore the Intimate Meanings of Food and Cooking*, ed. Arlene Voski Avakian (Boston: Beacon, 1997; reprint, New York: Berg, 2005). Reprinted by permission of Shirley Geok-Lin Lim.

"13/16" by Sherman Alexie, from *Sustenance & Desire: A Food Lover's Anthology of Sensuality and Humor* (Boston: David R. Godine, 2004). Reprinted by permission of Hanging Loose Press.

Excerpt from *Mastering the Art of French Cooking*, volume 1 by Julia Child and Louisette Bertholle, Simone Beck, copyright © 1961 by Alfred A. Knopf, a division of Random House LLC. Used by permission of Alfred A. Knopf, an imprint of the Knopf Doubleday Publishing Group, a division of Random House LLC. All rights reserved.

"The Vegetable Gardens at Bilignin" (pp. 263–280) from *The Alice B. Toklas Cook Book* by Alice B. Toklas. Copyright 1954 by Alice B. Toklas. Copyright renewed 1982 by Edward M. Burns. Foreword copyright © 1984 by M. F. K. Fisher. Publisher's Note copyright © 1984 by Simon Michael Bessie. Reprinted by permission of HarperCollins Publishers.

"Potatoes and Love: Some Reflections," from *Heartburn* by Nora Ephron. Reprinted by permission of International Creative Management, Inc. Copyright © 1983 by Nora Ephron.

"Repulsive Dinners: A Memoir," from *Home Cooking: A Writer in the Kitchen* by Laurie Colwin, copyright © 1988 by Laurie Colwin. Used by permission of Alfred A. Knopf, an imprint of the Knopf Doubleday Publishing Group, a division of Random House LLC. All rights reserved.

"The Demystification of Food," from *Vibration Cooking: Or, The Travel Notes of a Geechee Girl*, copyright © 1970 by Vertamae Smart-Grosvenor, published by Doubleday and Company. Granted by permission of Marie Brown Associates.

"How to Cook Moong Dal, Bengali Style" by Deborah Thompson first appeared in *Alimentum: The Literature of Food* 10 (Summer 2010): 24–25. Reprinted by permission of Deborah Thompson.

"Food and Belonging: At 'Home' and in 'Alien-Kitchens'" by Ketu H. Katrak, from *In Through the Kitchen Window: Women Explore the Intimate Meanings of Food and Cooking*, ed. Arlene Voski Avakian (Boston: Beacon, 1997; reprint, New York: Berg, 2005). Reprinted by permission of Ketu H. Katrak.

Excerpts from *Chez Panisse Menu Cookbook* by Alice Waters, copyright © 1982 by Alice L. Waters. Used by permission of Random House, Inc. Any third party use of this material, outside of this